Traditional Cooking *of*

IRELAND

Traditional Cooking *of* IRELAND

150 Classic Recipes from an Irish Home Kitchen

BIDDY WHITE LENNON
AND GEORGINA CAMPBELL

Photography by Craig Robertson

LORENZ BOOKS

This edition is published by Lorenz Books
an imprint of Anness Publishing Ltd
info@anness.com

www.lorenzbooks.com
www.annesspublishing.com

A CIP catalogue record for this book is available from the British Library.

Publisher: Joanna Lorenz
Senior Editors: Doreen Gillon, Susannah Blake and Felicity Forster
Photographer: Craig Robertson
Home Economist: Emma MacIntosh
Assistant Home Economists: Fergal Connelly and Lisa Harrison
Stylist: Helen Trent
Designer: Simon Daley

COOK'S NOTES

Bracketed terms are intended for American readers.

For all recipes, quantities are given in both metric and imperial measures and, where appropriate, in standard cups and spoons. Follow one set of measures, but not a mixture, because they are not interchangeable.

Standard spoon and cup measures are level.
1 tsp = 5ml, 1 tbsp = 15ml,
1 cup = 250ml/8fl oz.
Australian standard tablespoons are 20ml. Australian readers should use 3 tsp in place of 1 tbsp for measuring small quantities.
American pints are 16fl oz/2 cups. American readers should use 20fl oz/2.5 cups in place of 1 pint when measuring liquids.

Electric oven temperatures in this book are for conventional ovens. When using a fan oven, the temperature will probably need to be reduced by about 10–20°C/20–40°F. Since ovens vary, you should check with your manufacturer's instruction book for guidance.

The nutritional analysis given for each recipe is calculated per portion (i.e. serving or item), unless otherwise stated. If the recipe gives a range, such as Serves 4–6, then the nutritional analysis will be for the smaller portion size, i.e. 6 servings. The analysis does not include optional ingredients, such as salt added to taste.

Medium (US large) eggs are used unless otherwise stated.

Contents

Ireland – the food island

Ireland is an island on the outermost edge of Europe. On the map its western coastline follows the line of Europe's continental shelf, united by the Atlantic Ocean, from Cadiz in the south of Spain to Bergen in Norway.

On this green, fertile island everything that is grown, all the animals that are reared, everything caught in the fishing grounds and all that is eaten are influenced by a temperate climate. Ireland is only rarely influenced by the cold of Northern Europe but always, especially along the western seaboard, by the warm, wet westerly winds that blow in over the warm Gulf Stream.

It is often said that Ireland does not have a climate, it has weather. For a small island the climate is extremely varied, going from sunshine to rain within minutes. Rainfall is not excessive: 1,400mm/55in in the south and west and less than 700mm/27in in the "sunny south-east". Numerous rainy days and infrequent droughts mean high humidity, which brings cloud cover and so less bright sunshine than in much of Europe.

The siren call, "Ireland the Food Island", is more than just a recent clever sales slogan. Ireland is a fast-growing food-exporting nation. Its grass-fed beef and lamb and its dairy produce are exported all over the world. Stand in any Irish fishing port and observe how foreign trawlers and fish buyers covet the fresh seafood, caught in clean Atlantic waters.

All over Ireland similar crops are grown and the same foodstuffs produced: however, the best grassland for cattle is in the counties of Kildare, Meath and the Golden Vale; and the best mountain lamb is found in the mountains of Connemara and Wicklow. Wexford and the north of County Dublin on the east coast are famous for producing high-quality soft fruits.

How Ireland's food culture developed

When trying to unravel the gradual development of Ireland's food culture, the climate, geography and the history of the people merge. Plants and animals certainly existed in Ireland before the last great ice age, when ice covered most of the island and much of northern Europe. As the ice retreated, 13,000 years ago, there was a massive re-invasion of plants and animals, including the giant deer known as the great Irish elk. It is also known that over no more than a thousand years, a large number of new plants and animals appeared in Ireland, so a land bridge must have existed at a crucial time. As the ice melted, two things happened: the land started to rise and sea levels also rose.

About 7,500 years ago Ireland finally became detached from mainland Europe, limiting the varieties of flora and fauna that are indigenous – Ireland

Left *There are 32 counties within Ireland and Northern Ireland. Dublin is the capital city of Ireland and other main regional towns include Cork and Galway. Belfast is the capital city of Northern Ireland.*

Left *Harvesting cultivated mussels on a fish farm in the clean, clear waters of Killary Harbour, County Galway.*

has only about 70 per cent of British plants and about 65 per cent of freshwater insects and invertebrates found in Britain.

Man then took over. The island's food culture was created by successive waves of settlers. The earliest were happy to find a land rich in seafood and edible nuts, fruits and plants. In their footsteps each successive group introduced new plants and animals.

Ireland's favourite food and drink

What emerges through time is that, while the Irish are always ready and willing to take what they like and make it their own, they rarely abandon a favourite food. Still deeply ingrained in Irish society is a love of the fish, shellfish and the wild plants and animals that first brought humans to the island; the beef and *bánbhianna* (white foods made from milk) and the Celts' love of feasting; the grains, fruits and vegetables of the early Christian tradition; the game birds, animals and fish brought by the Normans.

Prevented by the climate from growing vines and producing wine, the Irish became expert brewers of distinctive ciders and beers. When the secret art of distillation was brought to Ireland from the Mediterranean the Irish discovered *uisce beatha* – whiskey – the water of life.

Even the potato, which eventually brought the misery of great famines, still has pride of place on every Irish table. Around the beginning of the 20th century, German families, who came to Ireland to escape persecution, influenced and greatly expanded the number of pork dishes, which were, for many generations, the ordinary Irish people's main fresh source of meat.

For even longer the Irish have welcomed chefs, home-grown or incomers, trained in the classic tradition. Now many talented young Irish chefs returning from "a stint abroad" are inspired to put a new spin on the traditional foods and in doing so offer essential support to a new wave of speciality food growers and producers.

Right *The pagodas and the warehouse of the Old Bushmills Distillery viewed over the dammed St Columb's Rill, which is the pure water source for the whiskey production at Bushmills, County Antrim, Northern Ireland.*

The first settlers

About 9,000 years ago, the first settlers found an island full of plants and trees, mainly hazel groves and pine, but there were also juniper, willow, oak, elm, birch, alder, ash and apple trees. The climate was a little warmer than it is today. These early settlers were hunter-fisher-gatherers and dwelt mainly on the shores of lakes, rivers or by the sea, in skin huts which they packed up and moved with them. The abundance of native timber may have been an attraction for these nomadic people. As well as providing the raw materials for fuel and building, and for making containers of bark, dense woods allowed them to build dugout canoes in which the early settlers could penetrate the otherwise inaccessible countryside using the navigable rivers and lakes.

From archaeological remains, particularly kitchen middens (rubbish heaps), we know that these early settlers knew much about edible plants, nuts, berries and roots. More importantly, they understood the seasonal movements of fish and animals. They used small flint hand-axes typical of European hunter-fisher-gatherers and hunted fish with a primitive harpoon-like tool made from a microlith – a tiny flint blade that is set in a bone or wooden handle. Archaeological examination also suggests they did not roam aimlessly over the island but moved between three or four campsites in a yearly pattern governed by the seasonal migrations of fish, birds and animals, and the seasonal availability of plants, seeds, nuts and berries.

Above *A reconstruction of a mesolithic hut, in the Ulster History Park, Omagh, County Tyrone, Northern Ireland.*

Moving with the seasons

Early spring would find the settlers camped on the coast near the estuaries of rivers where they harvested shellfish, including oysters, mussels, clams, cockles (small clams), limpets and seaweed. They caught fish such as tope (a type of shark), cod, pollack and coley, and ling and sole from offshore rocks on the incoming tide. They also caught nesting seabirds (mainly auks and puffins) and often took their eggs, and they fished the first-run salmon.

In summer the people followed the salmon up river to the lakes where they also caught other fish and harvested fruits and berries. There were large stocks of eels in the lakes too, but these were easier to catch as they began to shoal in late summer to swim downstream again in the autumn.

Left *Ancient trees such as the hawthorn with red berries and the rowan provided food for early settlers.*

Left *Hares and other small mammals were a valuable source of meat for early settlers.*

The settlers probably followed the eels down into the river valleys in the autumn and set up their winter camps well above the flood plains of the rivers. At this time they harvested wild hazelnuts, which were an important winter food and widely available in the indigenous forests.

During the winter season the people hunted and trapped game and wildfowl. Wild pig seems to have been the most important source of meat, along with hare and the occasional red deer. They ate birds, too (woodpigeon, duck, red grouse and capercaillie were most common), and a bird of prey, a goshawk, may have been used for falconry rather than food, although this is speculation.

While archaeological excavation can tell us a great deal, it cannot tell us everything. We do not know, for example, how early people cooked their food. They had no pots that have been discovered, so it is probable that much of their food was eaten raw or cooked over an open fire.

Mesolithic settlers

However, archaeological evidence does show us that some time after these earliest settlers, a second group arrived who had stronger, heavier tools with which they began to create small clearings in the woods. But they did not sow crops or keep domestic animals. They possessed pronged spears and possibly fish hooks. It has been suggested that these Mesolithic people probably preserved meat and fish, particularly by smoking and drying on racks in much the same way as it is done in Iceland today.

Many of the foods still most favoured in Ireland today were among the very first foods eaten here – wild berries, such as blackberries and rowan berries; fish, such as salmon and trout; and shellfish, such as oysters and mussels.

The hazel, significantly called the Tree of Knowledge, has long had an almost mystical reputation that may go right back to these early hunter-gatherers. The stems of the hazel provided rods for their weirs – fences set in a stream for catching fish. They are still used today in the River Bann to make wattle fences to guide migrating eels and salmon into nets. One of the many legendary tales of the Salmon of Wisdom tells us that it attained its knowledge by eating the nuts that fell from a hazel tree growing beside a well that fed the sacred River Boyne.

Right *The river Boyne, revered in many ancient Irish cultures, flowing past Newgrange, County Meath.*

The first farmers

About six thousand years ago another wave of settlers arrived: they were semi-nomadic farmers. It is not known where they first landed, or if they reached Ireland from Britain or from continental Europe. It seems likely that they arrived in small boats made of skins stretched over wood, craft not unlike the *curraghs* which are still used today in the west of Ireland.

Their arrival coincided with a change in climate and a decline in forest cover. By clearing the land for grazing and tillage they activated the growth of nettles and sorrel. They brought grains and other plants with them and animals unknown in Ireland: the horse (at that time no bigger than a pony), mountain sheep, goats and small cattle – predecessors of the hardy little Kerry cow of today.

The farming people brought pottery vessels for storage and cooking. They built wooden houses with hearths and pits for storage of their seed grain. They used polished stone axes to fell trees and, when mounted as a mattock (a kind of pickaxe for loosening soil), for cultivation of the soil. Wild foods remained important, and the herding of animals and cereal cultivation were integrated with fishing, hunting and gathering. The lack of querns for grinding and the abundance of cattle bones on dwelling sites suggest an emphasis on grazing rather than cereal cultivation. They ate sheep, goats and a domesticated pig, as well as wild animals such as boar, birds and occasionally even seal and bear.

Above *A curragh at sea on the Dingle peninsula, County Kerry.*

An organized society develops

Over a period of more than a thousand years, these early farmers developed a remarkable society. The most visible mark they left on the landscape is their tombs. There are three distinct types. Court graves were the earliest, of which over three hundred have been identified, mostly north of the central lowlands. There are about 300 passage graves, mainly on hilltops in eastern

Below *An exterior view of the vast tomb at Newgrange, in the valley of the River Boyne, County Meath.*

***Left** An overhead view of the tombs at Knowth, a national historic monument in County Meath.*

Ireland. The crowning achievement of this early society is the great series of gigantic tombs in the valley of the River Boyne at Knowth, Dowth and Newgrange in County Meath. These are vast structures, pre-dating the Egyptian pyramids, and are unquestionably the work of an advanced and highly organized society.

As many as four thousand people may have been needed to provide the workers to build these great monuments, to farm the valley and provide the food to feed them. But their shallow cultivation methods quickly exhausted the soil, so they moved on, clearing more woodland. Their old sites, allowed to lie fallow, regenerated themselves over about three hundred years. Over thousands of years successive cultures occupied the valley of the River Boyne. It remains some of the most fertile grazing land on the island. Then the climate became colder and wetter. Much of the old woodland was gradually engulfed by bogs, which crept outwards and upwards, covering many of the stone-walled field systems of the settlements. These were rediscovered when the bogs were cut away for fuel.

The early Bronze Age

The next wave of settlers brought Ireland into the early Bronze Age. These Beaker Folk were named after the elaborate decorated pots found in their burial places, called gallery graves, along with bronze axes and jewellery; these distinguish their owners from the earlier farmers of the island. They introduced new plants and animals into Ireland. Discovering and extracting metals meant a wider range of implements could be made, resulting in the introduction of new farming techniques.

***Right** Poulnabrone dolmen tomb, near Ballyvaughan, County Clare.*

It was these Bronze Age prospectors, roaming in search of metal-bearing rock formations, who first built *fulachta fiadh*, ancient cooking sites scattered over the countryside. A sunken trough lined with stones or wood was built near water; the troughs varied greatly in size, but one, made out of a recycled, hollowed-out canoe, held about 977 litres/215 gallons of water. A fire would have been lit nearby and large stones heated in it. The hot stones were then thrown into the trough and brought the water to the boil. Large joints of meat were wrapped in straw and put into the water. Recent experiments show that the meat cooked in 20 minutes to the pound weight – about standard modern cooking time! The stones often split when they were thrown into the water and were then thrown on to a pile on the far side of the trough.

Many of these ancient cooking-sites were discovered because of the characteristic horseshoe-shaped mounds made by the discarded stones. Sites are widespread; in County Cork alone there are over 2,500. *Fulachta fiadh* remained in use into early medieval times.

Celtic cattle culture

About 2,600 years ago, during the late Bronze Age, farming activity was advanced by the development of farm implements. More domestic animals, especially cattle, were kept and wheat, barley and flax were grown.

Another group of settlers arrived in Ireland, most likely seeking copper. They slowly replaced the hunting spear with swords and shields and also brought massive cauldrons, horses, wheeled carts, saddle querns, musical instruments and the ard plough. This wooden plough must have seemed miraculous then, because deeper penetration of the soil meant that exhausted land could bear crops again. However, it was susceptible to damage from buried stones that had to be removed. This labour tended to fix the early farmers to one place, quickly exhausting the newly enriched soils.

However, a rising population living on less fertile land seems to have caused unrest on Irish soil for the first time. During this period the first defensive dwelling sites appear: lake dwellings (*crannogs*) and hill-forts provided protection for farmers and their domesticated animals. These hillside settlements, and the appearance of distinctive bronze artefacts, are the first signs of Celtic intruders on the island.

A farming Dark Age

It is tempting to speculate that a race of warlike Celts plundered the island bringing about the collapse of an organized society. However, there is very little real evidence of this.

Sophisticated pollen-counting techniques suggest that the Celtic period ushered in a dark age for farming, caused by soil exhaustion, which was to last for about 600 years. About 2,250 years ago, in a period known as the Pagan Iron Age, there is evidence of a gradual disappearance of agriculture: the weeds of cultivation disappear first, followed by cereals as the soils became increasingly unproductive. Tillage farming declined and semi-nomadic pastoral farming re-emerged.

The coming of the iron plough brought to Ireland by later Celts would have allowed the re-establishment of tillage in some areas because of its ability to rip up the top layer of the acid heathlands and reveal the richer subsoils beneath. The only evidence for this is a few early ploughshares found near *crannogs*, which are thought to have been the permanent dwellings of kings or clan leaders. Generally, however, for many centuries, great herds of cattle reigned supreme. The Celts' way of life depended on cattle. Herding and protecting cattle from animal and human predators was a full-time occupation. Cattle raiding became the national pastime. A person's social standing and worth was reckoned in cattle units – a man or woman "of six heifers", or of "two milch cows", became a commonplace.

Above *The double-headed Celtic figure of Janus (meaning two-faced), near Lough Erne, Boa Island, County Fermanagh, Northern Ireland.*

Religious festivals

The great pagan religious festivals, their myths and their rituals, mainly centred around cattle. There were four seasons in the Celtic year. The festival of *Samhain* marked the end of one year and the beginning of the next, the end of the grazing season when the herds were brought together. Grass being in short supply in the winter months, only beasts fit for breeding were spared from slaughter. Some were salted

Left *Set in superb landscape and in the middle of Doon Lough, County Donegal, are the remains of Doon Celtic fort.*

Right *The Broighter ship, found at Broighter, County Derry, represents a ship intended for high seas. It has moveable oars and a mast for a sail. Celtic merchants and traders travelled around the coasts of western Europe in boats like this. It may have been an offering, possibly to Manannan mac Lir, King of the Ocean. The Celts valued gold highly and often went in search of it.*

for winter food. The whole extended family, or *tuath*, assembled and feasted for days on end.

The festival *Imbolc* (St Brigid's Day) was associated with sheep and means "sheep's milk". *Bealtaine*, the May feast, marked the time when the herds could once again be driven out to open grazing. Two great bonfires were lit and the cattle driven between them to protect them against disease. At *Lughnasa* sacrifices were made to the god *Lug* to ensure a good harvest of grain. These great rituals were supervised by the Druids of the tribe.

The Celtic influence

The need to keep cattle safe and productive initiated the development of Celtic farmsteads and farming practice. As well as *crannogs* the Celts built isolated ring forts, big enough to contain a house, and a *souterrain* for underground storage and protection from raiders. A stone fort was a *cathair* or *cashel* or *dun*; those with just an earthen bank were called a *rath*.

Approximately 40,000 forts existed, and today's Irish place names reflect this, such as Cahir, Cashel, Rathkeel and Dundrum. In winter, the cattle grazed near the fort, but in summer the Celts drove their cattle to summer pastures and set up a *buaile* – a temporary milking shelter, anglicized as "booley".

The Celts dominated Ireland for a thousand years. When other cultures challenged their supremacy they resisted and absorbed the invaders for many hundreds of years more. Despite its semi-nomadic, pastoral nature, theirs was a developed and organized society with an enlightened, structured code of law, art and great oral traditions in literature and genealogy. For the ordinary Irish people, this cattle culture would survive the coming of Christianity, the Normans, and Cromwell and his devastations, right up to the threshold of the 18th century. Nowadays the cultural and culinary devotion to cattle is still strong and vibrant.

1,700 years ago Ireland emerged from the historical darkness of the Iron Age. Agricultural activity and the population increased. The Romans had not invaded Ireland and as their power began to crumble in Britain, Irish tribes began to settle in Scotland, Wales, Cornwall and the Isle of Man.

Left *Crannogs were used from the Bronze Age to medieval times. This replica is by the lake at Craggaunowen. They consisted of palisaded buildings on an artificial island or a platform raised on stilts over water.*

Bánbhianna

In Celtic times the Irish developed their passion for *bánbhianna* – white meats made from milk. This passion persisted for over a thousand years. *Bánbhianna* fascinated visitors and in 1690 an Englishman wrote, "The people generally are the greatest lovers of milk I ever saw which they eat and drink about twenty several sorts of ways and what is strangest love it best when sourest."

The sagas and the Brehon Laws, written down about AD600, were the expression of the lore and laws of a much earlier period and contain much of value in reconstructing the Irish way of life before the arrival of Christianity. *Bánbhianna* divided into summer and winter types. No doubt milk was drunk fresh but the Irish passion for "soured" milk is apparent. The winter types were the bog (preserved and flavoured) butter and the hard cheeses, and the summer types included fresh butter, milk drinks and soft, fresh cheeses.

"Twenty several sorts of ways"

Treabhantar was a mixture of fresh milk and buttermilk (*bláthach*), the liquid left after butter-making and a drink in its own right. It was this buttermilk the Celts liked most, as country people do today. These souring methods were ways of increasing the supply of buttermilk they obtained in limited quantities from butter-making. Today, buttermilk is widely available in Irish supermarkets and is the "secret ingredient" in the Irish soda breads tourists rave about.

In summer *Imúr*, fresh butter, was the greatest symbol of plenty in this society. When heavily salted, sometimes flavoured with wild garlic or leeks, it was also stored in wicker baskets buried in the peat bog to provide a "high taste" for winter. Baskets of "bog-butter" buried in ancient times have been discovered – although not in an edible condition.

Bainne clabair was a "thick" milk soured naturally or by putting fresh milk into a vessel that had contained sour milk. Sometimes this separated out into a liquid cottage cheese.

Grutha were curds of various types – a summer food when cows were in full milk. *Cáis* is now the Irish-language word for cheese of all types but it seems originally to have referred to one specific type: *fáiscre grotha*, a pressed curd. *Tanach* was a hard cheese; how

Below *Cattle grazing on verdant pastures with a variety of natural herbage at Clogher Head, Co. Kerry.*

Left Ewes and lambs grazing in the spring on lush grass provide excellent milk for cheese.

hard it was is shown by the fact that Furbaide, Queen Maeve's nephew, used a piece in his sling, instead of a stone, when he killed her!

"The Vision of MacConglinne", a 13th-century poem in Irish, has many descriptions of foodstuffs. It refers to "sleek pillars of ripe cheese" supporting the roof of a building. The poem also describes *maethal* as a "smooth, sweet, soft cheese". It was a large cheese because another writer, referring to a person of formidable girth, says "his buttocks were like half a *maethal*."

Grús was soft curd (farmer's) cheese made from soured buttermilk, kneaded but not pressed. *Millsén* was a semi-liquid curd cheese made from whole milk set with rennet. *Mulchán* was another hard cheese, one of the last to die out. This was probably because it was exported in large quantities and made in Waterford until 1824, when an English writer, anglicizing the name to "Mullahawn", says it was "a cheese made from skimmed milk ... but of such a hard substance that it required a hatchet to cut it".

Whey, the by-product of cheese-making, was valued as the drink *meadhg*. Mixed with water (on Christian fasting days) it was known as *meadhguisce*; skimmed-milk whey was *liommeadghuisce*. These *bánbhianna*, along with those made from sheep's and goat's milk, make up the "twenty several" of that 17th-century visitor.

Left Making butter in a traditional way. *Right* An ass and cart bringing milk to the creamery in the old way in Arigna near the Shannon River, County Leitrim.

Scattering cattle herds

The dominance of *bánbhianna* in the Irish diet is apparent from reports of campaigns of successive English generals against the native Irish – as much against their cattle as against the Irish themselves. In 1580 "great preys of cattle were taken from the Irish and so has brought them to the verge of famine". In 1600 the Lord Deputy "forced all the cows from the plains into the woods so that for the want of grass they would starve and O'Neill's people would starve for the want of milk".

Having scattered the great herds, the English tried to change the Irish way of life that so irritated them. They thought able-bodied Irishmen should have more to do than "follow a few cows grazing ... driving their cattle continually with them and feeding only on their milk and white meats". The sting comes at the end, "... if they were exhausted by working in the fields and gardens they would have less energy for raiding."

Grains, fruits and vegetables

About 1,500 years ago Christianity reached Ireland. A monastic tradition, governed by abbots of foundations rather than diocesan bishops, characterized this early Christian period. The monastic diet, with its emphasis on grains and vegetables rather than meat and *bánbhianna*, led to a much wider development of arable farming and the cultivation of fruits and vegetables.

Above *Barley is still one of the main agricultural crops in Ireland and is used for beer and whiskey production.*

Grains and vegetables

Barley, wheat and a little rye were grown, and oats were introduced. Although soft wheats can be grown in Ireland, oats and barley are much better suited to the damp climate. Oats gradually became the principal grain crop and over centuries oaten bread became the common bread of the people. It remained so in large areas of rural Ireland into the 19th century.

Barley bread was associated with the deliberately spartan diet of the monks. Barley was also used for making beer. In early Christian times bread was leavened with barm. Wheaten bread was always regarded as the greatest delicacy – the bread of feast days and the tribute of chieftains and kings. Outside the monasteries, relatively little bread was eaten; as late as 1533 the King's Council in Ireland comments that the Irishry "can live hardily without bread or other good victuals".

However, a great deal of grain was eaten in the form of various types of porridge, which is still a traditional breakfast food today. As with milk, the Irish served porridge in various thicknesses made from a variety of grains and flavoured in several different ways – it is only in recent times that the word "porridge" has come to mean solely oat porridge. The grains were boiled in water, in sheep's or cow's milk, and then flavoured with butter, salt, cream or honey.

Early written sources distinguish between wild and newly introduced cultivated vegetables. The most prominent were strongly flavoured ones: leeks (*foltchép*), onions (*cainneann*, a shallot type), garlic (*creamh*) and celery (*imus*). Non-native vegetables, including cabbage (*braisech*), arrived about this time along with various root crops, and peas and beans.

Left *A series of "lazy beds" or raised beds at Slea Head on the Dingle peninsula, County Kerry.*

Right *Early orchards were established by monks and apples have now become a commercial crop – this large apple orchard in blossom is in County Armagh, Northern Ireland.*

Lazy beds

The traditional way of growing vegetable crops was in raised beds or ridges called "lazy beds", developed by the first farmers 4,500 years ago. The method has nothing at all to do with being lazy. It is a sophisticated way of coaxing the best out of thin, wet soils and was widely used, especially in the west of Ireland, until the end of the 19th century. You can often see the pattern of these beds both on and under the surface of the ground on mountainsides at heights much higher than are cultivated now.

Using only a spade, two cuts of topsoil folded back on themselves towards a central line to create a thicker, dryer ridge with drainage trenches down each side. The shape of this bed could be adjusted to the needs of individual crops at various stages of growth. The fertility of the bed and the texture of its soil were improved by the regular addition of manure, sand and seaweed. When a bed had been cropped regularly for a period it was divided down the central ridge and the soils thrown outwards over a layer of manure and seaweed to form two new beds drained by a central channel.

Orchards

The monks established many orchards in Ireland. Early illuminated manuscripts differentiate the sour sloe and the cultivated plum and between wild and sweeter cultivated apples. The Brehon Laws name the apple as a fruit of the chieftain class and say: "fragrant in smell, delicious in taste, and delectable in colour". The monks were protective of their orchards. St Comgall is said to have blessed a garden from which thieves were stealing the apples of his brethren: the culprits were struck blind.

Monastic annals record the apple harvest each year and monastic rules specify the amounts monks were allowed to eat: "If they be large, five or six of them with bread are sufficient; but if they be small, twelve of them are sufficient." Kings, it seems, ate more. A chieftain entertaining King Cathal MacFinguine had, amongst other things, to provide a bushel of apples to take the edge off the king's appetite.

Left *An ancient beehive hut on the Dingle peninsula, County Kerry.*

The Brehon Laws

Irish laws, religious rituals, genealogy and heroic tales were passed down by oral transmission through Druids, lawyers, poets and musicians in prodigious feats of Celtic memory. The Brehon Laws, ancient Irish law texts, were written down about 1.200 years ago but were taken from a much earlier period. Brehon law comes from the Irish word *breithearnh*, meaning 'a judge', and is the term used for the system of law in use in Gaelic Ireland. The Brehon Laws continued as the rules of conduct for the Irish living outside the English-governed area of The Pale until the late 16th century. They covered every aspect of life from land values and ownership, feasting and farming practices to food lists and their value as tribute.

Land was the property of the *derbhfhine* – all descended from the same great-grandfather. Each member of a king's *derbhfhine* was eligible to succeed him if elected by the freemen of the *tuath* (tribe). Each tribal king was bound by personal loyalty to a superior king who, in turn, was subject to a provincial king. In return for a stipend the lower-ranking kings had to render tribute: hostages, slaves, calves, sheep, pigs, salted meat, white meats, grains, malt and herbs. Virtually everyone was a client of someone; even an independent farmer had to render food rent to his chieftain. The food rents the king received from his clients allowed him to fulfil his duties to provide regular "mead feasts" to those of similar status, and a wild garlic feast at Easter. Clients were obliged to feast their lord along with others appropriate to his status.

Fostering and food

Links between *derbhfhine* were strengthened by fostering. Some children were sent into fosterage aged one and stayed until they were old enough to marry: 14 for a girl and 17 for a boy. They were educated for their place in life and, although foster parents cared for them like a member of their own family, by law the foods they were given reflected their place in a highly stratified society. This demonstrates that some foods had a higher status than others:

> *The children of the inferior grade are fed to a bare sufficiency on stirabout made of oatmeal on buttermilk or water, and it is taken with stale butter. The sons of chieftain grades are fed to satiety on stirabout made of barley meal upon new milk taken with fresh butter. The sons of kings are fed upon stirabout made of wheaten meal upon new milk taken with honey.*

The laws covered everything, even grazing-trespass of domestic animals: a farmer whose cows strayed had to

Left *Brian Boru, the High King of Ireland, at the Battle of Clontarf, Dublin in AD1034.*

***Right** Reconstruction of a Viking house and boat at the Irish National Heritage Park, Ferrycarrig, County Wexford.*

hand over a bushel of wheat and a milch cow for every 24 hours the trespass continued. Stranger still, until you take account of the importance of honey, bees came under the law. If a bee stung a passer-by who was not interfering with the bees in any way the beekeeper had to provide the victim with a meal of honey.

Cattle raids

Laws or not, the Celtic joy in cattle raiding and faction-fighting between tribes continued. Monasteries were raided in the same way as farmsteads belonging to a tribe; food, livestock, treasures and people were carried off. When the raiders were another Irish tribe, the despoiled *tuath* had, in theory, recourse to the law. The threat of judicial sanctions involving loss of status or honour, such as the exclusion from ritual sacrifices, was often sufficient to control an offender, for a time.

Vikings in Ireland

The Vikings, however, were not inhibited by such threats. These fierce raiders began to threaten Ireland from the 8th century onwards. Many Vikings settled quickly, established bases (*longphorts*) along the eastern and southern coasts of Ireland, and had a great impact on the everyday life of the country. They were traders who plied the seas from Russia to the Mediterranean and were responsible for the introduction of many new foods into the country. They exported slaves, metalwork, wool, hides and skins from Ireland and imported plums and other fruits, wines, olive oil, herbs and spices.

Their initial settlements grew in size and developed into the first real urban settlements in the country. Dublin (*Dyflin* or *Dubh Linn*, Black Pool) was an immensely important Viking stronghold. The Vikings of Dublin paid a levy to the Irish King Brian Boru of 150 vats of wine a year and another commentator wrote of the abundance of wine in Ireland which was paid for by "the return to Poitou of hides of animals and skins of wild beasts".

***Below** A mount with twin head terminals, probably from a horse bridle. It was almost certainly the work of a Hiberno-Norse craftsman working in Viking Dublin during the 9th century AD.*

***Below** Ratoo round tower in Ballyduff, County Kerry.*

The Normans in Ireland

The Normans did not actually invade Ireland. Dermot McMurrough, the Irish king of Leinster, bribed the Norman Strongbow to come to his aid against rebellious chieftains by offering his daughter in marriage and the Province of Leinster as Strongbow's inheritance.

The English suffered more than the Irish from the Norman presence. In the Domesday Book there is no trace of the families who ruled England before 1066. In Ireland, however, leading Irish families' names were still prominent in society four hundred years later. The Normans intermarried with the Irish at the highest level, the cultures intermingled and, just as the Vikings had done before them, they became "more Irish than the Irish".

The Normans profoundly influenced agriculture and land tenure. The pre-Norman Irish farmed contentedly at subsistence levels; there was land enough for all if you counted wealth in cattle. Food was grown to feed the family and for agricultural by-products, mainly skins and hides, that were traded for more exotic items like wine, spices and olive oil. The Normans, from mainland Europe where agriculture was highly developed, counted wealth in acres of land held and valued ploughed land for the rich soil that grew corn crops for the markets of Europe where huge profits could be made. However, once farming depends upon cash crops it is in serious trouble if the market fails through wars or fluctuating demand caused by falling population in times of pestilence. After the Normans, Irish farming got into grave difficulties time and time again.

Agricultural change

To the Normans, Ireland must have seemed under-populated and under-exploited. Although few in number, they altered agricultural practice in the country, and many of the Irish chieftains were happy to change because they recognized the wealth the changes might bring. The Normans settled in the richer agricultural lands of the eastern part of the island. Within a continually shifting line they built their fortified farms and enclosed land in a manner unknown in the country.

They introduced the open-field system and three-crop rotation. The feudal system of land tenure was enforced within the Norman sphere of influence. Irish kings and chieftains were displaced and their lands granted to tenants who supported the feudal lord. Some of these tenant farmers were foreigners but numbers of the old Irish tenant farmer class (*biatach*) stayed put. The day-to-day life of ordinary people changed little at first: instead of food "tributes" to their chieftain they paid food "rents" to their new master. If you were already of the old Irish "unfree class" (Irish euphemism for "slave") you became a feudal serf.

Above *A 14th-century effigy of the Norman knight Thomas de Cantwell at Kilfane Church, County Kilkenny.*

New animals are introduced

Norman settlement coincided with a rising European population and with warmer, drier weather favouring crops of wheat to feed a growing market and the supply of wool to clothe it. Sheep were important to the Normans:

Left *Trim Castle, County Meath, in the province of Leinster, one of the places where the Normans set up markets.*

Above left *Sheep were an important flock to the Normans for providing wool, meat and milk.*
Above right *A Norman Tower house at Dunguaire, Kinvara, County Galway.*

manuring arable land, and supplying wool for export, milk for cheese (for winter food) and meat.

As well as greatly increasing the sheep flock, the Normans brought many other animals and plants to Ireland. They brought freshwater (coarse) fish to breed in ponds, rabbits to breed in great warrens, doves to breed in dovecotes, the common hare to "course" (hunt with dogs) and the fallow deer to supplement the dwindling stocks of the native red. Peas and beans, and flax for linen were more widely grown. Markets were also established in towns.

Like the later Tudors, the Normans were passionate about hunting – hawking for game birds, coursing hare, or hunting deer and wild boar. The Irish had hunted and trapped for thousands of years but there is little evidence to suggest that they saw it as "sport". The Irishman's belief that "a dinner is only an excuse for one" if it does not contain a "plate of mate" appears to date from the Norman period.

In the Middle Ages the climate became wetter and colder, making good wheat hard to grow. The Black Death decimated the population of Continental Europe, and Britain and Irish urban centres. By the time of the Tudor plantations there were already two distinct Irelands: the well-kept, farmed lands of The Pale (much diminished from its early boundaries) and "beyond The Pale". This included large areas of undrained bog, lakes, mountains and secondary woods of "the mere Irish". It was land fit only for the old Irish way of farming (which the Tudors despised) called *creaghting*, where whole communities moved constantly, raiding and drifting from the protection of one lord to another.

Right *The Normans introduced fallow deer to Ireland. This herd is grazing in Phoenix Park, Dublin.*

Domestication of the pig

Neolithic farmers introduced the domestic pig to Ireland. In Celtic times a visitor recorded that pigs were allowed to run wild and were noted for their height, pugnacity and swiftness. They were fertile too: a Celtic pig was expected to rear a litter of nine piglets in the first year. Some were paid as food rent and others kept for home consumption. A prosperous farmer was expected to keep two breeding sows and have a bronze cauldron large enough to boil a boar, which was always served at feasts. Protocol demanded that the King receive the leg and his queen the haunch, and that the head of the boar go to the charioteer.

Above *A painting of a traditional thatched cottage with domestic pigs, c.1925, County Donegal.*

Acorns

In native tree lists, placed in order of importance, the oak comes top, followed by the hazel. Records show that the mast (the yield of acorns) from a single oak was enough to fatten a pig. Just how important this annual harvest was can be seen from a description of the great plain of Macha in the sagas: "and no mast was ever like its mast for size and fragrance. When the wind would blow over it the odour thereof would be smelt throughout Erin, to what point soever the wind would carry the scent, so that it was a heartbreak to the swine of Ireland when it reached them."

Pig meat, whether fresh (pork) or salted (bacon), was the favourite meat of the native Irish. The earliest sagas, the ancient laws, the monastic rules, even the granting by the Normans to their tenants of rights of pannage (grazing of the woods) for their pigs, all attest to the centrality of the pig in the Irish diet.

Cattle and sheep were kept for *bánbhianna* like milk and butter and for other products such as hides and wool, but from ancient times the pig was kept for meat only. Domesticated pigs, long-snouted, lean and muscular, were crucial to the farming economy. In time, when the great woods were long gone, it was the domestic pig's ability to survive on roots and scraps that ensured the continued availability of pork and bacon from the family pig, the only meat ordinary Irish people had to eat.

Left *An Empire Marketing Board poster dated 1929 promoting pig meat produced in the Irish Free State.*

The pig round

Before slaughter, a pig was fattened on mashed corn and milk. Some of the meat was eaten fresh, but most was salted, or cured and smoked at home. It was often shared in a "pig round" with neighbours – particularly the parts unsuitable for preservation. In 1600 the divisions made were described: the head, tongue and feet to the "smith, the neck to the butcher [the man who killed the beast], 2 small ribs that go with the hindquarters to the tailor, the kidneys to the physician, the udder to the harper, the liver to the carpenter and the sweetbreads to her that is with child". Children delivered the parcels and were rewarded with the bladder to make a football.

Every bit of the pig is still used in Irish cooking. Then, the fillets, called "pork steaks", were eaten fresh along with the heart, liver, brain, sweetbreads and stomach; the head was garnered for the cheeks (a delicacy), the ears, (pickled, then cooked) and the tongue, and the rest used after cooking to make brawn (sometimes called the head cheese); the trotters or *crúibíns*; the griskins, ribs and kidneys for stews; the blood made black puddings (blood sausages). White puddings, a peculiarly Irish delicacy, used up the scraps, mixing them with grains, onion and spices. The hams were treated separately for curing.

The flitches (loins) were cured as bacon, usually by rubbing with salt, sugar and saltpetre over two weeks, and then dried and (usually) smoked over a mixture of juniper berries, turf and oak chips. Hung from the rafters, they kept for months. An enthusiastic reference in the food poem "The Vision of MacConglinne" refers to the "rich juicy lard of a well fed choice boar".

Unlike France, Spain or Italy, the damp Irish climate was not suitable for the air-drying of sausages or hams and the Irish passion for bacon meant that as much as possible of the carcass was cured. We know, however, that sausages were made in early Christian times because two fascinating types are referred to in "The Vision of MacConglinne": *maróc* and *indrechtán*. They are intriguing simply because we have no way of knowing what they contained or how they were made.

***Above** After a period of intensive rearing of pigs, organic farming methods are being reintroduced around Ireland.*

***Left** Pigs' trotters, or* crúibíns, *are still eaten and are considered a delicacy in many parts of Ireland.*

The potato

It is not recorded in history how the potato reached Ireland, and it was slow to establish as a crop. Tradition has it that Sir Walter Raleigh, who had Irish estates near Youghal, brought it back from South America and introduced it to Ireland. This is probably unfounded. What we know is that towards the end of the 17th century it had already afforded relief when the grain harvest failed. In the early 18th century there were famines caused by the failure of the oat crop, and during many following winters any potatoes that were stored above the ground were destroyed by freezing. In 1770 a cultivar was found that stored well in damp conditions and this was the key to the potato's establishment as the staple food of the Irish poor.

Other historical factors played a part. By the 16th century, the Normans had gone native. Europe was divided by religion and the English control of Ireland was placed in Protestant hands. The old English colonizers were replaced by the "new English". This involved a massive transfer of lands, known in Ireland as "plantation". The ensuing wars ended in English victory, and the native Irish and most of the "old English" lost their lands.

The "planters" came to Ireland to make money. For a century or so most of the land was under pasture, rearing huge herds of sheep and cattle for export. But, following decades of war in Europe and the collapse of European agriculture towards the end of the 18th century, an enormous market for Irish grain opened up. In the south-east of Ireland a vast acreage was put to tillage, providing work for labourers who were given small patches of land. The "mere Irish" were reduced to smallholdings on poor land. Most of their produce went in rent. The potato became the staple food of these labourers.

Now the potato, with milk, some vegetables and some occasional meat or fish, provides a relatively healthy diet. Some historians believe this caused an increase in health and fertility. In a century (1741–1841) the population of the island increased from three million to eight million people. In good years the crop lasted a family eleven months. July was the time of want. Those with means bought oats or barley; those without lived on wild herbage like nettles and charlock which, taken as an only food, turned their complexions yellow – July became known as "the yellow month".

Above *A 19th-century illustration of* Solanum tuberosum, *the potato.*

After the battle of Waterloo in 1815 the markets for Irish grain contracted rapidly. Landlords reverted to production of sheep and cattle. Demand for labour lessened, forcing wages down. Peasant workers, unable to pay rent, saw their holdings and the grazing for their cow become smaller and smaller. Eventually, cut off from milk and any income from butter and pigs, they were forced to rely more and more upon the potato. In 1834 William Cobbett, the English journalist and agricultural reformer, spoke bluntly about the danger. He did not consider the potato a fit food for a working man. But potatoes, in the Irish climate, yielded nine tons an acre, enough to feed six adult men for a year.

Left *Potatoes are still one of the main cultivated vegetable crops in southern and Northern Ireland and fields of potatoes can be seen all over the countryside, such as those here in Trassy Road, Mournes, County Down.*

Famines

Potato blight, in the days before anti-fungal sprays and resistant varieties, resulted in crop failure and frequent famines. Cobbett spoke with passion of Irish people starving while vast quantities of cash crops were exported:

> *Hundreds of thousands of living hogs; thousands upon thousands of sheep and oxen alive; thousands upon thousands of barrels of beef, pork and butter, thousands upon thousands of sides of bacon and thousands upon thousands of hams; ship loads and boat loads coming daily and hourly from Ireland ... we beheld this while famine raged in Ireland amongst the raisers of this very food.*

And this was before the Great Famine of 1845–9. Then, coastal communities fared much better than those living inland. They ate shellfish, seaweed and the inshore shoaling fish. Inland lakes teemed with fish but the poor lacked the means to build boats and were prosecuted by landowners enforcing savage game laws. A poacher of hares or rabbits, if caught, faced seven years transportation to the colonies.

It is difficult today to imagine how the countryside looked just before the Great Famine of 1845–9. Outside the great estates the countryside had been stripped of anything that might be burnt as fuel. Endless potato ridges stretched as far as the eye could see.

Yet the Irish have never abandoned their love of the potato. It was in the years following the famines that the development of distinctive Irish potato dishes happened. 100 years later, with the population reduced to less than four million, Patrick Kavanagh, the Irish poet, could still describe the potato fields of his County Monaghan as a thing of beauty:

> *The flocks of green potato-stalks*
> *were blossom spread for sudden*
> *flight, The Kerr's Pinks in a*
> *frivelled blue, The Arran Banners*
> *wearing white.*

Above *Local vegetables, champ, butter and potatoes have been staple food for the Irish as shown in this Irish farmhouse kitchen.*

Left *S.J. Donoghue's cabin at Ardcara – the whole family, pigs and all, are grouped together by the fire during the potato famine. By an unnamed artist in the* Pictorial Times, *7 February 1846.*

Landowners and farmers

Once Ireland had been "planted", it divided into two societies, by culture, legal system, language and religion. There were landowners with large estates, and the rest included "strong farmers", some tenant farmers (albeit with little tenure), many people on tiny smallholdings, labourers and craftsmen.

Two distinct food cultures emerged. Behind demesne walls in "the big house" landowners, well supplied with meat, game and fish, grew fruit and vegetables in walled kitchen gardens. The big house had cooking-ranges, bakehouses, storerooms and the wherewithal to store stocks of food.

In marked contrast, the vast majority lived in small thatched cottages and cabins and, by and large, ate only the food they could grow on a tiny patch of land and cook in one pot over a turf fire set in an open hearth wide enough for smoking meat and fish. The rich diversity of native Irish food culture withered slowly, but the recipes for simple dishes survived through word of mouth and the tradition of hospitality. An unexpected guest would be invited to "take pot luck".

Strong farmers bred animals and arable crops (and their wives and daughters reared poultry); they sold these for profit at seasonal markets and fairs, allowing them to purchase expensive imported spices, dried fruits and tea leaves. It was the wives of the strong farmers who developed many of the rich breads and baking traditions that the Irish take for granted today. Although traditional baking is on the plain side, the subtle variations in flavour and texture make it a tradition to be proud of when you take into consideration the limited range of equipment and ingredients.

Above *Muckross House in Killarney, County Kerry. The elegantly furnished rooms portray the lifestyles of the landed gentry, while downstairs in the basement one can experience the working conditions of the servants employed in the house.*

Left *Old cottages set in farmland at Malin Head on the Inishowen peninsula in County Donegal.*

Basic cooking equipment

The three-legged iron pot was central to the food of the common people. Suspended from the "crane" (an upright pivot with an extending arm) two or three pots could be raised or lowered over the turf fire in the hearth. The bastable (an iron pot with a lid, handles and three short legs) was used for baking bread, tarts and cakes. The bread dough was set into the pot and the lid heaped with glowing turf embers giving even heat top and bottom. The lec (a bake stone) or a lan (a flat griddle with two lugs for lifting) could be set on a trivet or hung from the crane and used to cook potato cakes, scones and griddle breads. Hard, dry oatcakes were baked on a wooden or metal stand, which was simply set in front of the fire.

Huge iron frying pans were used for pancakes and cooking rashers (strips of bacon), eggs, and fish. A "muller" was a small pot with a long handle for heating drinks, such as mulled ale, or a hot punch made from *poitín* or whiskey. Strong farmers with access to regular joints of meat had a roasting spit: a 1.2m/4ft iron bar with a crank at one end for turning.

The poor had to be content with a small amount of pig meat, fish or seaweed, or a poached rabbit boiled with "pot-herbs" (root vegetables) as a relish for potatoes. Boiled in a large pot, potatoes were drained and tipped into a skib (osier basket) to allow moisture to escape. In the "big house", delicately worked silver rings, lined with a linen napkin, were used for the same purpose.

Given the cooking equipment and limited foods available to the poor, their ingenuity was admirable. They invented scores of potato recipes and used tiny amounts of fresh or preserved meat and seafood to add savour to one-pot stews and soups. They also added relish to oats and potatoes with wild foods.

Below *Cooking oatcakes on a griddle in an old Irish farmhouse kitchen with basic cooking equipment.*

Changing cuisine

There was some crossover between the different traditions. Strong farmers sent their daughters into service in the big house to learn fine cooking skills and enhance their marriage prospects, since the wealthier landowners employed classically trained cooks.

Landowners and strong farmers occasionally, at "high seasons" such as Christmas, Michaelmas or some other feast day, gave a gift of corned (salted) beef to their tenants. Emigrants, in particular those who went to America, took this tradition with them and created the myth that corned beef was a food of "feasting".

Industry developed belatedly, work became available in the cities, and country people brought their cooking traditions into urban areas. At the turn of the 20th century, before they might have been lost forever, pioneers like Florence Irwin travelled through Ulster learning traditional recipes from country women. Irwin published them in her famous book *The Cookin' Woman*. Later, Theodora FitzGibbon researched in southern Ireland, delving into the handwritten receipt books of the big houses. The work of these and later pioneers awakened new interest in both the food of the ordinary people and Irish country-house cooking, classic in technique but, nonetheless, essentially Irish.

Feasts and festivals

The Irish have a long tradition of celebrating festivals – mainly influenced by the seasonal Celtic pagan rituals and Christian feast days. Most festivals involve food and drink of some variety and there is always singing, dancing and playing musical instruments.

Imbolc

Originally, *Imbolc,* the first day of spring, was associated with the Celtic earth goddess, Brigit, a "mother goddess". The Christian church then transformed her into St Brigid and gave her a mythical past. Like the goddess she replaced, Brigid was given the patronage of cattle, the dairy, and food.

Traditionally at *Imbolc*, presents of freshly churned butter and buttermilk were made to the poor. The festive meal was *sowans* (fermented oat gruel), dumplings, apple cake, cider cake, colcannon and barm brack. A *Brídeóg* (an effigy fashioned from a churn dash – the wooden pole with a wider head inverted through the lid of the churn – and dressed in women's clothing) was carried from house to house by young people wearing ferocious masks. They made a collection for "the Biddy" – the anglicized name of the *Brídeóg*. Today there is no festival for *Imbolc*; it is simply the first day of spring.

Shrove Tuesday

A Christian festival, Shrove Tuesday was the day before Ash Wednesday, the start of the six-week Lenten fast, which forbade the eating of meat, milk, butter, eggs and sugar. Pancakes were cooked to use up these foods, preventing temptation during Lent. Shrove Tuesday is now commonly known as Pancake Day, when pancakes are traditionally served with butter, lemon, sugar or honey. However, chefs now produce ever more exotic fillings.

Left *The Celtic earth goddess, Brigit, a "mother goddess", who was given the patronage of cattle, the dairy and food.*

St Patrick's Day

The Lenten fast was set aside for St Patrick's Day, Ireland's national holiday – a day for feasting on fresh pig meat and strong drink, the *pota Pádraig* (Paddy's pot), to "drown the shamrock". The shamrock, worn as a symbol of the Trinity, was placed in the last of many such pots and, after a toast, plucked from the glass and thrown over the left shoulder for luck.

Easter

On Easter Eve, to mark the end of the Lenten fast, the Whipping of the Herring was performed by butchers' boys. Herrings were whipped with sticks, then thrown in a river, and a young beribboned lamb decorated with flowers was carried in procession to the market place. Easter replaced the Celtic celebration of fertility, so decorating and eating eggs became traditional.

Left *A postcard showing a patriotic Irishwoman on St Patrick's Day, 1916.*

Right *Dressed up as St Patrick at a parade to celebrate the saint's day of celebration on 17 March in Dublin.*

Nowadays young children are given chocolate eggs as a symbol that the fasting is over. Spring lamb is now eaten at Easter, but veal and goat kid were once equally popular. The poor received gifts of corned (salted) beef.

Echoes of fertility rituals lingered in the Cake Dance, where a cake of barm brack (decorated with birds, animals and fishes) provided by an ale-wife was set on top of a 3m/10ft high pike. Courting couples danced around it wildly until exhausted; the last couple still dancing "took the cake" and divided it up amongst them all.

Bealtaine

May Eve, or *Bealtaine*, is the start of summer when traditionally the cattle were sent to the *buaile* (booley) hill pasture. *Bealtaine* was untouched by Christianity but rich in pagan customs to guard against evil intended by the *Síóge* (malevolent fairies).

Most customs concerned cattle and their *bánbhianna*, to ensure they would survive until harvest time. Even during the 19th century, farmers drove cattle between two fires to protect them from disease. Cattle were also driven into abandoned raths and ring forts; they were bled, some of the blood was drunk, and the rest poured on the earth as a libation. Nothing was loaned or gifted on May Day lest luck "go with it". Stirabout, or hasty pudding (sweet milk thickened with flour), was prepared to show that winter supplies had held out.

Midsummer

Originally Midsummer was an ancient festival associated with the Summer solstice. Small, family fires were lit to appease the fire god, and their smoke, drifting over the crops, was believed to protect the plants from blight and rust. Cattle driven though the smoke were protected from natural ailments or magical influence. Big communal bonfires accompanied merrymaking, eating and drinking (*poitín* and beer) and food was contributed by all who could spare it.

The Twelfth of July

Of more recent origin are celebrations in Ulster commemorating King William of Orange's victory against James II at The Battle of the Boyne in 1690. At marches held by lodges of the Orange Order, spectators eat strawberries straight from the punnet. In the evening, participants have a drink or two to inspire singing and music at the great bonfires.

Lughnasa

A major Celtic festival, *Lughnasa* is now held on the first Sunday of August. Originally great assemblies and offerings were made to the god *Lug* to thank him for the first wild fruits of the summer harvest. The pagan practice of climbing hills to gather *fraughans* (wild blueberries or bilberries) became a day of feasting, courting and fairs. The people feasted on meat, the first of the potato crop with summer butter, then followed this with *fraughans*, wild strawberries and raspberries with cream. Unmarried girls made garlands using wheat to honour the goddess Ceres, and baked *fraughans* into cakes eaten at the bonfire dance that night.

The day is known by many names, which highlight its various aspects and traditions: Height, Garland or Fraughan Sunday and, in Northern Ireland, Lammas (an anglicization). This is the only surviving memory of an *óenach* (an ancient assembly) at which there would be a fair, chariot racing and games of strength.

An Auld Lammas Fair is held annually in Ballycastle, County Antrim during the last week of August, where the traditional treat is "yellowman", a sticky toffee pulled with the hands to produce a honeycomb texture.

Above *Vendors selling yellowman and dillisk at an Auld Lammas Fair in County Antrim.*

Puck Fair

Held annually in August, this three-day festival takes place in Killorglin, County Kerry. On Gathering Day stalls are opened to sell food and drink and booths are opened for trade and barter. On this first day a large billy goat is decorated with ribbons and paraded through the streets. The goat is crowned "King of the Fair" and placed on a three-storey platform in the middle of town. The second day of the fair features a livestock show. Travelling people and farmers sell and trade horses, donkeys, wagons and carts. On the evening of the third day, King Puck is led out of town by a piper to the accompaniment of traditional Irish music. This signifies the end of the fair.

Michaelmas

The goose harvest, Michaelmas, dates back to Norman times when, within The Pale, 29 September was one of two annual rent days. Geese born in spring were ready for killing and some of the flock would be paid as rent. "Green geese", young birds under six months, were considered a delicacy because they were lean and less fatty (most geese were not killed until they had grazed on the remains of the grain harvest). Michaelmas coincided with the apple harvest, so cider was brewed for the feast. Goose, sometimes par-boiled to render the fat, was stuffed with potato, onions, celery, bacon, sage and apples and roasted in a bastable oven. In County Cavan it was covered with blue marl clay and put into the fire to bake.

Harvest Home

In grain-growing areas, a harvest supper (harvest home) was held for the farm labourers. Potato dishes such as boxty were served with meat, cabbage and home-brewed beer.

Samhain (Hallowe'en)

Samhain marked the end of the Celtic year. Herds were gathered in and animals not to be kept for breeding were killed. Many were feasted upon, but most were preserved by salting, or cured by smoking. A sacrifice to the gods gained good fortune for the following year and care was taken not to anger the Celtic gods; the Irish people took care to appease the *Sióge*. In mythological literature this was a time when barriers between the natural world and "the otherworld" were removed and mortals encountered fairies. Despite Christian efforts to make it a day for praying for all souls, *Samhain* remained essentially pagan.

Right up to the middle of the 20th century the main dish was *banb samna* (the piglet of *Samhain*) and until quite recent times country people left out food for dead ancestors and to ward off fairies, especially the *púca* (Shakespeare's Puck). No wild fruits were gathered after Hallowe'en because the *púca* was believed to spit and urinate on them.

Divination customs were performed which are echoed by the charms still placed in dishes eaten at Hallowe'en: apples, roasted nuts, Hallowe'en pudding, fadge (potato apple cake), boxty pancakes, and the other two dishes that are eaten to this day – colcannon (potatoes and curly kale mashed with butter) and barm brack. In any of these traditional dishes, finding a ring meant marriage before the spring, a dried pea meant spinsterhood, a bean offered riches, a rag poverty, and a matchstick meant your husband would beat you!

Martinmas (11 November)

The Martinmas feast was supposedly established in gratitude to St Martin, who is credited with conferring the monk's habit and tonsure on his

Left *Musicians playing at the Puck Fair in Killorglin, County Kerry. The fair is one of Ireland's oldest and is held on 10–12 August every year.*

Above *Eating oysters and drinking a glass of Guinness at the Galway oyster festival held annually in September.*

nephew, St Patrick, Ireland's patron saint. In honour of his uncle, Patrick killed a pig for every monk and nun in Ireland. (It seems, though, that the pig was only offered to the monks in his monastery.) Martinmas was traditionally one of four days in the year when a pig was killed. This made agricultural sense, as six- to eight-month-old pigs, well fattened by harvest gleanings, were ready for slaughter and curing by November.

Midwinter (Christmas and St Stephen's Day)

Although a Christian festival, its 12 days relate directly to pagan traditions associated with the Midwinter solstice and the turn of the year. The Celtic celebration of the return of the dead was therefore replaced by a celebration of the birth of Christ.

Preparations begin in November. Rich puddings (using beef suet, mixed dried fruit, stout and/or whiskey), and whiskey-fed fruit cakes are made and matured. Christmas dinner begins with smoked fish, followed by roasted stuffed goose (now, it is more commonly turkey) and boiled, or baked, ham. Christmas pudding with whipped cream is followed by "mince" (suet and mixed dried fruit) pies.

Spiced beef is traditionally served on St Stephen's Day, when "wren boys" in fantastical costumes play Hunt the Wren. They go round the locality singing and prancing on hobby-horses. Food is offered to the boys and money is collected to pay for a "hooley" (a party) in a local hostelry; this is still done in the south-west.

New Year (Scottish Hogmanay) has few traditions in southern Ireland but, in Dublin, church bells ring, foghorns hoot, and people "see the New Year in" at a party.

Nollaig na mBan (6 January)

Women's Christmas – *Nollaig na mBan* – is still celebrated in rural areas, especially in the south and west, with a dainty feast of scones, cream, preserves, gingerbread, iced sponge cakes and tea (rather than strong drink).

Other festivals

Two less ancient, but well established, festivals are the The Wexford Strawberry Festival which is held out of doors in June when the renowned, intensely flavoured, locally grown strawberres are at their best, and the Galway Oyster Festival, held to celebrate the start of the native oyster season (they are harvested only when there is an 'r' in the name of the month). The latter takes up a whole week in September. Huge marquees are thronged with visitors from all over the world. There are oyster eating competitions and vast quantities of raw oysters are consumed, washed down with the traditional accompaniment – a glass of Guinness stout.

Below *Traditional dishes are still popular and are often served at special occasions. From left to right, Michaelmas goose with apple stuffing, Colcannon and Spiced beef.*

Irish farmhouse cheesemaking

Once an essential element of the Irish "white meats" food culture, economic policies during the 16th and 17th centuries gradually forced the decline of traditional cheesemaking. Despite extensive grasslands and dairy herds, cheesemaking was practised less and less during the 18th century, and by the early 19th century an agricultural writer could state "cheese is not an article of Irish produce; it is brought to the table of the affluent as an indulgence". The early 20th century saw dairy co-operatives (which made excellent butter for export) revive cheesemaking; but what they made was, in the main, factory-produced generic Cheddar.

The revival of handcrafted cheesemaking began on smallholdings in the 1960s. Families, many seeking "the good life" in peaceful rural Ireland, wished to use up surplus milk from their animals. A few wanted to make more interesting cheeses than were then available; they were joined by families who had farmed the same land for many generations but were seeking viable alternative farm enterprises to supplement mainstream income in difficult times. The 1970s also saw an influx of young people from Continental Europe who bought smallholdings in Ireland; and, missing their native cheeses, some of them made their own.

Modern Irish handcrafted farmhouse cheesemaking began in earnest on the isolated Beara Peninsula of west Cork in the 1970s, when Veronica Steele began using surplus milk from her husband's few cows to make cheese. Today, her great cheese, Milleens, is revered as the cheese that created the modern Irish cheesemaking revival. There are now about 65 farmhouse cheeses made all over the island – all are unique.

The formation of CÁIS (the Irish Farmhouse Cheesemaker's Association – the word for cheese in Irish is *cáis*) by some of the early cheesemakers allowed networking, and very quickly they evolved from enthusiastic amateurs to professionals. In doing so, they began to enter their cheeses in international competitions. The astonishing success of their cheeses in those competitions won them the respect of the international food community – chefs, retailers and distributors across the world – who marvelled at the distinctive personality of each cheese.

One farm, one cheese

European neighbours, with an unbroken cheesemaking tradition, find it hard to believe that in Ireland each

Below *A selection of Irish farmhouse cheeses including Milleens, Durrus, Cratloe Hills, Gubbeen and Lavistown.*

Left A worker checking a vat of curds and whey, during the production of Gubbeen cheese.

cheese is unique to its producer, made on only one farm, the result of the passion and dedication of one farm family. The concept of a named regional cheese (like Camembert, or Parmesan) made on many farms within a given area is unknown in Ireland. Irish cheesemakers came fresh to the craft. Most of them knew little about the old traditions, none tried to reproduce a lost cheese; history had given them the freedom to be innovative. Terroir, grass and natural herbage, and the personality of the cheesemaker, came together to astound visiting cheese lovers. New cheesemakers embrace diversity and endeavour to develop a cheese that stands out because it is different.

What makes Irish cheese so flavoursome?

Irish cheeses have a common secret ingredient – the exceptional quality of the milk. Travellers through the countryside quickly realize that grass is Ireland's principal crop. The land on which it grows is extremely rich, the natural herbage varied, and it is well watered all year. The temperate climate allows herds to spend spring, summer and autumn at pasture; even while housed for the short winter they are fed natural grass fodder. Whether you desire a cheese made from cow's, sheep's or goat's milk, whether you prefer a soft, a semi-soft, or a hard cheese, whether you seek mild, fresh cheeses, or pungent, matured, washed-rind cheeses, or blue cheeses, or smoked cheeses, you will, today, find an Irish farmhouse cheese to your taste.

Many Irish people buy their cheeses at farmers' markets. They buy them by name, a little of this and a little of that. Although Irish supermarkets now stock farmhouse cheeses, in the early days they showed little interest. However, leading chefs and speciality food stores in Ireland and abroad did. Irish farmhouse cheeses are now sold in over 20 countries. Traceability is crucial. In Ireland, traceability is not to a region but to a family; their farm and the townland hill or valley in which the herds, which provide the milk, graze: Cratloe Hills, Gabriel, Durrus, Ardrahan, Gubbeen. Farm cheesemaking in Ireland has, without doubt, a good future. Thirty years on, the parents who began it all are already passing on their skills and knowledge to their children who will continue to make the family cheese on the family farm.

Below Gubbeen cheese maturing in a stone room at Gubbeen House on the south-west tip of Ireland.

Artisan food producers

Traditionally, Ireland always exported vast amounts of food. Most of it was live animals, sheep, cattle and pigs (even elderly horses to France and Belgium), as well as corned (salted) beef and pork. Vast numbers of fish and shellfish caught in the rich fishing grounds surrounding the island were also sold abroad. This export trade continued even during the great potato famines of the mid-19th century, while people died of starvation in the country.

Until relatively recent times little value was added, in the main, to most exported foods. Whiskey went to Scotland for blending, and stout (Guinness) and beer were manufactured for the UK market. During World War I and after, large amounts of factory-made Cheddar-type cheese and then creamery butter began to be sold into the UK market. Factory production of "traditional" products for export was increased enormously and these were marketed using the genuine concept of Ireland as a green, unpolluted food island, but this resulted in the steady loss of the skills and the handmade quality of many of these products (particularly ham, bacon and other smoked foods). Traditional skills became increasingly discounted, even endangered.

The economic boom of the 1980s to the early 2000s caused an explosion of fine-dining restaurants run by chef-patrons. Instinctively, these chefs, in a typically "Irish" manner, began to develop a "modern Irish cuisine" by seeking out genuine handmade, traditional products – many of them now to be obtained only from artisan food producers.

Above *An attractive display of freshly caught fish and seafood, including Dublin Bay prawns.*

Left *Specialist butcher's shops in the city of Limerick.*

Speciality food producers

Recent years have seen real growth in the number of small businesses producing speciality foods. Small food producers have seen their sales increase rapidly in line with increasing consumer demand for the variety and pleasure which authentic speciality foods offer. Speciality foods are usually defined by exclusive or limited distribution through independent fine food stores, delicatessens, food halls and local farmers' markets.

Many of these products started out when someone had a desire to save traditional artisan production skills and

products, others are innovative, many are organic. Most of these small producers espouse the principals of the international Slow Food Movement whose goal is to spread and stimulate awareness of food culture, flavours and ancient techniques, to safeguard the food and agricultural heritage (biodiversity and artisanal techniques), to protect the heritage of traditional eating places, and resist the worldwide standardization of tastes.

A dedicated arm of Bord Bia (the Irish Food Board) now markets Irish-made speciality foods. It enables many small producers to market their products more widely at home and to export them for sale in fine food outlets abroad.

Markets

Farmers' and small producer markets are now held weekly, fortnightly or monthly throughout the island, from Temple Bar in central Dublin to the furthermost extremities of rural Ireland. Not all the speciality producers go to

Right *Harvesting apples in a small orchard in County Armagh.*

Left *Shopping for fish, fruit, meat and vegetables in the covered English market, Cork City.*

all markets but most regularly attend the markets in their local area. Some have invested heavily in Continental-style refrigerated trailers, which open out into retail stores on site. You will find many interesting and fine speciality products, including farmhouse cheeses, stunning smoked products, traditional handcrafted meat products, organically grown meats and meat products, pre-prepared foods, organically grown fruit and vegetables, breads, oatcakes, cakes and biscuits (cookies).

Handmade chocolates

There are now about a dozen or so Irish firms making chocolates for the home and export markets. Some are relatively long established and others are recent arrivals, but all make distinctive, mostly handmade, rich dark chocolates, often with fillings based on Irish whiskey, and other traditional flavourings.

Apple juices and ciders

Although there is a large international cider-making industry in Ireland, there are also a number of smaller apple growers, based in apple-growing areas, such as in Counties Armagh, Carlow and Kilkenny, who use their own organically grown apples to make superb fresh apple juices and ciders, and even a distilled apple brandy.

Mustards and preserves

This is now a thriving sector with many fine specialist producers supplying the home market and a growing export market. Look out in particular for coarse-grained mustards (some of them whiskey-flavoured) and traditional fruit-based chutneys. Fostered by regional competitions held by The Irish Country-women's Association, there was a strong home-based tradition of jam and preserve making using locally grown, or gathered, fruits and berries. This tradition has now developed into a thriving artisan-based industry with some companies exporting their goods.

The new Irish cuisine

The development of modern Irish cooking coincided with the startling economic growth and the creation of the so-called Celtic Tiger economic boom that took place over the 1980s and 90s.

For generations, Irish chefs trained in Ireland in the classical tradition, then went abroad to complete their training and broaden their experience. When they returned, as surely as the settlers and invaders of earlier times, they brought back foreign culinary influences and new ideas and flavours.

The process continues to this day; the youngest generation of chefs often do a stint in the New World and Australasia. The result has been the creation of a contemporary Irish cuisine that is, at its best, unique.

Above *The award-winning* Chapter One *restaurant in Dublin. The chef and owner, Ross Lewis, is the Commissioner General of Euro-toques and a successful advocate of modern Irish cooking.*

The Irish style of cooking

Fortunately, the thrust of modern Irish cooking is less towards fusion food and more towards allowing a natural mingling of traditional Irish food culture with an innovative approach to the cooking and presentation of long-established foods. The finest Irish chefs now combine classic and international techniques and influences with local produce. What has emerged is a lighter modern style, but one still firmly based on Irish foods and themes.

The style is best illustrated by describing some signature dishes offered by top chefs: roast loin of bacon with a clove and Irish Mist jus, served on a bed of braised cabbage leaves and potato cake; rack of lamb with a whiskey marmalade crust, leek confit and caramelized kumquat jus; a gratin of crayfish and asparagus with a tomato and avocado salsa; bacon and frisée salad with Parmesan crisp and a poached egg; a seafood tapas plate of Dublin Bay prawns (jumbo shrimp), ceviche of John Dory, (bell) peppers stuffed with brandade of salt ling and crab claws, each with its own sauce or dressing; grilled (broiled) monkfish with boxty potatoes and a saffron and langoustine sauce.

Starting in many chef-owned restaurants (which are not confined to cities but found in every corner of the country) this style of cooking was encouraged by the growth of the

Left *The lakeside* Wineport Lodge *in Glasson, County Westmeath – the rooms are named after wine 'regions'.*

Left *Enniscoe, a Georgian heritage house, on the shores of Lough Conn, Mayo, offers superb country cooking.*

tourist industry, the expectations of discerning visitors and the increasing number of Irish people who could afford to eat out regularly.

That contemporary cooking has trickled down into home cooking is the result of a fruitful interaction between leading chefs such as Myrtle Allen (who built the reputation of Ballymaloe Country House with her daughter-in-law Darina Allen) and her fellow members of the Irish Food Writers' Guild, who write widely about these new ways with traditional foods. In families that enjoy cooking, you will encounter dishes cooked in the classic way and, sometimes at the same meal, a traditional food given a modern spin.

Euro-toques

Another factor has been the number of Irish chefs who are members of Euro-toques, the European Community of Cooks. There are over 200 enthusiastic members in Ireland, from Michelin-starred restaurants, country house hotels, farm guesthouses, restaurants in cities and in the depths of the country – even some bars serving pub-grub. Euro-toques believes that diversity is the future of food production and members are encouraged to avoid the danger of fashionable but bland internationalism and to maintain a real flavour of Ireland.

Their charter commits them to supporting the quality of natural foods, maintaining classic dishes, the ways of preparation, and regional differences. They take the nurturing of young talent seriously, selecting and coaching Ireland's representatives at international chefs' competitions, such as the Bocuse d'Or, but they are not elitist: all chefs are invited to join providing they follow the code of honour and use fine-quality, non-genetically modified foods and support local craft and artisan food producers. In an era when handcrafted foods produced using time-honoured methods were seriously threatened by large-scale factory production, the support of Euro-toques, in buying these products and reawakening in consumers an appreciation of and interest in real food, has been crucial to artisan and craft food producers.

Right *A signature dish by the chef Kevin Dundon of the Dunbrody Country House Hotel, County Wexford.*

Identifying local food

The Irish highly value quality, locally produced foods. They like to know where their food comes from. Increasingly, the name of a product, producer or locality in which the food was produced will be incorporated into the menu description of a dish. The celebration of local food, be it a style of black pudding (blood sausage), lamb bred on an upland area that lends a particular flavour, beef from a local farmer, dry-cured bacon from a butcher or fruit from a local grower, has led to more interaction between chefs, artisan food producers and consumers and has been of great value in the development of contemporary Irish cuisine.

The Irish kitchen

"Let the food be fresh and the drink be aged."

The Irish are opinionated about food and they have a tradition of great hospitality. They prefer things cooked simply, be it meat, fish or dairy produce. They favour fresh food, in its natural season, and they like to know how it reached the table – who reared it and who killed it, and who grew it or made it.

Wild harvest

The Irish love walking and often roam the countryside at weekends. As they walk, many of them still forage. Foraging is a seasonal activity. Traditionally, St Brigid's Day (1 February), the first day of spring, was when foraging began. Nowadays, three plants are harvested during February and March: the stinging nettle (*neanntóga*), the dandelion (*caisearbhán*) and *praiseach* (charlock), a wild cabbage. These are noted for their cleansing, purgative properties. Nettle soup, made on a potato base, is still a favourite in country homes and often appears on menus of fine-dining restaurants. A late-spring treasure is the common morel mushroom (*Morchella vulgaris*).

Above *Wild garlic, or ramsoms, growing under the trees in Killarney, County Kerry.*

Summer harvest

In May the broad, tender, spear-like leaves of wild garlic (*Allium ursinum*), which the Irish call ramsoms, carpet damp woodland floors, especially in County Wicklow. Traditionally used fresh in salads, the puréed leaves today can be preserved in olive oil to add a pungent, unique flavour as a plate dressing or decoration for strong meats and fish, as a pesto-type sauce for pasta or in salad dressings.

Carrageen is the seaweed most used for flavouring and for thickening soups and desserts, such as puddings. *Dillisk* or dulse was an important flavouring for potato dishes; it is now also used to flavour cheese and bread. *Sloke* (laver) was served as a vegetable with lamb and used to flavour oatcakes. Samphire and seakale (*Crambe maritime*) are still eaten as vegetables.

Green leaf summer salads were always important in the diet; the fields and hedgerows supplied dandelion, sorrel, wild garlic, watercress, cowslips, wild thyme and marjoram, mint and lavender (these last four were dried for winter use) and any other green leaf that presented itself was used.

Autumn riches

The richest harvest still arrives in autumn: the hedgerow fruits, the hazelnut and walnut, wild field mushrooms and other fungi. The *fraughan* (wild blueberry) arrives first. Traditionally collected on Fraughan Sunday, the first Sunday of August, its fruits were used for pies, sauces, jams, preserves and jellies and for flavouring *poitín* (an illegal spirit drink distilled from barley and potatoes) and other spirits, such as whiskey and gin. Purple elderberries are still widely used for jam- and wine-making. The great harvest for home liqueur-making is the sloe (*áirne*), the bitter fruit of the blackthorn tree and a relative of the wild plum. Sloe gin liqueur is still made in Irish homes.

Left Dillisk *or dulse is often served with potato dishes.*

Right *Blanched seakale.*

Left to right Irish sloes, hazelnuts and rowan berries.

Wild strawberries are harvested for eating but also to flavour spirits; vodka is still flavoured with them today. Blackberries (brambles) are often eaten fresh and cooked in tarts, but mainly preserved in jams and jellies, or combined with sour crab apples that provide the pectin to set the jelly. The abundant red berries of the rowan tree are jellied to make the favourite traditional accompaniment to venison. Rosehips, which are rich in vitamin C, are often gathered to make a valuable health-giving syrup.

Below left *Blackberries or brambles grow wild in the late summer.*
Below right *A selection of freshly picked mushrooms.*

The Irish were never dedicated gatherers of mushrooms and fungi. However, they did dry the field (portobello) mushroom when they found a group and made a ketchup by salting mushrooms in layers, then pouring off the liquor. There is a revival of interest in fungi, and tutored mushroom hunts produce harvests of ceps, chanterelles, *trompettes des morts*, parasols, milk caps, oysters, blewits, puffballs and beefsteaks.

Throughout history the hazelnut was the most important annual wild crop. The hazel tree still grows in vast groves, particularly in the west, such as in the Burren, County Clare, and the harvest for home use is enormous and widespread. The Irish always knew how to dry and preserve the nuts and even today the sweet milky kernel is a standard ingredient in wholemeal breads, cakes, puddings, ice creams and farmhouse cheeses.

Honey

Irish honey, gathered wild, was a natural sweetener for drinks, and is still an essential ingredient in Irish cooking. It is now produced mainly by many small beekeepers who sell to local delicatessen and health food shops. The local herbage and flora give their honey its distinctive flavour.

Vegetables, herbs and fruits

Above *Cabbage is the second largest vegetable crop in Ireland.*

The Irish have no great tradition of vegetable cookery, but vegetables and potatoes were important in their diet. A limited range of species thrives outdoors: the potato, onion, leek, carrot, parsnip, cabbage, Brussels sprout, cauliflower, swede (rutabaga) – known in Ireland as turnip – and beetroot (beet). Vegetables were usually plain boiled and dressed with butter.

Even today vegetables are most often served as a mixed side dish. Traditional soups and stews depend upon a high vegetable and herb content but this (and the tradition of one-pot cooking) encouraged the cooking of vegetables for too long. Modern transport allows out-of-season vegetables to be imported from many parts of the world, but the Irish still eagerly await the arrival of home-grown new season's potatoes and field vegetables.

Organic vegetable growing in Ireland is increasing. Growers, countrywide, supply local towns using several ways: wholesale markets, growers' markets, health food shops, farm gate selling and weekly box-delivery systems. Many chefs now source organic vegetables locally.

Below *Potatoes and carrots are two of the most commonly eaten vegetables.*

As well as accompanying main dishes, vegetables are used in soups, in first courses, as garnishes for entrées, as vegetarian dishes, and in many savoury dishes. Carrot, onion, celery, leek, parsnip, swede, with fresh parsley, thyme, garlic and bay leaf, are known in Ireland as "pot-herbs" – a basic ingredient in many stews and soups, and as "the bed" that absorbs juices when roasting red meats.

Potato Apart from "first earlys" such as Homeguard or Ulster Sceptre, the Irish prefer floury potatoes, such as Maris Piper, Golden Wonder and Kerr's Pink. They eat them in huge quantities, boiled or steamed "in their skins" (jackets) (removed at table on a side plate) and dressed with butter. Potatoes are also mashed with milk (or cream) and butter, with added herbs or other mashed vegetables. Traditional dishes like boxty, colcannon, poundies, champ, stampy, potato cakes, breads and potato pastry are popular, and in some restaurants they can contain surprising additions.

Cabbage Eaten all year round, cabbage is the largest horticultural crop grown in Ireland after potatoes. Most types are cultivated: white, green and red (when stewed with apple, red cabbage is a favourite accompaniment for goose and venison). The Irish prefer pointed-hearted, fresh, soft green-leafed types. Cabbage can be eaten raw, boiled, steamed and stir-fried.

Carrot Irish-grown carrots are available from June until April. Young pencil-thin ones are eaten raw or boiled until just tender, then buttered and sprinkled with fresh parsley.

Onion, leek and spring onion (scallions) The Irish adore onions, and they are also an essential cleansing, health-promoting, element in their diet. They can be eaten raw in salads, fried in butter, boiled in milk, roasted (sometimes with a cheese topping) or chargrilled.

No Irish person regards beefsteak as correctly presented without a serving of butter-fried onion. Leek is often used with fish in the same way as onion with meat. Spring onions (scallions) are used to flavour traditional potato dishes such as champ or colcannon, and in salads.

Celery An essential pot-herb, celery is eaten raw (as crudités), braised (especially the hearts *au gratin*), with cheese or as an ingredient in a soup.

Parsnip A sweetener for stews and soups, young parsnips are also eaten blanched or plain roasted. Older ones are boiled, mashed, creamed and often mixed with mashed carrots or turnips. They also make a delicious spiced soup.

Swede Known as turnips, the firmer textured, less bitter-tasting swede (rutabaga) is preferred to the white turnip. It is usually served as a mash (with cream and chives) or par-boiled then fried in bacon fat.

Below Sun-ripened gooseberries.

Cauliflower and broccoli These popular vegetables can be cooked in similar ways. Favourite dishes are the classic *au gratin* and a soup incorporating cheese and cream.

Globe artichoke and Jerusalem artichoke The globe artichoke flourishes in the warmth of the south-west and its hearts are greatly appreciated. The Jerusalem artichoke grows easily in Ireland and is used for a popular soup and often added to potato mashes. It has a special affinity with game meats.

Fresh herbs Parsley, thyme, chives, basil, sage and mint still remain the most widely used fresh herbs in Irish home cooking, but almost all herbs are commercially grown and readily available and used. Leaves of tansy, a common weed, were once an essential ingredient in black puddings (blood sausage) but are now rarely used in this way except by artisan speciality producers.

Fresh fruits Apples are an important crop for cider-making, home eating and cooking. The Bramley, fluffy in texture, is generally preferred for cooking. Pears are no longer a commercial crop but are still available locally. Wexford strawberries are seasonal, luscious, eagerly awaited and sold by growers from stalls at the side of main roads throughout the summer. They are eaten fresh with cream (sometimes whipped) and a sprinkling of sugar.

Left Raspberries – deep red fruits, with a wonderfully intense flavour.

Gooseberries, named because they "cut" the fat taste of goose, are used to make sauces and chutneys that "break" fat-rich and fatty-tasting foods like pork, goose, mackerel and fresh herring. Rhubarb is also used in this way as well as in tarts, crumbles and pies.

Raspberries, strawberries, loganberries, blackberries, tayberries, blueberries, fraughans (bilberries), red and blackcurrants, and rhubarb are commercial crops, eaten fresh and now used by artisan producers to make jams, compotes and sauces. Contemporary breakfasts increasingly go for healthy options and these compotes are eaten with natural yogurt or porridge, or spread on freshly baked home-made bread and scones. Sauces for desserts feature fresh fruit as an alternative to cream.

Below Home-made fruit compote.

Fish and shellfish

There was a long period when the Irish displayed an ambivalent attitude to fish. From the arrival of Christianity 1,600 years ago until very recently, the lengthy fasts of Lent and Advent and the many other "fast days" (including Friday every week) meant the majority of the population was obliged to abstain from eating meat and dairy foods for a good part of the year. Consequently fish became associated in the minds of the ordinary people with denial and penitence.

Above *Atlantic salmon has fatty, deep pink flesh with a superb, rich flavour.*

Fasting was a harsh regime for the common people who lived inland without access to fresh fish. During the period when potatoes were the dominant food, the consumption of fish, mainly salt herrings and ling, was reduced in poor homes to tiny quantities, used in much the same way as seaweed – as a relish to add flavour to potatoes or oatmeal.

The long Christian fasts are no longer widely observed and over the past 30 years the bounty of the sea has once again regained its place as a prized, if increasingly expensive, everyday food.

The seas around Ireland are rich and heavily fished, some say overfished, by fleets from many other countries. Not all the fish caught are landed in Ireland but many are eagerly bought for immediate export to the capitals of Europe. In the better Irish restaurants, some specializing in fish, there is usually a fish "special of the day" – outside Dublin this usually means that it has been caught locally and landed in the last 24 hours.

Non-migratory freshwater fish, such as pike, perch, carp and bream, are not native to Ireland and were, in the main, introduced by the Normans. Known as "coarse" fish they are not really rated by the Irish and nowadays are rarely eaten. They do, however, provide enormous tourist revenue from the large numbers of anglers from England and Europe who come to fish Ireland's lakes, canals and rivers.

Migratory fish, such as salmon, white (sea) trout and eels are highly prized. When an Irishman asks an angler if he has caught "a fish" he does not mean any fish, he means a salmon – a usage found in written sources as far back as early in the 10th century.

Left *Salmon fishing in beautiful Lough Inagh, Connemara, County Galway.*

Fish cooking

On the whole, Irish people prefer their fish simply cooked. In restaurants, it tends to be served with classic (mainly

Left *Fly fishing is enjoyed throughout Ireland's huge number of rivers.*

French) sauces. Shellfish, such as crab, lobster, crayfish and Dublin Bay prawns (jumbo shrimp) are usually treated with greater imagination by many chefs. Fishcakes, fish pâtés, terrines and galantines feature widely on restaurant menus and will often be served with spicy international-style jams and salsas.

There is no great tradition of fish soups, but one, universally known as seafood chowder, is widely available and much enjoyed in pubs at lunchtime. There is no standard recipe, but a good one can be truly sublime and may contain everything from white fish and salmon to shellfish, prawns (shrimp), crab claw, mussels, clams, scallops or scallop corals, and even tiny rings of baby squid and matchsticks of crisp bacon.

Freshwater fish

Salmon (*bradán*) Fresh salmon appears on the menu of almost every Irish wedding, restaurant and party. It is usually poached whole with butter, white wine or cider and herbs, such as dill or fennel leaves. If served cold, the skin is often replaced by overlapping, paper-thin slices of cucumber. Whole, cooked farmed salmon is available in supermarkets. Most restaurants will serve salmon steaks (darns), sometimes briefly marinated, then pan-seared.

Buttered baby new potatoes with watercress or wilted baby spinach leaves with a wine and cream-based sauce are a classic accompaniment.

Sea (white) trout (*breac geal*) Because of its increasing scarcity, this migratory trout is currently even more highly prized than the salmon. It is rarely seen on restaurant menus – any angler lucky enough to catch one will bear it home in triumph! Sea trout is always cooked whole with dill, just lightly poached.

Brown (river) trout (*breac*) There is no better breakfast or supper than one or two of these freshly caught, small fish. Simply gut them, dust in seasoned flour and pan-fry whole in butter for a quick meal. Pink-fleshed fillets of farmed rainbow trout are widely available.

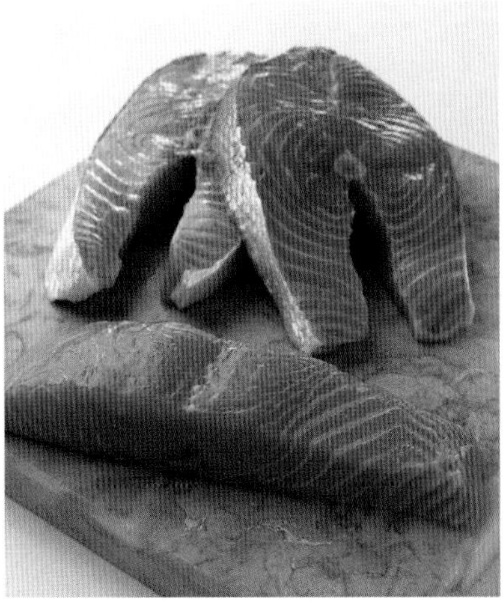

Above *Fillets and steaks are one of the most popular ways of cooking salmon. Both types are perfect for making light and colourful Irish dishes.*

Below *Brown (river) trout and rainbow trout are delicious when simply pan-fried with a spoonful of butter.*

are less expensive and the latter is probably the fish eaten most regularly in Irish homes. Much of the haddock catch is smoked.
Sea bass (*bas*) Although sea bass is now rare in the wild, farmed bass are imported and feature widely on restaurant menus.

Less common fish

Tusk (*torsca*), John Dory (*deorai*), red gurnard, red and grey mullet, and orange roughy are more regularly available than they used to be, as cod becomes scarcer and more expensive.

Left *Fishing boats at Dingle Harbour, County Kerry.* ***Below, from top*** *Turbot flesh is creamy white in colour with a firm, dense texture. Monkfish tails are sweet and taste similar to lobster.*

Oil-rich and cartilaginous sea fish

Mackerel (*ronnach*) An Irish favourite, sold whole or filleted. Usually pan-fried fresh and served with a gooseberry sauce. Increasingly whole fillets are now hot-smoked by artisan producers.
Herring (*scadán*) The Irish do everything to the herring that their northern European neighbours do. Traditionally, fresh fillets are coated in crushed oatmeal and pan-fried in butter. Many are kippered (cured and smoked).
Tuna (*tuinnín*) Albacore and bluefin tuna cut into thick "steaks" are pan-seared and served with a sauce.
Ray (*roc*) Ray wings are a great Irish favourite (even in takeaway meals); they are most often simply seasoned, floured, pan-fried and served with a nutty black butter or caper sauce.

Flat white sea fish

Turbot (*turbard*) and black sole (*sól*) are the Irish favourites; but brill (*broit*), megrim (*scoilteán*), white sole (*leathóg bhán*), lemon sole (*leathóg mhín*) and plaice or flounder (*leathóg ballach*) are all popular; the last two are frequently offered for breakfast. They are usually cooked in butter, and (depending on the size) offered whole on the bone or filleted, and served with a herb- or lemon-based sauce.

White sea fish

Monkfish (*láimhineach*) Popular and widely available, meaty monkfish tail fillets are simply cooked and served with a sauce.
Hake (*colmóir*) A great favourite with Irish chefs, hake is expensive because most of the catch is exported to the rest of Europe.
Cod (*trosc*) Because of overfishing, cod is now a seriously endangered species. However, other dryer-fleshed members of the cod family, such as pollack (*mangach*), coley (*glasán*) and mora (*trosc domhainmhara*) are less favoured. Haddock (*cadóg*) and whiting (*faoitín*)

Left, below and right *Dublin Bay prawns or scampi, scallops and mussels.*

Shellfish

The Irish eat any shellfish that comes their way with great enjoyment: clams, winkles, whelks, cockles, limpets, sea urchins, crabs, mussels, oysters, squid, Dublin Bay prawns (jumbo shrimp), crayfish, lobsters and scallops. Many of these are exported in very large quantities to the capitals of Europe with the result that most of them are now expensive luxury foods in Ireland. There is a traditional lobster dish called The Dublin Lawyer, and the joke is that "you'd need to be a lawyer to afford lobster"! This traditional Irish dish is lightly boiled to kill the lobster, then flavoured in a cream sauce and flamed in whiskey.

Molluscs

Even though they are exported in vast quantities, the mussel and the oyster are probably the most enjoyed and plentiful shellfish today, as they were in the past. Mussels and the non-native Pacific oyster are now extensively cultivated. Mussels are enjoyed everywhere, cooked in the shell in an unthickened white wine, cream and garlic "broth", sprinkled with parsley and eaten with wholemeal (whole-wheat) brown soda bread and butter.

Oysters are mostly eaten raw, usually from the shell, with just a squeeze of lemon, or maybe a splash of Tabasco sauce, and traditionally accompanied by a pint of stout. The opening of the native oyster season (September to April) is celebrated annually in Galway. Thousands of oysters are consumed, and countless pints downed during one riotous week. The farmed Pacific oyster is available almost all year round.

Scallops are a great favourite and appear on almost every restaurant menu. The corals, once removed, are now prized, and this delicately flavoured muscle is usually just flash-fried or briefly poached and served with a wide variety of sauces.

Dublin Bay prawn

The Dublin Bay prawn (jumbo shrimp) is not unique to Dublin Bay at all. It is usually fished in the Irish Sea and is actually a widely distributed species (*Nephrops norvegicus*) known as the Norway lobster, or langoustine. Most restaurants serve them as a first course, cooked in the shell (or removed from the shell and coated in breadcrumbs) with a tasty chilli jam or other fusion-style accompaniments.

Right *There are over 100 different varieties of oyster worldwide, but the Irish Galway oyster is one of the finest.*

Smoked and cured foods

The Irish tradition of smoking food, like that of many northern European countries, was dictated by the damp, humid climate which makes air-drying of fish, even small ones, difficult and meat all but impossible. In woodlands, plenty of oak and beech grew, and these were burned to smoke foods.

Since the 14th century, Ireland has exported vast quantities of pickled salmon, herrings and corned (salted) beef. The need to salt-cure foods grew out of the need to preserve shoaling summer fish like herring and mackerel, and grass-fed animals which were usually killed at the beginning of winter.

In pre-Norman times salt was most likely produced by burning seaweed and boiling up the resulting ash with water. The Brehon Laws refer to using *murláith* (sea ash) for salt. There are references from the 12th century to *salann Saxanach* (English salt) so it is probable that salt was imported into Ireland after the arrival of the Normans.

Need has turned into love and, from ancient times to this day, the Irish have salt-cured or smoked almost anything. There is now a global market for Irish premium products from companies such as Belvelly Smokehouse, Woodcock Smokery and Burren Smokehouse.

***Above** Smoked salmon and Irish brown bread make a flavoursome traditional combination.*

Smoked fish

Smoked wild Atlantic salmon is the premium product. The cure is mild (about 3 per cent salt) and the fish is cold-smoked. There are many different smoking recipes, each closely guarded by the maker. Wild salmon is almost always sold as a whole side fillet, vacuum-packed rather than pre-sliced. To be sure of getting the genuine product and value for money (because it is more costly than farmed salmon) look for the words "Wild Irish" on the label (wild, without Irish, means Pacific).

"Irish Smoked Salmon" usually denotes farmed salmon, cheaper and more often sold pre-sliced. Farmed salmon can, however, be of very high quality, especially those certified as organic and farmed in cages far out to sea in the ocean where they develop a firm texture from swimming against the current.

***Left** Salmon being smoked in a traditional way.*

Left to right *Smoked mackerel fillets, smoked eel and kippers.*

Smoked salmon is commonly served with sliced lemon, ground black pepper and wholemeal (whole-wheat) bread and butter, as a light meal or first course, but it is also used as an ingredient in many dishes. Salmon is also cured as gravadlax, or hot-smoked and called "barbecued salmon".

Sea (white) trout (farmed off the west coast – no one would dream of smoking a wild one) are usually dry-salted then cold-smoked. Rainbow and, very occasionally, brown (river) trout are hot-smoked whole.

There are still extensive eel fisheries, particularly in Northern Ireland, and there is a large export trade to Europe of live eels. Eels processed in Ireland are gutted but not skinned, and smoked whole. They are expensive and eaten as part of a mixed smoked seafood platter. This will normally include mackerel, processed as fresh as possible, filleted then hot-smoked (therefore fully cooked); cold-smoked wild mussels (an artisan product); and thinly-sliced smoked salmon and eel. The platter is eaten simply, with wholemeal bread and butter and small, delicious garnishes (lemon or capers), or sauces which complement the fishes – creamed horseradish, gooseberry or even a delicate chilli jam.

Salted herrings were once the food of the poor and exported in vast quantities. Herrings were pickled or soused. To split, lightly salt, and then smoke a herring is to "kipper" it. Kippers are eaten for breakfast, just warmed in boiling water, or grilled (broiled), and served with or without a poached egg. Superb kippers (without dye) are available from artisan producers and are a pale copper colour. Other smoked seafoods include haddock, cod, tuna, sprats, albacore, oysters and scallops.

Ling, a member of the cod family, was once widely filleted, salted and dried. It is still available in the deep south of Ireland where it is soaked overnight to remove the salt before simmering in onion-flavoured milk.

Salted and smoked meats

Corned beef is the Irish name for salted beef. Brisket was the traditional cut, but the leaner silverside and topside are more popular today. It is cooked slowly in water with pot-herbs, stout such as Guinness or Beamish, or cider and traditionally eaten with cabbage.

Smoked bacon and ham (also eaten "pale" and unsmoked), are so popular that Irish stores always offer both. Craft butchers and artisan producers use wood for smoking: oak or beech or a mixture of the two. Such is the Irish love of smoked foods that in recent times artisan producers have expanded the range of meats they smoke. The list now includes lamb, pork, duck, chicken and speciality sausages.

Many Irish farmhouse cheesemakers offer a smoked cheese. One fine restaurant even smokes mushrooms in an in-house smokery.

Below *A tasty dish of corned beef, cabbage, potatoes and carrots is traditionally served on St Patrick's Day.*

Beef

In Brehon Law the standard unit of currency was the milch cow. This cow "should be docile, of attractive appearance and loving towards her calf. She should not be a gorer, a bellower, or a kicker, or have a misshapen udder. She should not be lame, blind in one eye, prone to break out of the cattle enclosure, or hostile towards the bull."

Kerry cattle

Such a cow could have been a Kerry. One of the oldest breeds in Europe, the Kerry is now thought to be derived from the little black Celtic shorthorn cow, which was dominant in Ireland until the end of the 18th century. Kerry cows are hardy, growing a good coat of hair when out-wintered and they are easy calving. Their milk is light to digest, having small globules of butterfat, and it is most suitable for cheese and yogurt production.

It has been argued that *Bos longifrons* or *brachyceros* was the original Celtic breed of cattle, imported from Asia via continental Europe in the late Stone Age. These animals were supposedly even smaller than the present-day small Kerry breed, which may be their successor. Although the Kerry is no longer a significant commercial breed in Ireland, its survival as a genetic resource of native stock is widely recognized and it allows breeders to respond to changing consumer demand.

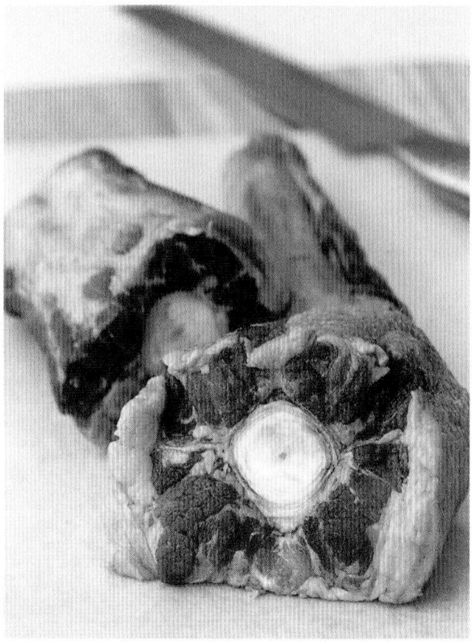

Above *Oxtail is excellent in stews.*

Herds of Kerry cows can be seen grazing within the vast National Park in County Kerry and also at the official state guesthouse at Farmleigh in the Phoenix Park in central Dublin (said to be the largest city park in Europe). Farmers involved in the European environmental scheme (REPS) receive a payment whenever they register a female Kerry cow.

Irish cattle breeds

The dairy industry in Ireland dictates that the main source of calves for beef production is from the national cow herd. Extensive exports of beef to markets with varying demands means that two broad types of beef cattle have emerged: lean, late-maturing beef bred from Continental sires (Charolais, Simmental, Limousin, Blonde d'Aquitaine) and early maturing beef, well-marbled with fat and much tastier, bred from Hereford, Angus and shorthorn sires.

The most prized pedigree beef breeds are Irish Hereford and Irish

Left *Cows grazing by Kilmacduagh monastic site, near Gort, Galway.*

Left Cattle feeding on top of the magnificent coastal cliffs at Ballybunion, County Kerry.

Angus. The Hereford was introduced in 1775 and farmers quickly recognized the merit of using a Hereford sire on Holstein cattle. For the home market, 80 per cent of craft butcher kills are Hereford or Hereford crosses. The Irish, disliking the lean, dry meat of Continental breeds, appreciate the red, marbled beef of the Hereford. The same eating quality applies to the Angus, a breed that has undergone a revival since the 1960s.

Grass-fed beef, like Irish lamb, has great flavour. Historically, quantity mattered most, but now quality is paramount. The use of hormones has, therefore, been banned in Ireland for many years. Irish farmers now breed to meet the specified requirements of the top end of foreign markets.

How the Irish eat beef

For an Irishman dining out, a thick, juicy steak is the heart of a good dinner. No restaurant, no matter how creative or Michelin-starred its chef, would dare omit a plain simply cooked beefsteak (fillet, T-bone, or sirloin) from its menu. The Irish attitude to beef is very sensible – if the beef is good enough it needs no embellishment. In the home, the Irish eat beef (and other meats) two ways: slowly wet-cooked, or quickly dry-cooked.

Rib and sirloin roasts are served with a sauce of horseradish, slaked with cream to temper its fiery flavour. Steaks and home-made beefburgers are accompanied by pan-fried mushrooms and onions. Slow-cooked wet dishes include winter warmers, such as a stew of shin (shank) of beef simmered with stout and root vegetables. Oxtail stew and soup, steak and kidney puddings and pies, steak and oyster pie are popular. Ox tongue is delicious lightly brined, slow-cooked with pot-herbs, then skinned, rolled, pressed and eaten cold. New additions to the wet-cooked repertoire include slow-cooked minced (ground) meat sauces to eat with pasta, and lean strips of beef stir-fried Asian-style.

Right Rib and sirloin cuts of beef.

Goats and sheep

The sheep kept by early settlers in Ireland are thought to have been dark-fleeced antecedents of the Soay breed, still found on the Hebrides in Scotland, which provided wool by moulting. Goats may also have been common but goat remains can be difficult to distinguish from those of sheep. Wild goats still roam the Burren in County Clare and it is likely that goats rather than cows were the primary grazing animal of early farmers.

Curiously, although goat kid (the meat of young male goats) was traditionally the meat used to make the famous Irish stew, it fell from favour many years ago. Kid meat is now hardly ever eaten in Ireland even though there are some quite large herds kept and bred for milk and farmhouse cheesemaking. Significantly, there has been a quite recent development: the organic feeding of young male goats for supply to specialist restaurants.

Above *Goats resting on the Dingle peninsula, County Kerry.*

How the Irish eat lamb

The Irish love lamb. Mint, thyme and marjoram are the common herbs used to add flavour to everyday family meals, such as stews, chops, steaks, lamb-burgers and speciality sausages. It is becoming ever more highly regarded among those who place a high value on naturally reared meat that has a fine flavour because the animal has grazed on hill pastures. In restaurants, menus usually name the hills on which the lamb to be served has been reared. Preparation still remains simple. The most frequently featured dishes are slow-cooked lamb shanks or rump of lamb, and fast-cooked rack of lamb, often with a herb crust, served with intense sauces flavoured with red wine or port and redcurrants or other berries.

Specialized lamb production

Early lamb production is targeted at the Easter market when a roast of tender, pale-fleshed spring lamb is traditionally the festive meat. Spring lamb is normally about 100 days old and

Left *Herding sheep at Dunquin, Slea Head, Dingle peninsula, Kerry.*

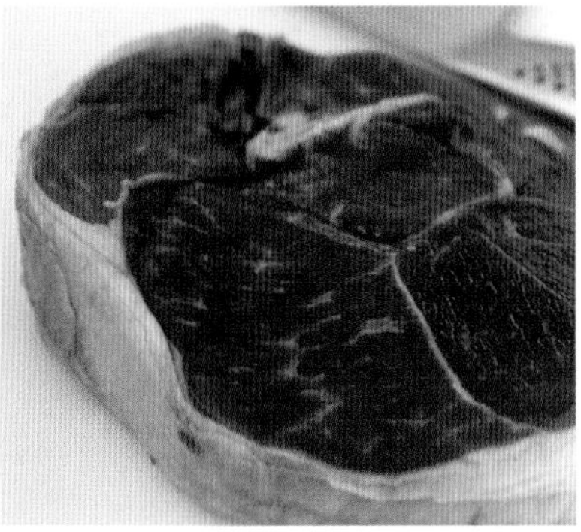

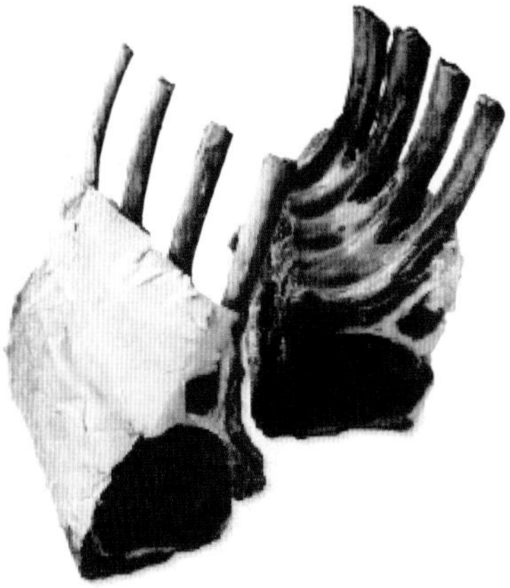

Far left *Lamb steak and* ***left*** *racks of lamb are two of the most popular cuts of lamb in Ireland.*

weighs about 18kg/40lb. The main product in Ireland is mid-season lamb, which fits in with seasonal grass growth.

Far more lamb is grown than the Irish can eat, and the Irish sheep industry is very much export-orientated with 75 per cent of lamb leaving the country. Although Ireland exports lamb to almost all EU countries, France is by far the main outlet. In 1998 Irish sheep meat exports totalled 58,000 tonnes (tons), of which 43,000 tonnes went to France, 5,000 tonnes to Germany and 4,500 tonnes to the UK.

Sheep farmers aim at the top end of the market and are becoming sophisticated at breeding, feeding and finishing lambs to the individual requirements of potential markets. In more recent years, market outlets have developed in Mediterranean countries for light lamb carcasses of 9–12.5kg/20–28lb, ideally with pale meat colour. These lambs are fed concentrates indoors for a period of six to seven weeks before killing to provide sufficient fat cover and to lighten the redness of the meat, which is rich red in grass-fed lambs.

Connemara mountain lamb

In Ireland, native and visitor alike seek out a particular speciality: Connemara mountain lamb. These animals graze an extensive but well-defined mountain area in the west of Ireland. In famine times (the mid-19th century) black-faced lambs from the Scottish border region were introduced to Connemara. A combination of higher terrain and higher rainfall than those in the region from which the breed originated meant that the animal that has evolved in the last 150 years is smaller and leaner than the original stock.

However, it is probably the variety of the local herbage and flora that makes the most difference and ensures the very special flavour of this mountain lamb. There is an amazing range of natural herbage. Walk on the wild side in the company of a western hill farmer and he will proudly call out scores of names of the plants that grow on his particular mountain.

Mountain lamb is a seasonal treat. The lambs are born in March and April and allowed to grow naturally and slowly. The first ones reach the market in August at about five months old; then the high season is September and October with some late-born arrivals killed as late as November. In the past, lambs surplus to local needs would have been brought down to the lowlands for fattening and finishing.

Today there is a growing realization that this meat is very special, and a number of craft butchers in Connemara and Galway specialize in supplying the demand for this seasonal treat. *Bord Bia* (The Irish Food Board) has now taken an interest and promotes it as a speciality food.

Right *Sheep grazing in the hills – Irish lamb is exported all over Europe.*

Pork

Once known as the "gentleman who paid the rent", pigs were as numerous as people. Traditionally done at home, pig rearing and production is now a combination of large-scale manufacturers (for both home and export markets), artisan producers and many craft butchers specializing in pork.

Pork, fresh and cured, could be eaten at every meal of the day. Breakfast, known as "the full Irish" in southern Ireland, and "an Ulster fry" in Northern Ireland, consists of rashers (strips of bacon), breakfast sausages, black (blood sausage) and white pudding, served with tomato, mushrooms, potato cakes and wholemeal (whole-wheat) soda bread. Ham, salamis, brawn and haslet feature in lunchtime sandwiches.
At dinner, pâtés, terrines and black pudding are served as first courses. Main dishes include chops, roasted loin leg and belly, boiled (and then baked) ham and bacon. Ham and bacon are used as ingredients to flavour salads, stuffings, mashed potato dishes and even bread.

Black and white pudding

The main ingredient of black pudding (blood sausage) is pig's blood mixed with diced back fat, onions, herbs and spices, and oatmeal or barley, and encased in intestines. It is then boiled for an hour. It can be served sliced, grilled (broiled) or fried, and as an ingredient or garnish in dishes from salads to stews and casseroles, and it is sometimes served with fish or shellfish.

Above *A pig in County Limerick.*

Left *Black and white pudding from Clonakilty, County Cork.*

Drisheen A unique blood pudding from County Cork, drisheen is locally made with a critical mixture of sheep and beef blood serum poured into intestines. It is grey in colour and moist, with a wobbly blancmange-like texture.
White pudding This is made with chopped off-cuts of pork and bacon and offal (innards). Though it has similar flavouring ingredients to black pudding, white pudding contains no blood.

Bacon, gammon and ham

The rear leg is removed from the side of pork for curing separately as ham. After brining, the rest of the side is divided into gammon (shoulder and collar joints) and back and belly bacon for rashers (strips). Traditionally both were dry-cured but since wet-curing by injecting brine into the meat was introduced in 1862, that method has been popular with bacon manufacturers. Traditional dry-cured bacon and ham are sought after by discerning consumers and are still available from craft butchers and small food producers. Each curer has his own secret refine-ments. The basic process is to rub regularly with salt (flavourings, such as sugar or juniper berries, may be used) to draw out moisture. Matured over a period of weeks, some is then smoked. During dry-curing bacon and ham lose weight and so this is more expensive. Traditional ham cures include Limerick (mild and moist) and Belfast (salty and dry). Most Irish bacon and ham is cooked before eating, but a few craft butchers now produce air-dried hams, similar to European hams, to eat raw.

Bacon and ham are widely used in Irish cooking as the main constituent of a dish and as a flavouring ingredient for soups, salads, vegetables and sauces.

The Irish breakfast sausage

A fine-textured fresh sausage, the Irish breakfast sausage contains about 65 per cent ground pork meat and fat, rusk or cereal and some water. Each producer has his own recipe for spicing and flavouring. The breakfast sausage is now a popular breakfast and snack food and an essential ingredient of Dublin Coddle, a popular stew made by simmering of bacon and sausage with potatoes, onions and parsley, eaten with soda bread and stout. Sausages were rarely made in the home because the solitary pig of the cottager class would not have provided enough intestine for casings after the black puddings had been made.

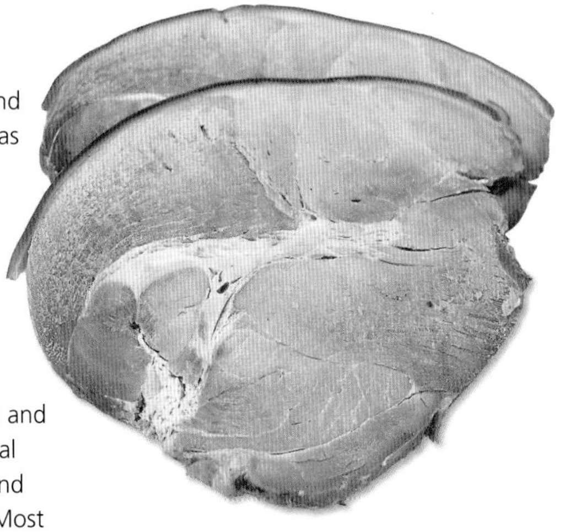

***Above** Slices of cooked Irish ham.*

Speciality sausages

Many craft pork butchers and artisan producers make speciality sausages for cooking at home. They use (singly or in combination) pork, lamb, beef, venison and other game, with combinations of herbs, seasonings and other ingredients, such as vegetables. Some are great, others perhaps are ill-conceived.

Brawn The old name for brawn was collared head, or head cheese. It is made from various boiled and cooked cuts of pork, pigs' cheeks, tongue and feet set in aspic.

Kidney A beloved delicacy, kidney is eaten grilled (broiled), often with a spicy devilled sauce.

Liver Pig's liver is mainly used in blood puddings and pâtés.

***Left** A typical Irish breakfast sausage.*
***Right** Kassler – smoked pork.*

Crubeen Once sold freshly cooked as a street food and associated with drinking sessions and wakes (funeral feasts), crubeen is the lightly brined foot of a pig. Eaten with the fingers, crubeens are favoured not for the meat, for there is little, but the rich gelatinous skin and fat. Having fallen from favour, they are now a popular food at stag parties. Chefs in fine-dining restaurants delight in putting a modern spin (and a high price) on this food of the people.

Bodices/spare ribs The traditional name for bacon or pickled pork ribs is bodices. Today they are more usually fresh pork ribs.

Haslet Haslet probably arrived in Ireland from Germany via the north of England. In Dublin this popular ready-to-eat, cooked "loaf" is now made from sausage meat (bulk sausage) and onion.

Kassler Brought to Ireland at the beginning of the 20th century by a number of German family pork butchers, Kassler, when made correctly, is highly regarded. It is made from prime cuts of pork, loin and fillet, lightly brined and briefly smoked.

Game

Unlike their European neighbours, the native Irish have rarely hunted animals "for sport"; they hunted for food. Most today are reluctant to kill any creature (except for food) that does not pose a threat to crops or livestock.

Game originally included river fish, shellfish, birds, deer, boar, wild (escaped domestic) cattle, sheep and goats, as well as wolves, badgers, foxes, wild cats, martens, otters, hares, rabbits and squirrels. The tradition of seasonal "huntin', shootin' and fishin' for game" within great estates (and the employment of gamekeepers) became part of mainly upper-class Irish life during the 18th and 19th centuries. Rigid gun-licensing laws enforced recently have now made it largely a tourist activity.

Norman kings declared game their private property. Surviving forest animals – red deer, roe deer, imported fallow deer and wild boar – became "beasts of the forest" reserved for hunting in enclosed, managed royal parklands. Their meat was "venison". The swan, extraordinarily, was a "bird of the forest" and therefore the king's venison. Great landowners were granted "warrens" with similar game rights on lands outside royal forests. Poachers were mutilated or executed when caught. Today only deer meat is called venison.

The practice of hanging or burying meat or game for many days so that partial corruption took place and tenderized the meat was disliked in Ireland, but this pratice was adopted later in the kitchens of some of the big Irish houses.

Above *Deer are often farmed for export.*

Left *In the 11th and 12th centuries, wild boar were imported into royal parklands and hunted for their meat.*

Venison

Wild deer – the native red, the introduced fallow and sika, and all their crossbreeds – roam Wicklow, Kerry and other highland areas. In some counties they have almost become a pest, as they invade kitchen gardens and damage commercial crops, and they are now regularly culled (but never red deer in the National Park in County Kerry). There are different open seasons for hunting stags and hinds. Stags may be hunted from September until February. Hinds may be hunted only between November and January.

The saddle and the rear haunch are usually marinated in red wine, oil and fresh herbs and root vegetables (pot-herbs) before being larded with pork

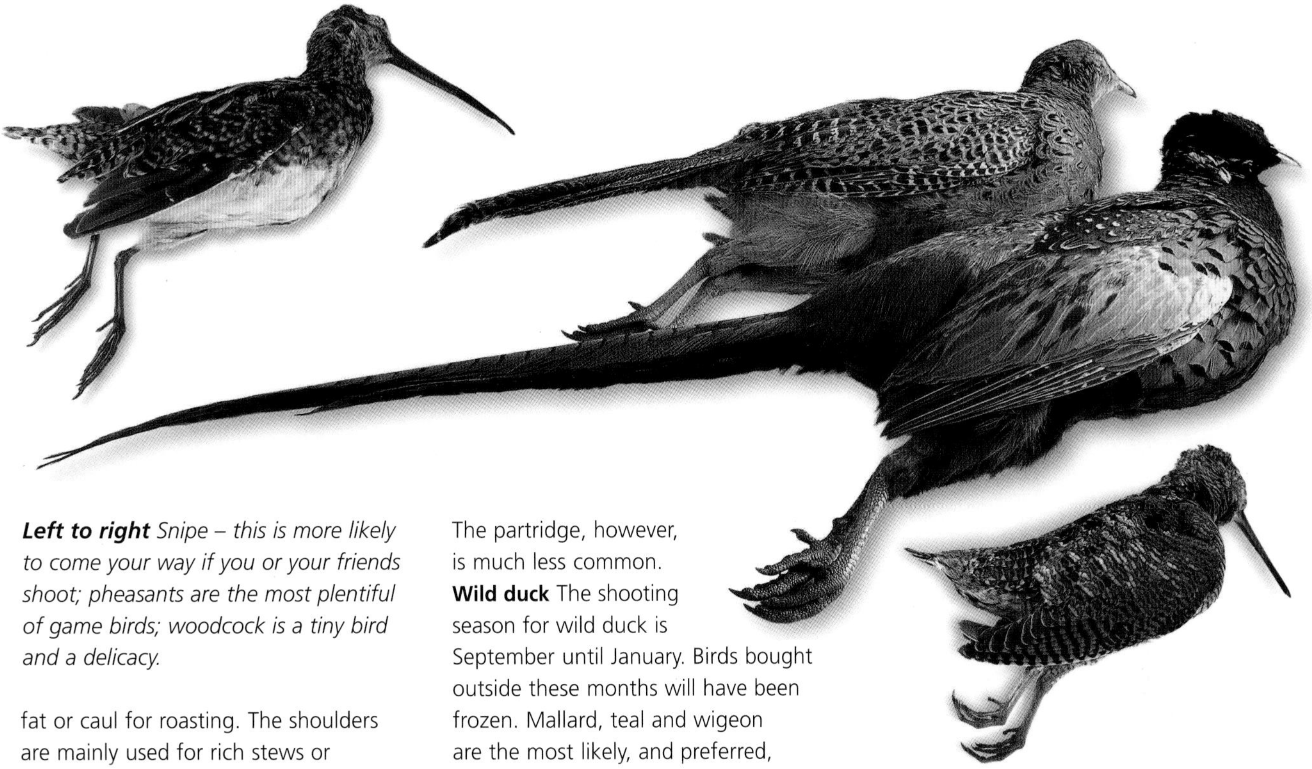

Left to right *Snipe – this is more likely to come your way if you or your friends shoot; pheasants are the most plentiful of game birds; woodcock is a tiny bird and a delicacy.*

fat or caul for roasting. The shoulders are mainly used for rich stews or casseroles, or ground for use in terrines or coarse pâtés and, increasingly, in speciality sausages.

Deer are also extensively farmed, largely for export (butchered young and tender), and farmed venison is available all year round in many Irish supermarkets, as steaks, chopped for stewing or in speciality sausages both fresh and smoked.

Game birds

Many game birds are available in Ireland from specialist butchers.

Woodcock and snipe The most valued and increasingly rare Irish game birds in restaurants. Available from November to January. If you see one, order it!

Red grouse Available fresh only in September, red grouse is now extremely rare in Ireland.

Cock pheasant and red-legged partridge Both pheasant and partridge are available fresh from November until January. Pheasant is the most commonly available game bird nowadays. Bought fresh it is used mainly in classic English recipes and as one ingredient in game pies, made particularly at Christmas. The partridge, however, is much less common.

Wild duck The shooting season for wild duck is September until January. Birds bought outside these months will have been frozen. Mallard, teal and wigeon are the most likely, and preferred, species offered.

Wild goose Restricted shooting seasons, "fishy-tasting" flesh and the need to treat it differently when cooking have removed wild goose (Canada and grey-lag) from most home and restaurant menus. However, it is still hunted and appreciated in some homes. The season is limited: the Canada goose may be shot from October until January, the grey-lag from 1 September to 15 October.

Wood pigeon Now a pest, farmers shoot wood pigeons every day of the year. Local supplies are always available. The official hunting season is June until January. Only the breasts are roasted; the legs are added to terrines, pâtés, game pies, stews, casseroles and the stockpot.

Rabbit and hare

Originally trapped, rabbits are now shot wild all year round but they are also farmed on a small scale. They are usually dusted in flour, lightly browned in butter or bacon fat, and then stewed gently in apple cider or a dry white wine, with fresh herbs and bacon-flavoured dumplings. Rabbit is an essential ingredient in game terrines and pies.

The hare is no longer as widely available as it once was. It was never trapped or shot but only hunted with dogs. There is a restricted hunting season from 26 September until the end of February.

Above *The hare is a timid and swift animal, less common than the rabbit.*

Farmyard fowl and eggs

For rural families the keeping of fowl was vital to the household economy. Hens, ducks, geese, turkeys, sometimes guinea fowl and less commonly pigeons were kept and bred. Their flesh provided meat for the Sunday dinner. Eggs provided a nourishing breakfast and were widely used for baking the ever popular cakes and tarts.

An industrious woman could earn a good deal of "egg money" selling her produce at markets or to local stores. Farmyard fowl and eggs were always "women's business" – no decent man would dream of taking a share of the profits. These were reserved for luxuries women craved: tea (once known as "China ale"), dried fruit and spices, cloth for a dress or ribbons for their hair. From an early age girls were taught to care for fowl, given a few chickens to rear and allowed to spend their own "egg money".

Goose From September to Christmas goose was the festive food served at wedding feasts and, during those three months, was a regular Sunday roast for wealthy families. Michaelmas Day, 29 September, was once a great feast day and also rent day for many and goose was the traditional dish. In medieval times goose was stuffed with herbs and fruit, boiled with dumplings and served with apple or garlic sauce. In later times it was roasted, stuffed with onions, bacon and potatoes.

There is no great industrial production of geese today, so geese produced by artisan producers are a luxury food, but they are making a come-back as the bird for a special festive occasion.

Left to right *Corn-fed, free-range and organic chickens.*

Turkey The turkey was known in Ireland as early as the 17th century. Only in the 20th century, however, did it become the bird of choice for "the Christmas dinner" and oust the goose as the farmyard bird most likely to generate a good income. This is curious because turkeys are difficult to rear and more prone to disease than geese. Farmhouse, free-range turkeys are highly prized at Christmas, but intensive (industrial) production means that turkey remains a plentiful, cheap and popular white meat.

Duck Traditionally, a duck was cooked with turnips, parsley and juniper berries, and apples were often made into a sauce to accompany it. A real farmyard duck is relatively rare now, although excellent ducks are sold by medium and small producers. Smoked duck has become a popular restaurant first course. Fresh duck, cooked so that the skin is crisp and served with a variety of fruity sauces, remains popular in the home. In restaurants the leg is often served as a slow-cooked confit; the breast usually gets brief but high-heat cooking so that it remains rare and juicy.

Left *Free-range chickens feeding in a farmhouse yard.*

__Left to right__ A goose egg is twice the size of a hen's egg and weighs about 200g/7oz; a duck egg is about the same size as a very large hen's egg. A hen's egg is most common, a bantam's egg slightly smaller and a quail's egg is the smallest.

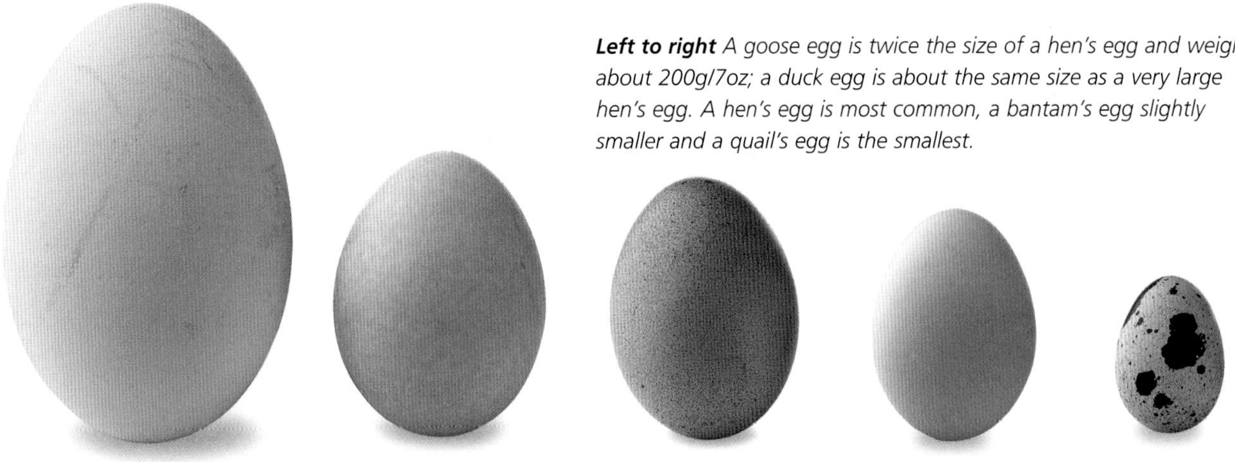

Chicken The Irish were relatively conservative when using chicken, content with a Sunday roast of stuffed chicken accompanied by boiled bacon and served with a bread sauce. Older hens, with their laying days behind them, used to be stewed with root vegetables or made into pies, but that was in the days when chickens ranged freely about the farmyard, fed on a variety of foods, grew slowly and developed a complex flavour. Now, intensively reared, industrially produced chicken dominates the market and has become a cheap, weekday, fast-food (usually pre-prepared) option. Organic, free-range farm chickens are available from good supermarkets, craft butchers and farmers' markets but are now an expensive treat. Smoked chicken, a fairly recent innovation, has become a tasty first course.

Quail The majority of quails eaten today are farmed by artisan food producers. They also sell the tiny eggs, sometimes hard-boiled and preserved in mild, lightly spiced wine vinegar. They are also served just lightly boiled, or as a garnish, or as a party nibble dipped in celery salt.

Egg production and cooking

Hens' eggs come from a two-tiered production system: commercial, or truly free-range (farm-fresh) and organic. Many still buy the latter because eggs, duck eggs too, remain an essential part of Irish food culture. Whether simply fried, poached or scrambled with butter then served with bacon, smoked salmon, or kippers (smoked herring) – eggs remain an essential element of the Irish breakfast. For light meals, they can be baked, or coddled in cream, or made into an omelette. Eggs are used to enrich sauces, in baking, and in desserts – mousses, meringues, crème caramel and crème brûlée are very popular. Duck eggs, once reserved for men (women and children ate hens' eggs), are sought after for baking because of their stronger flavour.

__Left__ Geese are reared on Irish farms as a luxury food to be enjoyed on festive occasions. __Above__ Turkey has become the most popular bird for eating on Christmas Day.

Dairy produce

As one of Ireland's major industries, dairy farming shapes the countryside, permanently covering much of the land in lush green pasture. Despite its small size, the island has diverse microclimates. The south and west are warmed by the Gulf Stream and have quite distinct plants from those in the sunny south-east, and they are different again from the rich "golden vale" of the southern midlands or of the Drumlin country, the northerly midlands. It is the rich grass that gives such consistent high quality to milk and butter, and the variation in herbage which enables so many varieties of cheese, each with a distinctive flavour, to be produced.

Milk and buttermilk

Full-fat (whole) milk is an essential ingredient in Irish cooking. It is produced by dairy farmers and collected daily by large co-operative creameries for pasteurization and distribution to retailers. Irish milk is not usually subjected to ultra-heat treatment so it retains its fresh flavour and is widely enjoyed as a drink.

Two varieties of buttermilk are available: cultured and natural. Originally, buttermilk was the liquid squeezed out of cream churned for butter. It looks like skimmed milk and has a slightly sour flavour as a result of the ripening of the cream before churning. Natural buttermilk produced in creameries is mainly used for making other products.

Natural buttermilk produced in smaller quantities by producers of farm or country butter is highly regarded. Cultured buttermilk made from skimmed milk is slightly fermented with cultures of the same organisms used to "ripen" cream for creamery butter. Heat-treated to kill bacteria and stop fermentation, it has a longer shelf life. Alas, it's not as good to drink as natural buttermilk and cannot be used as an ingredient where "live" buttermilk is required, such as in home-made curd (farmer's) cheeses, but it is perfectly effective for traditional Irish breads and baking.

Although buttermilk is no longer drunk as much as a thirst-quencher, or used as a traditional dressing for potatoes, there is a high consumption of buttermilk because it remains an essential ingredient in cooking. It is used by bakers for Irish soda breads and scones, and for the home baking of bread.

Left *A milking cow kept in a garden at Beaufort, Ring of Kerry.*

Opposite *The excellence of Irish milk means that Irish butter and cheese are of high quality and are widely exported in Europe.* ***Far left*** *Buttermilk.* ***Left*** *Irish butter is rich and creamy.*

Butter

Always found on an Irish table, butter is lavishly used on bread, potatoes, vegetables and cakes, such as scones. Most butter is produced in creameries. Irish milk has a high butter-fat content. Butter made from the cream has an excellent flavour and a rich colour. For centuries it has been exported in vast quantities.

Hormone-free, quality assured milk is processed to a consistent standard in large-scale creameries all over the island and marketed abroad under the brand name Kerrygold; it is acknowledged to be of the finest flavour and quality. Creamery butter is available salted and unsalted (sweet). Irish butter is also a constituent in a number of low-fat dairy spreads.

Country, or farm, butter Once, country butter was made on every dairy farm in the country. Local grasses and herbage determine its flavour. Now sold alongside "creamery" butter, butter made in the traditional way gets a longer ripening period (typically three days) before churning, and it is lightly salted.

Right *Plain yogurt is rich in nutrients.*

Cream and yogurt

Two types of cream are available: fresh and soured. Fresh cream – double (heavy) and single (light) – is by far the most popular, and large quantities are consumed on porridge, in coffee and as a "sauce" for fruit tarts, desserts and puddings. It is also used commercially and in the home for a vast range of cream-based desserts and for cream whiskey liqueurs. It features in many savoury dishes and sauces. Sour cream is used less but it is sometimes mixed with herbs to dress baked potatoes. Crème fraîche is catching on and is much in evidence in leading restaurants.

As yogurt is not a traditional Irish food, its production is of fairly recent origin. That said, it is a product in tune with the Irish taste for fermented and sour-milk products and it is very popular. A vast range is sold, with every level of fat content from zero per cent to full fat. Natural live yogurt, whole fruit yogurts, yogurt drinks, commercially produced yogurt desserts and many more ready-to-eat products are also offered.

Irish farmhouse cheeses

There are about 65 established artisan cheesemakers. Some make a single farmhouse cheese, others several varieties. All use the milk from their own herd of cows, sheep or goats, or milk from neighbouring farms.

Above Cheesemaking may be a relatively new industry in Ireland, but within a short space of time many award-winning Irish cheeses have been exported around the world.

Artisan cheesemakers

Each cheese is unique to the individual cheesemaker, and several Irish farmhouse cheeses have won awards at international food competitions. This exposure has extended their market to many countries of the world where they are available in gourmet food outlets and from specialist cheesemongers.

Much appreciated as a gourmet ready-to-eat food, farmhouse cheese is frequently eaten as a snack or luncheon dish, or used to add flavour and texture to traditional and contemporary dishes. It takes pride of place as a final dinner course eaten with bread, crackers or crisp oatcakes and accompanied by celery, pears, apples, grapes or chutney.

At family meals a farmhouse cheese chosen according to mood and season is served. In many restaurants a cheese board or a cheese plate will have a selection of four or five from the main cheese groups and always includes locally produced cheeses. There are a number of truly great cheeses, many from the Cork area, and several have won awards. These descriptive notes really give only a glimpse of the wide diversity of Irish farmhouse cheeses.

Cow's milk cheeses

Ardrahan: a semi-firm cheese with a washed rind and an earthy flavour that grows more robust and tangy as it ages.
Cashel Blue: this is original in flavour and texture. It is a modern blue-veined cheese from County Tipperary, sweet, tangy, rich and buttery.
Coolea: a semi-firm cheese made only from summer milk. It is matured for between six months and two years, becomes firm with a complex, grassy, herbal flavour that lingers and grows longer and stronger with aging.
Cooleeney: a soft white mould cheese – smooth, with robust flavours of oak and mushroom and a velvety texture.
Dilliskus: made with summer milk only, this is a firm cheese flavoured with dillisk or dulse (seaweed). It has a distinctive aroma with a great texture, and a sweet, tangy flavour.

Left Cooleeney (bottom), a soft white cheese from Tipperary, and Croghan (top), a vegetarian semi-soft cheese, made from goat's milk in the Wexford region.

Durrus: a semi-soft, washed-rind cheese; moist, with a sweet herbal, yet complex, earthy flavour.
Gabriel and **Desmond:** two exceptional cheeses, made from summer milk only, hard in the Swiss alpage style. Desmond has an intensely spicy, floral flavour that lingers. Gabriel is just as intense but has a sweeter, more subtle flavour. Both mature from a moist dense to a granular and flinty texture.
Gubbeen: a washed-rind cheese with a scented mushroom flavour and a firm, smooth, moist texture.
Knockanore: a hard-pressed cheese; well-aged and with a deep flavour that lingers.
Lavistown: a semi-soft, brushed-rind cheese made from skimmed milk. It has a clean buttermilk tang that is richer in flavour in winter.
Milleens: a soft, washed-rind cheese from Cork; matures to spilling cream with a complex flavour and a herby, spicy tang.
St Killian: a soft white mould cheese; fully ripe it has a rich, liquid interior.

Below, from top *Durrus and Gabriel.*

Right *Mine-Gabhar (back), a soft white goat's cheese from Wexford, and Milleens (front), a semi-soft white cheese from west Cork.*

Goat's milk cheeses

Blue Rathgore: a blue cheese from Northern Ireland, moist and crumbly, with a slightly burnt taste.
Boilie: a fresh cheese with a delicate, sweet flavour, that is presented packed in flavoured oil.
Corleggy: a natural rind, hard cheese. It has a fine smooth texture, with rich layers of complex flavours.
Croghan: an unpasteurized, organic, vegetarian semi-soft cheese, made from goat's milk in the Wexford area. The flavour suggests grass and hay, while the finish is aromatic without being pungent. It is made only from spring until autumn.
Mine-Gabhar: an organic, soft white natural rind cheese. It is deep and smooth, with oaky herbal flavours.
Oisin: made with organic milk; Ireland's only blue goat's milk cheese.
Old MacDonnells Farm: fresh, smooth with a light floral flavour.
Poulcoin: a brushed-rind, firm cheese; floral balanced by oak flavours.
St Tola: made with organic milk. It has a sweet, floral flavour which, as it matures, becomes even more pronounced.

Sheep's milk cheeses

Abbey Blue: a flavoursome, organic, soft white-blue cheese.
Cratloe Hills Mature: a hard cheese that at six months has developed a robust, fudge-caramel flavour.
Crozier Blue: from the same maker as Cashel Blue; rich ewe's milk results in a distinctive cheese, smooth and buttery, with a pronounced flavour.
Knockalara: a fresh, moist cream cheese with herbal, citrus flavours.

Smoked and flavoured cheeses

Many cheesemakers, including some whose cheeses have already been mentioned, make other varieties for smoking, or smoke some of their regular cheeses, usually lightly over oak or beech. Others, particularly those making hard-pressed cheeses and fresh cheeses, flavour some of their output. A wide variety of ingredients is used: cumin, garlic, sweet red (bell) peppers, green peppercorns, cloves, wine, porter, whiskey, hazelnuts, ham, nettles, chives and dill. Smoked and flavoured cheeses are gaining in popularity.

Below St Tola is a superb goat's cheese.

Grains, breads and baking

An old Irish rhyme perfectly describes the grains that the Irish grow and the hierarchy of each in the food culture, an order lasting from early Christian times until the last century:

Rye bread will do you good,
Barley bread will do you no harm,
Wheaten bread will sweeten
your blood,
Oaten bread will strengthen
your arm.

Clockwise from top *Flake meal (rolled oats), oatmeal, whole oats and oat bran.*

Rye, a winter-hardy cereal grown since the Bronze Age, was a useful winter-sown crop. However, it fell from favour perhaps because it was the bread of fasting in monasteries – penitential food. Next came barley bread; barley was wholesome for feeding animals and useful for humans in times of scarcity (and even more useful for distilling). Once a variety of wheat was found to suit the climate, it was always the most prized grain. Oats thrived in the Irish climate and made the bread of working people, and oatcakes remain popular. Yalla meal (maize) is not mentioned in older texts; it was an imported famine food, not relished by the Irish. Traditionally, at least as much grain was eaten as porridge, or stirabout, made using all available grains. Grains are still widely used in soups and puddings.

Below *Wheaten flour.*

Irish bread is different

Most Irish bread was leavened either with barm (a bye-product of brewing), sowans (fermented from oat husks), potato barm, sourdough or yeast. Towards the end of the 18th century bicarbonate of soda (baking soda) arrived. Used with buttermilk or soured milk, the action of one enhances the other; bicarbonate of soda interacts with the lactic acid of buttermilk to release carbon dioxide into the dough, making it rise.

Visitors love the taste and texture of Irish bread, and to this day wholemeal (whole-wheat) soda bread remains the bread of the nation, whether home-baked or produced commercially. In many parts of Ireland a loaf of this bread is called a "cake", going back to the old Viking word for a flattish round of bread, *kake* or *kaak*.

Although wholemeal soda bread (also called brown bread) is the most popular, the same combination is used for white soda breads, plain and flavoured, white and brown scones, and sweet teabreads. Other traditional baked goods include barm brack (with fruits and spices), griddle breads, potato cakes, crumpets, muffins and fruit tarts, as well as traditional sweet cakes, such as porter cake, carrot cake and ginger-bread (which is a cake, despite its name).

The Irish baking tradition

Home-baking still remains a living tradition for two main reasons: baking competitions at local agricultural shows and the work of the Irish Country Women's Association, whose members pass on traditional recipes and baking skills. Traditional Irish baked goods are also widely available in local bakeries and supermarkets.

The essential flavours of Irish baking

Dairy foods, the *bánbhianna* of ancient times, are essential in baking. Butter is still traditional, and only for economic reasons will any other fat be substituted. It is used in almost everything, and some cooks even add a smidgen to soda bread. Butter is always served with bread, barm brack, scones, teabreads and even porter cake. Hard cheeses are added to bread and scones, and soft fresh cheese is used in baked curd- and cheesecakes. Cream is served with tarts and puddings.

A wide variety of flavouring liquids is used. Buttermilk is used for breads, scones and some cakes; fresh (sweet) milk for cakes, pancakes and puddings. Porter cake – a robust fruitcake – is named after the liquid used: a dark brown, hopped and malty alcoholic drink. Cider is used in some sponge cakes and puddings. Whiskey is an essential ingredient in the rich, double-iced fruitcakes made for christenings and weddings and in Christmas cake and Christmas pudding (the latter usually contains stout as well).

Crystallized fruits are widely used, mainly lemon, orange, cherry and angelica stems; so are dried fruits, such as currants, raisins, sultanas (golden raisins), apricots, figs and prunes.

Fresh fruits used in tarts and cakes include cooking and eating apples, rhubarb, pears, blackberries, strawberries, raspberries, blueberries and *fraughans* (bilberries or wild blueberries), cranberries, lemons and oranges. Nuts, particularly almonds, hazelnuts and walnuts are used whole or crushed in almost everything from bread to cakes and meringues.

Left *Barm brack is one of Ireland's most delicious teabreads.*

Above *A selection of Irish soda breads and scones.*

Some oddities

Grated carrots are used in cakes and fruit puddings. The seaweed, dillisk or dulse, a traditional flavouring for potatoes, bread and scones, is currently undergoing a revival. Flavoured breads are popular; the addition of crisp bacon, diced black pudding (blood sausage), seeds, such as sesame and poppy, and pinhead oatmeal, shows that Irish bakers are willing to put a new spin on traditions.

Spices and sweeteners

The most common spices and flavourings used in baking are cloves, nutmeg, cinnamon, ginger, vanilla, caraway and, of course, honey. Most sugar is made from Irish-grown sugar beet, but dark cane sugar and treacle (molasses) are also used.

Brewing and distilling

The Irish have been brewing beer since Celtic times with distilling following much later. The climate is unsuitable for making wine, but it has been imported into the country for centuries.

Irish beers were brewed from barley (and some other grains) and flavoured with wild hops. Ale, porter and stout were all "top fermented". Ale, light in colour with a pronounced taste of hops, has a tartness that sets it apart. It is drunk cold or hot flavoured with spices. Porter, now made only in micro-breweries, is dark brown with a highly hopped, malty flavour. Stout is very dark with a distinctive, rich, malty flavour and a bitter taste of hops.

Today, Ireland's main breweries – Guinness, Murphy's, Beamish and Smithwicks – are supplemented by a number of microbreweries (such as Caffrey's, Biddy Early's and Porterhouse), who make traditional and contemporary brews. Stout and beer are the most popular alcoholic drinks, consumed in great quantities in the famous Irish pubs.

Apples are native and have been used from at least medieval times to make a fermented drink called *nenadmin*. The 16th century saw an expansion of cider-apple orchards and a growth in the popularity of cider. Naturally produced cider (made from 28 apple varieties) remains a vibrant industry, and cider is widely enjoyed.

Mead is a fermented honey-based drink made since Celtic times. Once a festive drink, it had fallen from fashion by the early 19th century. Revived about 25 years ago, it is now served at "medieval" tourist banquets and sold in airport stores.

Irish whiskey

Distilling was first used for perfumes and medicines. Written evidence for *uisce beatha* (water of life – whiskey) appeared in 1403 in *The Annals of the Four Masters*, where a man for whom a surfeit of *uisce beatha* became *uisce marbtha* (water of death) is mocked. The *Annals* are in Latin and historians argue whether this refers to distilled wine or to grain whiskey; however, we know *uisce beatha* from grain was widespread by the middle of the 16th century. Then, one Christmas Day, a tax of four pence a gallon was imposed. Folklore maintains the making of the illicit spirit *poitín* began the following day. By the 18th century 2,000 stills were in operation. Whiskey had become the spirit of the nation.

Irish whiskey differs from other whiskies. It is made only from kiln-dried barley (malted and unmalted), yeast and pure Irish water, by two methods: pot still and column

Below, left to right *Draught Guinness is a smooth, creamy stout with a refreshing, roasted flavour and a rich, black hue. Murphy's Irish Stout is a light, smooth stout – both are served cool. Paddy's and Jameson are two of the most popular Irish whiskeys. Baileys Irish cream can be drunk alone or with ice, or used to flavour recipes.*

Left *Whiskey barrels at the Jameson Distillery.*

still. The latter produces grain whiskey; it is more efficient (distilling constantly) but it removes some of the oils and aromatics that make pot still so flavoursome. There are three types of Irish whiskey: single malt (produced at one distillery only), pure pot stilled and a column-and-pot still blend of grain and malt. All are distilled three times and matured in oak barrels.

There are about 100 whiskey brands. Not all are exported and many are made to suit the Irish palate. The Irish do not ice whiskey; "breaking it" with water is optional (some experts say desirable) and it is often drunk neat. Whiskey lovers tend to have a lifelong attachment to one brand with a "nose", taste and "finish" to their liking.

Some, like Paddy, are soft and gentle, others, like Powers, "explode" in the mouth. Jameson (a blend) has achieved acclaim abroad. Matured in sherry and bourbon casks, it mellows to a golden colour and is smooth, complex and elegant. By no means bland, Jameson is designed to have wide appeal – it accounts for about 75 per cent of all Irish whiskey sold globally. Bushmills, the oldest distillery in Ireland, makes a range of single malts and blends valued at home and abroad. Premium whiskeys are matured for up to 21 years.

Whiskey liqueurs Recipes for whiskey liqueurs date from 1602; raisins, dates, aniseed, molasses, liquorice and herbs were used. Based on an ancient drink called heather wine, Irish Mist is made with heather honey, herbs and spices, aged whiskey and other spirits. It is mellow and distinctive.

Other Irish drinks

Irish cream liqueurs A modern invention (from the 1970s), cream liqueurs are made with whiskey, double (heavy) cream and honey. They are widely exported, and there are many brands, each subtly different. The biggest selling, Baileys, is the world's 15th largest spirit brand.

Gin Cork Dry Gin, the market leader, is made at a distillery founded in 1793. Triple-distilled grain spirit is flavoured with a secret recipe of berries and fruits. Gin is used as a base for home-made sloe gin liqueur.

In Irish food culture almost everything brewed or distilled is used in cooking: as a cooking liquid for meat, game, poultry or seafood, or as a subtle flavouring for savoury or sweet sauces. You will encounter all the products of Irish breweries and distilleries in cakes, puddings, desserts, ice creams, jams, preserves or handmade chocolates.

Irish coffee Invented in 1943 by Joe Sheridan, chef at Foynes flying-boat base in Clare, this combination of a full (Irish) measure of whiskey, black coffee and sugar, with lightly whipped cream floating on top, is a global favourite.

Right *Cork Dry Gin.*

Breakfasts

A traditional Irish cooked breakfast is far more than the sum of its parts. Bacon, sausages, mushrooms, tomato and egg are the basic ingredients, and you can use them all, or a selection if preferred. Freshly squeezed juice or fruit begin the feast, then yogurt, cereals or porridge herald the hot plate. Home-baked bread and preserves accompany – and all is washed down with tea or coffee. No wonder lunch is so often off the menu for visitors to Ireland!

Porridge

One of Ireland's oldest foods, porridge remains a favourite way to start the day, especially during winter. Brown sugar or honey, cream and a tot of whiskey are treats added for weekend breakfasts and to spoil guests in some of the best guesthouses and hotels.

Serves 4

1 litre/1¾ pints/4 cups water

115g/4oz/1 cup pinhead oatmeal

good pinch of salt

Variation Modern rolled oats can be used, in the proportion of 115g/4oz/ 1 cup rolled oats to 750ml/1¼ pints/ 3 cups water, plus a sprinkling of salt. This cooks more quickly than pinhead oatmeal. Simmer, stirring to prevent sticking, for about 5 minutes. Either type of oatmeal can be left to cook overnight in the slow oven of a range.

1 Put the water, pinhead oatmeal and salt into a heavy pan and bring to the boil over a medium heat, stirring with a wooden spatula. When the porridge is smooth and beginning to thicken, reduce the heat to a simmer.

2 Cook gently for about 25 minutes, stirring occasionally, until the oatmeal is cooked and the consistency smooth.

3 Serve hot with cold milk and extra salt, if required.

Per portion Energy 115Kcal/488kJ; Protein 3.6g; Carbohydrate 20.9g, of which sugars 0g; Fat 2.5g, of which saturates 0g; Cholesterol 0mg; Calcium 16mg; Fibre 2g; Sodium 304mg

Brown soda breakfast scones

These unusually light scones are virtually fat-free, so they must be eaten very fresh – warm from the oven if possible, but definitely on the day of baking. Serve with fresh, high-quality butter such as Irish Kerrygold.

Makes about 16

225g/8oz/2 cups plain (all-purpose) flour

2.5ml/½ tsp bicarbonate of soda (baking soda)

2.5ml/½ tsp salt

225g/8oz/2 cups wheaten flour

about 350ml/12fl oz/1½ cups buttermilk or sour cream and milk mixed

topping (optional): egg wash (1 egg yolk mixed with 15ml/1 tbsp water) or a little grated cheese

1 Preheat the oven to 220°C/425°F/Gas 7. Oil and flour a baking tray. Sift the flour, bicarbonate of soda and salt in a bowl, add the wheaten flour and mix. Make a well in the centre, pour in almost all the liquid and mix, adding the remaining liquid as needed to make a soft, moist dough. Do not overmix.

◀ **2** Lightly dust a work surface with flour, turn out the dough and dust the top with flour; press out evenly to a thickness of 4cm/1½in. Cut out about 16 scones with a 5cm/2in fluted pastry (cookie) cutter. Place on the baking tray and then brush the tops with egg wash, or sprinkle with a little grated cheese, if using.

3 Bake for about 12 minutes until well risen and golden brown.

Variation For a more traditional scone mixture that keeps longer, rub 50g/2oz/¼ cup butter into the dry ingredients. Increase the proportion of the soda to 5ml/1tsp if you like, as the scones will not be as light.

Per scone Energy 117Kcal/493kJ; Protein 3.8g; Carbohydrate 20.9g, of which sugars 1.5g; Fat 2.6g, of which saturates 1.4g; Cholesterol 6mg; Calcium 49mg; Fibre 1.7g; Sodium 72mg

Boxty potato pancakes

Said to have originated during the Irish famine, these delicious pancakes use blended potatoes in the batter mix and can be made as thin or thick as you like. They are delicious served rolled around a hot savoury filling such as cooked cabbage and chopped bacon bound in a light mustard sauce.

Makes 4 pancakes

450g/1lb potatoes, peeled and chopped

50–75g/2–3oz/½–⅔ cup plain (all-purpose) flour

about 150ml/¼ pint/⅔ cup milk

salt to taste

knob (pat) of butter

1 Place the peeled and chopped potatoes in a blender or in the bowl of a food processor and process until the potato is thoroughly liquidized (blended).

2 Add the flour and enough milk to the processed potato to give a dropping consistency, and add salt to taste. The milk and flour can be adjusted, depending on how thin you like your pancake. Heat a little butter on a griddle or cast-iron frying pan.

3 Pour about a quarter of the mixture into the pan – if the consistency is right it will spread evenly over the base. Cook over a medium heat for about 5 minutes on each side, depending on the thickness of the cake. Serve rolled with the hot filling of your choice.

Per pancake Energy 163Kcal/689kJ; Protein 4.8g; Carbohydrate 30.9g, of which sugars 2.7g; Fat 3.1g, of which saturates 1.7g; Cholesterol 8mg; Calcium 69mg; Fibre 1.9g; Sodium 236mg

Potato cakes

This is the traditional method of making potato cakes on a griddle or heavy frying pan. Commercial versions are available throughout Ireland as thin, pre-cooked potato cakes, which are fried for breakfast or (especially in the north) for high tea. Griddle-cooked potato cakes were traditionally buttered and eaten hot with sugar, rather like pancakes.

Makes about 12

675g/1½lb potatoes, peeled

25g/1oz/2 tbsp unsalted (sweet) butter

about 175g/6oz/1½ cups plain (all-purpose) flour

salt

1 Boil the potatoes in a large pan until tender, then drain well and mash. Salt well, then mix in the butter and allow to cool a little.

2 Turn out on to a floured work surface and knead in about one-third of its volume in flour, or as much as is needed to make a pliable dough. It will become easier to handle as the flour is incorporated, but avoid overworking it. Roll out to a thickness of about 1cm/½in and cut into triangles.

3 Heat a dry griddle or heavy frying pan over a low heat and cook the potato cakes on it for about 3 minutes on each side until browned. Serve hot with butter, or sugar, if you prefer.

Right *From top to bottom, Avalanche, a white-skinned early maincrop potato from Northern Ireland; Avondale, a beige-skinned maincrop from Ireland; and Barna, a red-skinned late maincrop from Ireland.*

Per portion Energy 1276Kcal/5392kJ; Protein 30.4g; Carbohydrate 249.1g, of which sugars 6.7g; Fat 24.1g, of which saturates 13.4g; Cholesterol 53mg; Calcium 282mg; Fibre 14g; Sodium 203mg

Oatmeal pancakes with bacon

These oaty pancakes have a special affinity with good bacon, making an interesting base for an alternative to the big traditional fry-up. Serve with traditional or home-made sausages, fried or poached eggs and cooked tomatoes.

Makes 8 pancakes

115g/4oz/1 cup fine wholemeal (whole-wheat) flour

25g/1oz/¼ cup fine pinhead oatmeal

pinch of salt

2 eggs

about 300ml/½ pint/1¼ cups buttermilk

butter or oil, for greasing

8 bacon rashers (strips)

Cook's tip When whole oats are chopped into pieces they are called pinhead or coarse oatmeal. They take longer to cook than rolled oats and have a chewier texture.

1 Mix the flour, oatmeal and salt in a bowl or food processor, beat in the eggs and add enough buttermilk to make a creamy batter of the same consistency as ordinary pancakes.

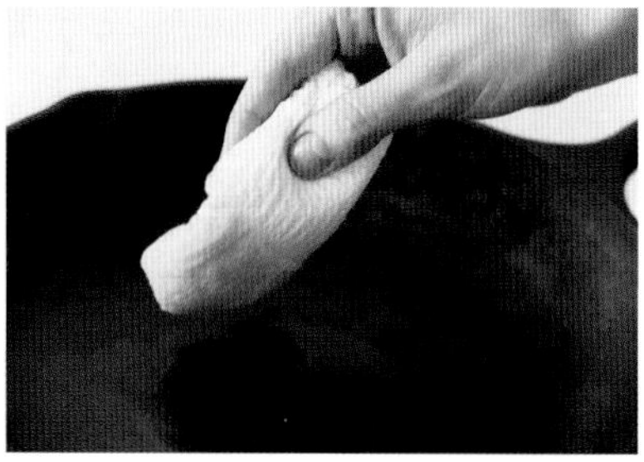

2 Thoroughly heat a griddle or cast-iron frying pan over a medium-hot heat. When very hot, grease lightly with butter or oil.

3 Pour in the batter, about a ladleful at a time. Tilt the pan around to spread evenly and cook for about 2 minutes on the first side, or until set and the underside is browned. Turn over and cook for 1 minute until browned.

4 Keep the pancakes warm while you cook the others. Fry the bacon. Roll the pancakes with a cooked rasher to serve.

Per pancake Energy 202Kcal/845kJ; Protein 11.9g; Carbohydrate 13.1g, of which sugars 2g; Fat 11.8g, of which saturates 4.8g; Cholesterol 87mg; Calcium 59mg; Fibre 1.5g; Sodium 654mg

Buttermilk pancakes

These little pancakes are made with buttermilk, which is widely available in Ireland, and they are quite like the dropped scones that are so familiar across the water in Scotland. They are delicious served warm, with honey.

Makes about 12

- 225g/8oz/2 cups plain (all-purpose) flour
- 7.5ml/1½ tsp bicarbonate of soda (baking soda)
- 25–50g/1–2oz/2–4 tbsp sugar
- 1 egg
- about 300ml/½ pint/1¼ cups buttermilk
- butter and oil, mixed, or white vegetable fat (shortening), for frying
- honey, to serve

1 In a food processor or a large mixing bowl, mix together the plain flour, the bicarbonate of soda and enough sugar to taste. Add the egg, mixing together, and gradually pour in just enough of the buttermilk to make a thick, smooth batter.

2 Heat a heavy pan and add the butter and oil, or white fat. Place spoonfuls of the batter on to the hot pan and cook for 2–3 minutes until bubbles rise to the surface. Flip the pancakes over and cook for a further 2–3 minutes. Remove from the pan and serve warm with honey.

Per portion Energy 1449Kcal/6098kJ; Protein 38.5g; Carbohydrate 214.2g, of which sugars 42.7g; Fat 54.9g, of which saturates 19.6g; Cholesterol 300mg; Calcium 695mg; Fibre 7g; Sodium 219mg

Cheese toasties

These savoury toasties, made with hard Irish farmhouse cheese such as Gabriel or Desmond, are a nice little snack for breakfast or anytime.

Serves 4

- 2 eggs
- 175–225g/6–8oz/1½–2 cups grated hard Irish farmhouse cheese, or Cheddar
- 5–10ml/1–2 tsp Irish wholegrain mustard
- 4 slices wheaten bread, buttered
- 2–4 halved tomatoes (optional)
- ground black pepper
- watercress or parsley, to serve (optional)

1 Preheat the oven to 230°C/450°F/ Gas 8 (the top oven of a range-type stove is ideal for this recipe). Whisk the eggs lightly and stir in the grated cheese, mustard and pepper.

2 Lay the buttered bread face down in a shallow baking dish and divide the cheese mixture among the slices, spreading it out evenly.

3 Bake in the oven for 10–15 minutes, or until well risen and golden brown, adding the halved tomatoes for a few minutes, if using. Serve immediately, with the tomatoes, and garnish with sprigs of watercress or parsley.

Variations

• A slice of cooked ham may be added to the sliced bread before the cheese mixture, if you like.

• Hard Irish farmhouse cheeses such as Lavistown from Kilkenny, or the semi-hard Orla from County Cork, can be used in this recipe.

Per portion Energy 452Kcal/1877kJ; Protein 29.8g; Carbohydrate 0.1g, of which sugars 0.1g; Fat 35.3g, of which saturates 20.9g; Cholesterol 313mg; Calcium 681mg; Fibre 0g; Sodium 717mg

Creamy scrambled eggs with smoked salmon

A special treat for weekend breakfasts, eggs served this way are popular in some of Ireland's best guesthouses and hotels and are a good alternative to the traditional fry-up.

Serves 1

- 3 eggs
- knob (pat) of butter
- 15ml/1 tbsp single (light) cream or milk
- 1 slice of smoked salmon, chopped or whole, warmed
- salt and ground black pepper
- sprig of fresh parsley, to garnish
- triangles of hot toast, to serve

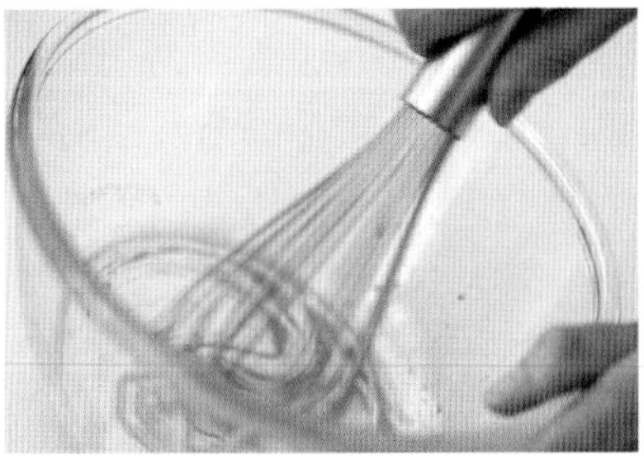

1 Whisk the eggs in a bowl together with the cream or milk, a generous grinding of black pepper and a little salt to taste if you like, remembering that the smoked salmon may be quite naturally salty.

2 Melt the butter in a pan and, when it is warm, add the egg mixture and stir until nearly set. Add the cream, which prevents the eggs from overcooking as well as enriching the dish.

3 Either stir in the chopped smoked salmon or serve the warmed slice alongside the egg. Serve immediately on warmed plates and garnish with the parsley and hot toast.

Below *Salmon are found in the clean Glenteenassig river, County Kerry.*

Per portion Energy 447Kcal/1862kJ; Protein 37.3g; Carbohydrate 0.4g, of which sugars 0.4g; Fat 33.6g, of which saturates 13.1g; Cholesterol 734mg; Calcium 128mg; Fibre 0g; Sodium 1.37g

Jugged kippers

The demand for naturally smoked kippers is ever increasing. They are most popular for breakfast, served with scrambled eggs, but they're also good at an old-fashioned high tea. Jugging is the same as poaching, except that the only equipment needed is a jug and kettle. Serve with freshly made soda bread or toast and a wedge of lemon, if you like.

Serves 4

4 kippers (smoked herrings), preferably naturally smoked, whole or filleted

25g/1oz/2 tbsp butter

ground black pepper

1 Select a jug (pitcher) tall enough for the kippers to be immersed when the water is added. If the heads are still on, remove them.

2 Put the fish into the jug, tails up, and then cover them with boiling water. Leave for about 5 minutes, until tender.

3 Drain well and serve on warmed plates with a knob (pat) of butter and a little black pepper on each kipper.

Per portion Energy 449Kcal/1859kJ; Protein 31.8g; Carbohydrate 0g, of which sugars 0g; Fat 35.7g, of which saturates 8.3g; Cholesterol 123mg; Calcium 96mg; Fibre 0g; Sodium 1.5g

Kedgeree

Of Indian origin, kedgeree came to Ireland via England and the landed gentry. It quickly became a popular dish using smoked fish for breakfast or high tea. This is a more manageable dish than the full Irish breakfast when feeding several people, and it is often served in guesthouses and restaurants.

Serves 4–6

450g/1lb smoked haddock

300ml/½ pint/1¼ cups milk

175g/6oz/scant 1 cup long grain rice

pinch of grated nutmeg and cayenne pepper

1 onion, peeled and finely chopped

50g/2oz/¼ cup butter

2 hard-boiled eggs

chopped fresh parsley, to garnish

lemon wedges and wholemeal (whole-wheat) toast, to serve

salt and ground black pepper

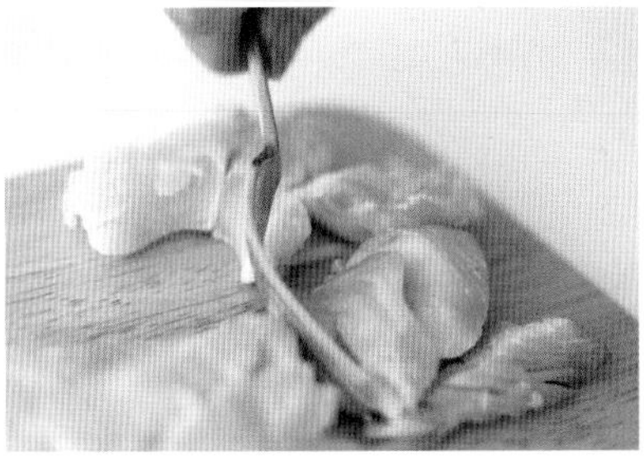

1 Poach the haddock in the milk, made up with just enough water to cover the fish, for about 8 minutes, or until just cooked. Skin the haddock, remove all the bones and flake the flesh with a fork. Set aside.

2 Bring 600ml/1 pint/2½ cups water to the boil in a large pan. Add the rice, cover closely with a lid and cook over a low heat for about 25 minutes, or until all the water has been absorbed by the rice. Season with salt and a grinding of black pepper, and the nutmeg and cayenne pepper.

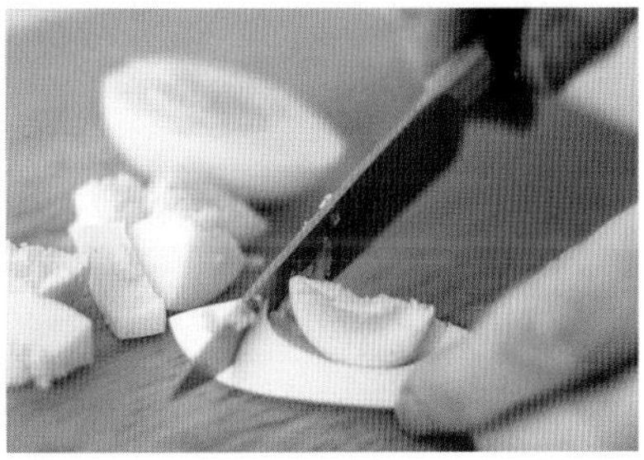

3 Meanwhile, heat 15g/½oz/1 tbsp butter in a pan and fry the onion until soft and transparent. Set aside. Roughly chop one of the hard-boiled eggs and slice the other into neat wedges.

4 Stir the remaining butter into the rice and add the flaked haddock, onion and the chopped egg. Season to taste and heat the mixture through gently (this can be done on a serving dish in a low oven if more convenient).

5 To serve, pile up the kedgeree on a warmed dish, sprinkle generously with parsley and arrange the wedges of egg on top. Put the lemon wedges around the base and serve hot with the toast.

Variation Try leftover cooked salmon, instead of the haddock.

Per portion Energy 399Kcal/1668kJ; Protein 28.9g; Carbohydrate 38g, of which sugars 2.2g; Fat 14.6g, of which saturates 7.6g; Cholesterol 181mg; Calcium 62mg; Fibre 0.5g; Sodium 974mg

Kidney and mushroom toasts

The traditional Irish breakfast treat of lamb's kidneys is most often encountered in the country or regional towns. This little dish makes an excellent alternative to the big "breakfast plate", or could be a light, tasty supper. Serve with tomato slices or wedges and parsley on hot herby-buttered toast or scones.

Serves 2–4

- 4 large, flat field (portobello) mushrooms, stalks trimmed
- 75g/3oz/6 tbsp butter
- 10ml/2 tsp Irish wholegrain mustard
- 15ml/1 tbsp chopped fresh parsley
- 4 lamb's kidneys, skinned, halved and cored
- 4 thick slices of brown bread, cut into rounds and toasted, or halved, warm scones
- sprig of parsley, to garnish
- tomato wedges, to serve

1 Wash the mushrooms thoroughly and gently remove the stalks.

2 Blend the butter, wholegrain mustard and fresh parsley together.

3 Rinse the prepared lamb's kidneys well under cold running water, and pat dry with kitchen paper.

4 Melt about two-thirds of the butter mixture in a large frying pan and fry the mushrooms and kidneys for about 3 minutes on each side. When the kidneys are cooked to your liking (they are best left a little pink in the centre), spread with the remaining herb butter. Serve with the tomato, garnished with parsley, on the hot toast or scones.

Per portion Energy 593Kcal/2480kJ; Protein 39.2g; Carbohydrate 26.3g, of which sugars 2.7g; Fat 37.7g, of which saturates 21.6g; Cholesterol 647mg; Calcium 145mg; Fibre 4.3g; Sodium 773mg

The traditional Irish breakfast

A hearty Irish cooked breakfast is far more than the sum of its parts, and its enduring popularity, at least for weekend brunches and holidays, may go a long way towards explaining why lunch is often off the menu for travellers in Ireland. Choosing the very best ingredients is a major part of this meal's success.

Serves 4

- 4 lamb's kidneys, halved and trimmed
- wholegrain Irish mustard, such as Lakeshore, for spreading
- 8 rashers (strips) back or streaky (fatty) bacon, preferably dry-cured
- 275g/10oz black pudding (blood sausage), such as Clonakilty, sliced
- 225g/8oz good quality sausages
- butter or oil, for grilling or frying
- 4 tomatoes, halved
- 4–8 flat field (portobello) mushrooms
- 4 potato cakes or potato bread
- 4 eggs
- sea salt and ground black pepper
- chopped fresh chives or fresh parsley sprigs, to garnish

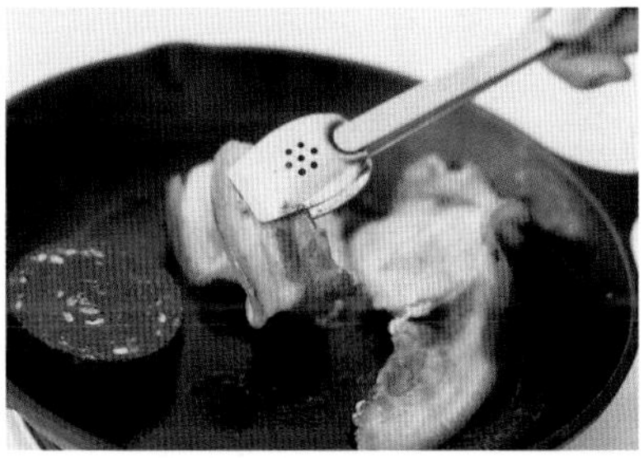

1 Spread the kidneys with a little mustard. Grill (broil) or fry the bacon, black pudding, kidneys and sausages with butter or oil, as preferred, until crisp and nicely browned. Season to taste, and then keep warm.

2 Meanwhile, fry or grill the halved tomatoes with knobs (pats) of butter, and fry or bake the flat field mushrooms, preferably in the juices from the bacon, kidneys and sausages, until they are just tender.

3 Fry the potato cakes or potato bread until warmed through and golden brown on both sides. Cook the eggs to your liking. Arrange everything on large, warm plates, and garnish with chopped chives or parsley sprigs. Serve at once.

Per portion Energy 894Kcal/3728kJ; Protein 50.6g; Carbohydrate 40.1g, of which sugars 5.5g; Fat 60.4g, of which saturates 20.1g; Cholesterol 618mg; Calcium 115mg; Fibre 3.5g; Sodium 2.25mg

Soups

Soups and broths (brotchán) hold an honoured position in traditional Irish cooking. Originally a simple but nourishing basic gruel made with oatmeal with added vegetables, typical Irish soups later developed into the "meal in a soup bowl" that use a wide variety of vegetables, fish and meat, and are enjoyed throughout the country today.

Potato soup

This most Irish of all soups is not only excellent as it is, but versatile too, as it can be used as a base for numerous other soups. Use a floury potato, such as Golden Wonder.

Serves 6–8

- 50g/2oz/¼ cup butter
- 2 large onions, finely chopped
- 675g/1½lb potatoes, diced
- about 1.75 litres/3 pints/7½ cups hot chicken stock
- sea salt and ground black pepper
- a little milk, if necessary
- chopped fresh chives, to garnish

1 Melt the butter in a large heavy pan and add the onions, turning them in the butter until well coated. Cover and leave to sweat over a very low heat.

2 Add the potatoes to the pan, and mix well with the butter and onions. Season with salt and pepper, cover and cook without colouring over a gentle heat for about 10 minutes. Add the stock, bring to the boil and simmer for 20–30 minutes, or until the vegetables are tender.

3 Remove from the heat and allow to cool slightly. Purée the soup in batches in a blender or food processor. Reheat over a low heat and adjust the seasoning. If the soup seems too thick, add a little extra stock or milk to achieve the right consistency. Serve very hot, sprinkled with chopped chives.

Below *Verdant Irish landscape, with fields of lush, agricultural land seen in the view across the gap on Mamore, on the Inishowen peninsula.*

Per portion Energy 178Kcal/746kJ; Protein 3.5g; Carbohydrate 26.1g, of which sugars 5.4g; Fat 7.4g, of which saturates 4.3g; Cholesterol 18mg; Calcium 29mg; Fibre 2.6g; Sodium 328mg

Parsnip soup

This lightly spiced soup has become popular in recent years, and variations abound, including a traditional combination of parsnip and apple in equal proportions.

Serves 6

- 900g/2lb parsnips
- 50g/2oz/¼ cup butter
- 1 onion, chopped
- 2 garlic cloves, crushed
- 10ml/2 tsp ground cumin
- 5ml/1 tsp ground coriander
- about 1.2 litres/2 pints/5 cups hot chicken stock
- 150ml/¼ pint/⅔ cup single (light) cream
- salt and ground black pepper
- chopped fresh chives or parsley and/or croûtons, to garnish

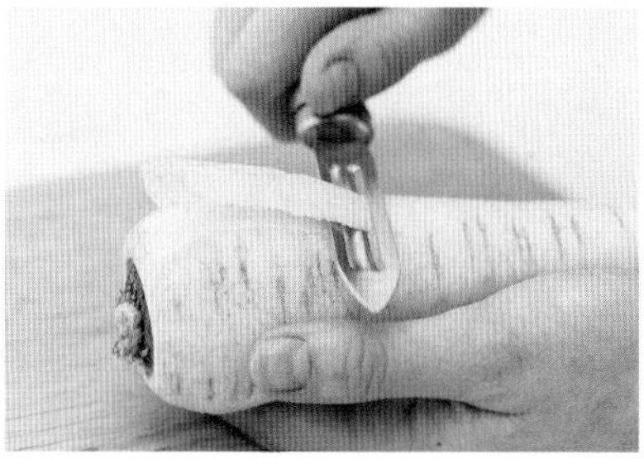

1 Peel and thinly slice the parsnips. Heat the butter in a large heavy pan and add the peeled parsnips and chopped onion with the crushed garlic. Cook until softened but not coloured, stirring occasionally. Add the ground cumin and ground coriander to the vegetable mixture and cook, stirring, for 1–2 minutes, and then gradually blend in the hot chicken stock and mix well.

2 Cover and simmer for about 20 minutes, or until the parsnip is soft. Purée the soup, adjust the texture with extra stock or water if it seems too thick, and check the seasoning. Add the cream and reheat without boiling.

3 Serve immediately, sprinkled with chopped chives or parsley and/or croûtons, to garnish.

Per portion Energy 325Kcal/1355kJ; Protein 5.9g; Carbohydrate 32.1g, of which sugars 15.9g; Fat 20.1g, of which saturates 11.5g; Cholesterol 47mg; Calcium 138mg; Fibre 10.9g; Sodium 233mg

Brotchán foltchep

This traditional leek and oatmeal soup is also known as *Brotchán Roy* and combines leeks, oatmeal and milk – three ingredients that have been staple foods in Ireland for centuries. Serve with freshly baked bread and Irish butter.

Serves 4–6

- about 1.2 litres/2 pints/5 cups chicken stock and milk, mixed
- 30ml/2 tbsp medium pinhead oatmeal
- 25g/1oz/2 tbsp butter
- 6 large leeks, sliced into 2cm/¾in pieces
- sea salt and ground black pepper
- pinch of ground mace
- 30ml/2 tbsp chopped fresh parsley
- single (light) cream and chopped fresh parsley leaves or chives, to garnish

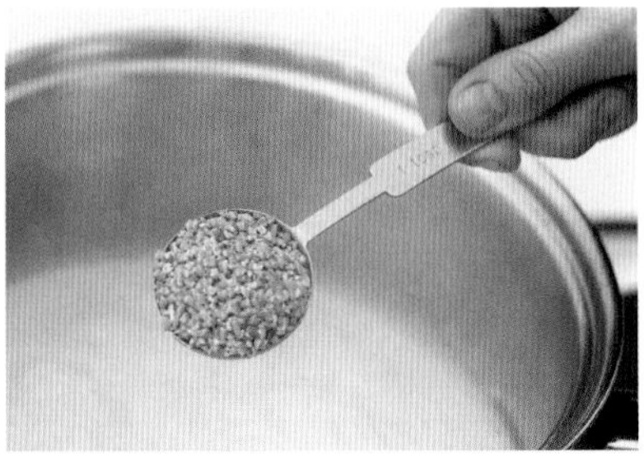

1 Bring the stock and milk mixture to the boil over medium heat and sprinkle in the oatmeal. Stir well to prevent lumps forming, and then simmer gently.

2 Wash the leeks in a bowl. Melt the butter in a separate pan and cook the leeks over a gentle heat until softened slightly, then add them to the stock mixture. Simmer for a further 15–20 minutes, or until the oatmeal is cooked. Extra stock or milk can be added if the soup is too thick.

3 Season with salt, pepper and mace, stir in the parsley and serve in warmed bowls. Decorate with a swirl of cream and some chopped fresh parsley or chives, if you like.

Variation Make nettle soup in the spring, when the nettle tops are young and tender. Strip about 10oz/275g nettle tops from the stems, chop them and add to the leeks. Continue as above.

Per portion Energy 199Kcal/834kJ; Protein 10g; Carbohydrate 19.5g, of which sugars 12.4g; Fat 9.6g, of which saturates 5.1g; Cholesterol 22mg; Calcium 243mg; Fibre 5.8g; Sodium 219mg

Leek and cheese soup

The cheese is an integral part of this substantial soup, which makes full use of ingredients that have always been important in Irish cooking. It can be a good way to use up cheeses left over from the cheeseboard. Serve with freshly baked brown bread.

Serves 6

3 large leeks

50g/2oz/¼ cup butter

30ml/2 tbsp oil

115g/4oz Irish farmhouse cheese, such as Cashel Blue

15g/½oz/2 tbsp plain (all-purpose) flour

15ml/1 tbsp wholegrain Irish mustard, or to taste

1.5 litres/2½ pints/6¼ cups chicken stock

ground black pepper

50g/2oz/½ cup grated cheese and chopped chives or spring onion (scallion) greens, to garnish

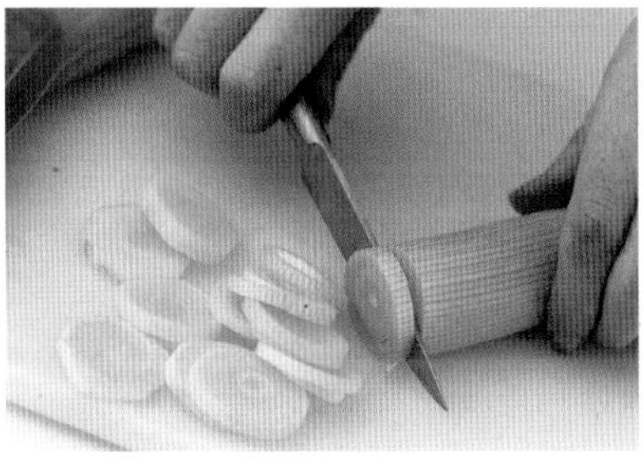

1 Slice the leeks thinly. Heat the butter and oil together in a large heavy pan and gently cook the leeks in it, covered, for 10–15 minutes, or until just softened but not brown.

2 Grate the cheese coarsely and add it to the pan, stirring over a low heat, until it is melted. Add the flour and cook for 2 minutes, stirring constantly with a wooden spoon, then add ground black pepper and wholegrain mustard to taste.

3 Gradually add the stock, stirring constantly and blending it in well; bring the soup to the boil.

4 Reduce the heat, cover and simmer very gently for about 15 minutes. Check the seasoning and serve the soup garnished with the extra grated cheese and the chopped chives or spring onion greens, and hand fresh bread around separately.

Variation Any melting cheese can be used instead of Cashel Blue, such as Cooleeney, a soft white cheese from County Tipperary, St Killian or Milleens, from West Cork.

Per portion Energy 187Kcal/773kJ; Protein 5.6g; Carbohydrate 4.3g, of which sugars 1.9g; Fat 16.6g, of which saturates 8.6g; Cholesterol 32mg; Calcium 118mg; Fibre 1.8g; Sodium 407mg

Mushroom soup

Using a mixture of mushrooms gives this soup character. This makes a flavoursome light meal served with fresh crusty bread.

Serves 4–6 as a light meal or 6–8 as a soup course

- 20g/¾oz/1½ tbsp butter
- 15ml/1 tbsp oil
- 1 onion, roughly chopped
- 4 potatoes, about 250–350g/9–12oz, roughly chopped
- 350g/12oz mixed mushrooms, such as Paris Browns, field (portobello) and button (white), roughly chopped
- 1 or 2 garlic cloves, crushed
- 150ml/¼ pint/⅔ cup white wine or dry (hard) cider

- 1.2 litres/2 pints/5 cups good chicken stock
- bunch of fresh parsley, chopped
- salt and ground black pepper
- whipped or sour cream, to garnish

1 Heat the butter and oil in a large pan, over medium heat. Add the onion and potatoes. Cover and sweat over a low heat for 5–10 minutes until softened but not browned.

2 Add the mushrooms, garlic and white wine or cider and stock. Season, bring to the boil and cook for 15 minutes, until all the ingredients are tender.

3 Put the mixture through a mouli-légumes (food mill), using the coarse blade, or liquidize (blend). Return the soup to the rinsed pan, and add three-quarters of the parsley. Bring back to the boil, season, and garnish with cream and the remaining parsley.

Per portion Energy 155Kcal/648kJ; Protein 3.3g; Carbohydrate 13.6g, of which sugars 3.4g; Fat 7.6g, of which saturates 3.1g; Cholesterol 11mg; Calcium 23mg; Fibre 2.1g; Sodium 117mg

Garlic soup

This interesting and surprisingly subtly flavoured soup makes good use of an ancient ingredient that is not only delicious but also has great health-giving properties.

Serves 8

- 12 large garlic cloves, peeled
- 15ml/1 tbsp olive oil
- 15ml/1 tbsp melted butter
- 1 small onion, finely chopped
- 15g/½oz/2 tbsp plain (all-purpose) flour
- 15ml/1 tbsp white wine vinegar
- 1 litre/1¾ pints/4 cups chicken stock
- 2 egg yolks, lightly beaten
- bread croûtons, fried in butter, to serve

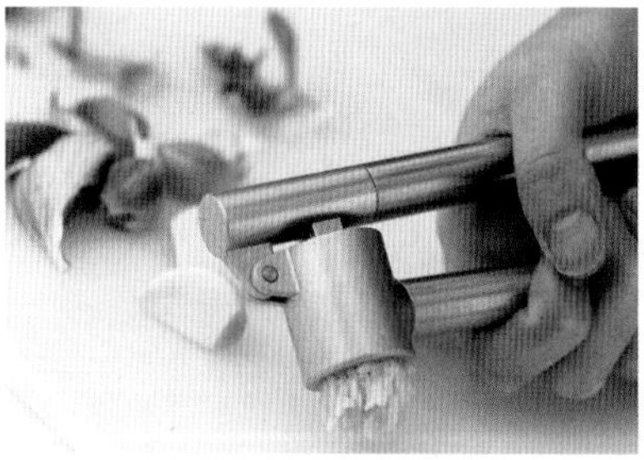

1 Crush the garlic. Put the oil and butter into a pan, add the garlic and onion, and cook them gently for 20 minutes.

2 Add the flour and stir to make a roux. Cook for a few minutes, then stir in the wine vinegar, stock and 1 litre/1¾ pints/4 cups water. Simmer for 30 minutes.

3 When ready to serve, whisk in the egg yolks and do not allow the soup to boil again. Put the croûtons into soup bowls and pour the hot soup over.

Cook's tip This garlic soup brings a great sense of well-being and is a real treat for garlic-lovers.

Per portion Energy 55Kcal/229kJ; Protein 1.3g; Carbohydrate 3g, of which sugars 0.5g; Fat 4.4g, of which saturates 1.6g; Cholesterol 54mg; Calcium 12mg; Fibre 0.3g; Sodium 50mg

Fish soup

With some fresh crusty home-made brown bread or garlic bread, this quick-and-easy soup can be served like a stew and will make a delicious first course or supper.

Serves 6

- 25g/1oz/2 tbsp butter
- 1 onion, finely chopped
- 1 garlic clove, crushed or finely chopped
- 1 small red (bell) pepper, seeded and chopped
- salt and ground black pepper
- 2.5ml/½ tsp sugar
- a dash of Tabasco sauce
- 25g/1oz/¼ cup plain (all-purpose) flour
- about 600ml/1 pint/2½ cups fish stock
- 450g/1lb ripe tomatoes, skinned and chopped, or 400g/14oz can chopped tomatoes
- 115g/4oz/1½ cups mushrooms, chopped
- about 300ml/½ pint/1¼ cups milk
- 225g/8oz white fish, such as haddock or whiting, filleted and skinned, and cut into bitesize cubes
- 115g/4oz smoked haddock or cod, skinned, and cut into bitesize cubes
- 12–18 mussels, cleaned (optional)
- chopped fresh parsley or chives, to garnish

1 Melt the butter in a large heavy pan and cook the chopped onion and crushed garlic gently in it until softened but not browned. Add the chopped red pepper. Season with salt and pepper, the sugar and Tabasco sauce. Sprinkle the flour over and cook gently for 2 minutes, stirring. Gradually stir in the stock and add the tomatoes, with their juices and the mushrooms.

2 Bring to the boil over medium heat, stir well and then reduce the heat and simmer gently until the vegetables are soft. Add the milk and bring back to the boil.

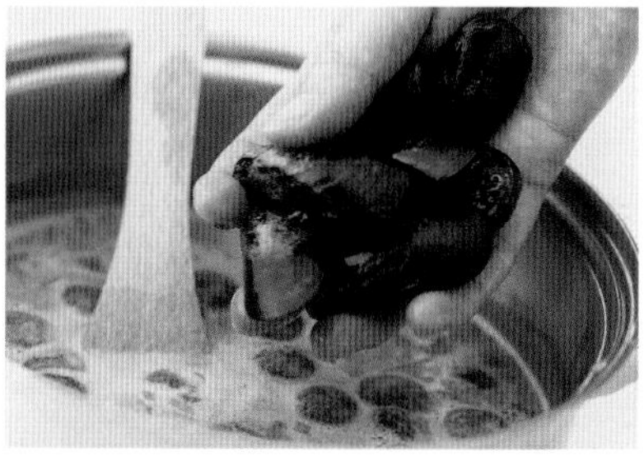

3 Add the fish to the pan and simmer for 3 minutes, then add the mussels, if using, and cook for another 3–4 minutes, or until the fish is just tender but not breaking up. Discard any mussels that remain closed. Adjust the consistency with a little extra fish stock or milk, if necessary. Check the seasoning and serve immediately, garnished with parsley or chives.

Per portion Energy 142Kcal/597kJ; Protein 13.9g; Carbohydrate 10.7g, of which sugars 7.1g; Fat 5.2g, of which saturates 2.9g; Cholesterol 36mg; Calcium 84mg; Fibre 1.7g; Sodium 91mg

Seafood chowder

This filling fish soup is infinitely adaptable according to the availability of fresh fish and shellfish. Hand around freshly made brown bread separately.

Serves 4–6

- 50g/2oz/¼ cup butter
- 1 large onion, chopped
- 115g/4oz bacon, rind removed, diced
- 4 celery sticks, diced
- 2 large potatoes, diced
- 450g/1lb ripe, juicy tomatoes, chopped or 400g/14oz can chopped tomatoes
- about 450ml/¾ pint/2 cups fish stock
- 450g/1lb white fish fillets, such as cod, plaice, flounder or haddock, skinned and cut into small chunks
- 225g/8oz shellfish, such as prawns (shrimp), scallops or mussels
- about 300ml/½ pint/1¼ cups milk
- 25g/1oz/¼ cup cornflour (cornstarch)
- sea salt and ground black pepper
- lightly whipped cream and chopped parsley, to garnish

1 Melt the butter in a large pan, add the onion, bacon, celery and potatoes and coat with the butter. Cover and leave to sweat over very gentle heat for 5–10 minutes, without colouring.

2 Meanwhile purée the tomatoes in a blender, and sieve them to remove the skin and pips. Add the tomato purée and fish stock to the pan. Bring to the boil, cover and leave to simmer gently until the potatoes are tender, skimming the top occasionally as required.

3 Prepare fresh prawns by plunging briefly in a pan of boiling water. Remove from the pan as the water boils. Cool and peel.

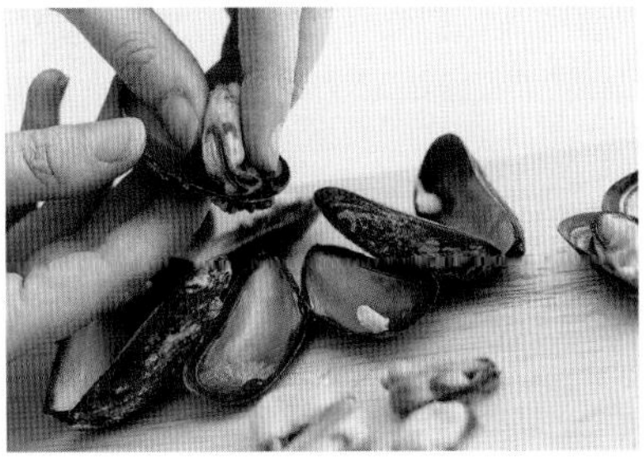

4 If using mussels, scrub the shells and discard any that do not open when tapped. Put the mussels into a shallow, heavy pan, without adding any liquid. Cover tightly and cook over a high heat for a few minutes, shaking occasionally, until all the mussels have opened. Discard any that fail to open. Remove the cooked mussels from their shells. Raw shelled scallops can be left whole.

5 Add the shellfish to the soup. Blend the milk and cornflour together in a small jug (pitcher), stir into the soup and bring to the boil again. Reduce the heat, and cover and simmer for a few minutes until the fish is just tender. Adjust the texture with milk or stock if necessary and season to taste with sea salt, if required, and freshly ground black pepper. Serve in warm soup bowls, garnished with a swirl of cream and some parsley.

Variation To make cockle and mussel chowder, replace the mixed fish and shellfish with 175g/6oz shelled cooked mussels and 115g/4oz shelled cooked cockles; include any liquor left from cooking the mussels and cockles. Reserve a few in their shells for garnish, if you like.

Per portion Energy 488Kcal/2050kJ; Protein 46g; Carbohydrate 36.2g, of which sugars 11.3g; Fat 18.7g, of which saturates 9.6g; Cholesterol 127mg; Calcium 163mg; Fibre 3.5g; Sodium 771mg

Bacon broth

A hearty meal in a soup bowl. The bacon hock contributes flavour and some meat to this dish, but it may be salty so remember to taste and add extra salt only if required.

Serves 6–8

- 1 bacon hock, about 900g/2lb
- 75g/3oz/⅓ cup pearl barley
- 75g/3oz/⅓ cup lentils
- 2 leeks, sliced, or onions, diced
- 4 carrots, diced
- 200g/7oz swede (rutabaga), diced
- 3 potatoes, diced
- small bunch of herbs (thyme, parsley, bay leaf)
- 1 small cabbage, trimmed, quartered or sliced
- salt and ground black pepper
- chopped fresh parsley, to garnish
- brown bread, to serve

1 Soak the bacon in cold water overnight. Next morning, drain it and put it into a large pan with enough fresh cold water to cover it. Bring to the boil, skim off any scum that rises to the surface, and then add the barley and lentils. Bring back to the boil and simmer for about 15 minutes.

2 Add the vegetables to the pan with some black pepper and the herbs. Bring back to the boil, reduce the heat and simmer gently for 1½ hours, or until the meat is tender.

3 Lift the bacon hock from the pan with a slotted spoon. Remove the skin, then take the meat off the bones and break it into bitesize pieces. Return to the pan with the cabbage. Discard the herbs and cook for a little longer until the cabbage is cooked to your liking.

4 Adjust the seasoning and ladle into large serving bowls, garnish with parsley and serve with freshly baked brown bread.

Per portion Energy 306Kcal/1284kJ; Protein 17.7g; Carbohydrate 33.5g, of which sugars 8.3g; Fat 12.1g, of which saturates 4.3g; Cholesterol 35mg; Calcium 74mg; Fibre 4.6g; Sodium 1.05g

Kidney and bacon soup

Although there is a modern twist in the seasonings, the two main ingredients of this meaty soup are still very traditionally Irish.

Serves 4–6

225g/8oz ox kidney

15ml/1 tbsp vegetable oil

4 streaky (fatty) bacon rashers (strips), chopped

1 large onion, chopped

2 garlic cloves, finely chopped

15ml/1 tbsp plain (all-purpose) flour

1.5 litres/2½ pints/6¼ cups water

a good dash of Worcestershire sauce

a good dash of soy sauce

15ml/l tbsp chopped fresh thyme, or 5ml/1 tsp dried thyme

75g/3oz/¾ cup grated cheese

4–6 slices French bread, toasted

salt and ground black pepper

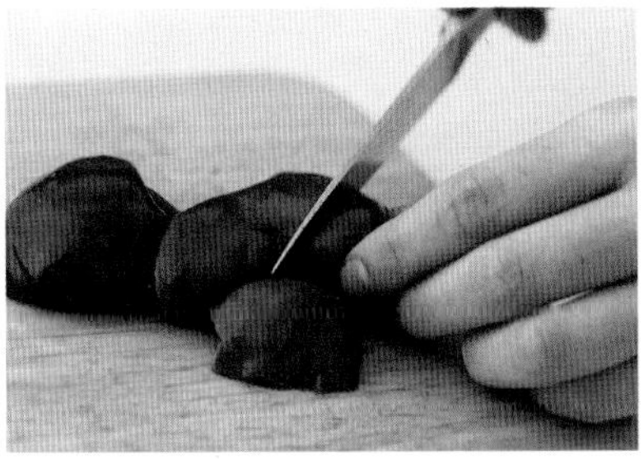

1 Wash the kidney in cold, salted water. Drain, dry well on kitchen paper and chop.

2 Heat the vegetable oil in a large pan over a medium heat. Add the chopped streaky bacon and sauté for a few minutes. Add the prepared kidney and continue cooking until nicely browned. Stir in the chopped onion and chopped garlic, and cook until the onion is just soft.

3 Add the flour and cook for 2 minutes. Gradually add the water, stirring constantly. Add the sauces, thyme and seasoning to taste. Reduce the heat and simmer gently for 30–35 minutes.

4 Sprinkle the cheese on to the toast and grill until it is bubbling. Pour the soup into bowls, and top with the toast.

Right *Cattle grazing above Sheephaven Bay, Muckish, Rosguill, County Donegal.*

Per portion Energy 445Kcal/1866kJ; Protein 26.8g; Carbohydrate 40.7g, of which sugars 5.4g; Fat 20.2g, of which saturates 8.1g; Cholesterol 192mg; Calcium 241mg; Fibre 2.4g; Sodium 1.18g

Lamb and vegetable broth

This is a good modern adaptation of the traditional recipe for Irish mutton broth, *Brachán caoireola*, and is delicious served with wholemeal bread.

Serves 6

- 675g/1½lb neck of lamb on the bone
- 1 large onion
- 2 bay leaves
- 3 carrots, chopped
- ½ white turnip, diced
- ½ small white cabbage, shredded
- 2 large leeks, thinly sliced
- 15ml/1 tbsp tomato purée (paste)
- 30ml/2 tbsp chopped fresh parsley
- salt and ground black pepper

1 Trim any excess fat from the meat. Chop the onion, and put the lamb and bay leaves in a large pan. Add 1.5 litres/ 2½ pints/6¼ cups water and bring to the boil. Skim the surface and then simmer for about 1½–2 hours. Remove the lamb on to a board and leave to cool until ready to handle.

2 Remove the meat from the bones and cut into small pieces. Discard the bones and return the meat to the broth. Add the vegetables, tomato purée and parsley, and season well. Simmer for another 30 minutes, until the vegetables are tender. Ladle into soup bowls and serve.

Per portion Energy 162Kcal/675kJ; Protein 13.1g; Carbohydrate 8.5g, of which sugars 7g; Fat 8.6g, of which saturates 3.8g; Cholesterol 44mg; Calcium 42mg; Fibre 3g; Sodium 55mg

Beef and barley soup

This traditional Irish farmhouse soup makes a wonderfully restorative dish on a cold day. The flavours develop particularly well if it is made in advance and reheated to serve.

Serves 6–8

- 450–675g/1–1½lb rib steak, or other stewing beef on the bone
- 2 large onions
- 50g/2oz/¼ cup pearl barley
- 50g/2oz/¼ cup green split peas
- 3 large carrots, chopped
- 2 white turnips, chopped
- 3 celery stalks, chopped
- 1 large or 2 medium leeks, thinly sliced
- sea salt and ground black pepper
- chopped fresh parsley, to serve

1 Bone the meat, put the bones and half an onion, roughly sliced, into a large pan. Cover with cold water, season and bring to the boil. Skim if necessary, then leave to simmer until required.

2 Meanwhile, trim any fat or gristle from the meat and cut into small pieces. Chop the remaining onions finely. Drain the stock from the bones, make it up with water to 2 litres/3½ pints/9 cups, and return to the rinsed pan with the meat, onions, barley and split peas.

3 Season, bring to the boil, and skim if necessary. Reduce the heat, cover and simmer for about 30 minutes.

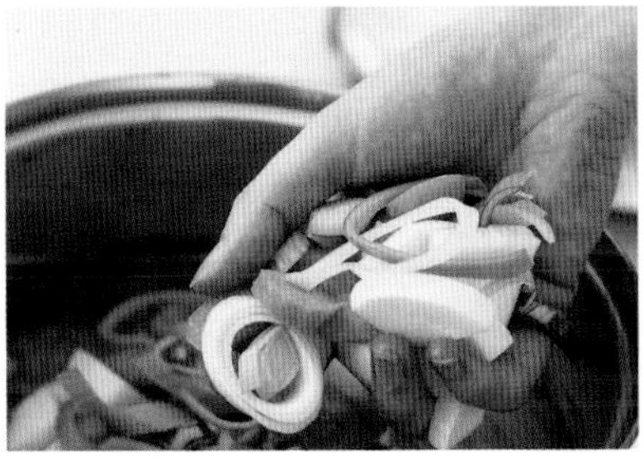

4 Add the rest of the vegetables and simmer for 1 hour, or until the meat is tender. Check the seasoning. Serve in large warmed bowls, generously sprinkled with parsley.

Above *A traditional Irish thatched roof cottage in Mooncoin village, Kilkenny.*

Per portion Energy 194Kcal/816kJ; Protein 20.3g; Carbohydrate 21.6g, of which sugars 12g; Fat 3.5g, of which saturates 1.2g; Cholesterol 50mg; Calcium 84mg; Fibre 5g; Sodium 88mg

First courses

Although such things would have been common enough in the "big houses" of yesteryear, starting a family meal in Ireland with a first course or appetizer is a modern notion, made popular through the huge recent increase in restaurant dining. Yet many would now cite these tasty little dishes as their favourite part of a larger meal – and they tend to make excellent light meals or snacks in their own right.

Goat's cheese salad with hazelnut dressing

The milder-flavoured goat's cheeses are popular in Ireland. Corleggy Quivvy (small chunks preserved in oil) and Boilié (little balls in jars of oil) are examples of excellent handmade soft cheeses, both from County Cavan and widely available from normal food stores.

Serves 4

175g/6oz mixed salad leaves, such as lamb's lettuce, rocket (arugula), radicchio, frisée or cress

a few fresh large-leafed herbs, such as chervil and flat leaf parsley

15ml/1 tbsp toasted hazelnuts, roughly chopped

15–20 goat's cheese balls or cubes

For the dressing

30ml/2 tbsp hazelnut oil, olive oil or sunflower oil

5–10ml/1–2 tsp sherry vinegar or good wine vinegar, to taste

salt and ground black pepper

1 Tear up any large salad leaves. Put all the leaves into a large salad bowl with the fresh herbs and most of the toasted, chopped nuts (reserve a few for the garnish).

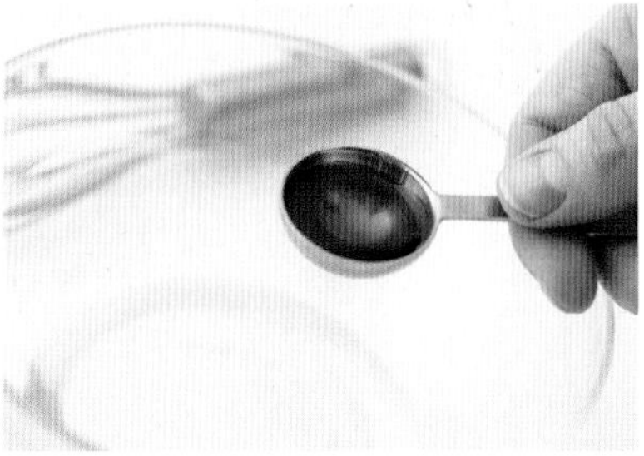

2 To make the dressing, whisk the hazelnut, olive or sunflower oil and vinegar together, and then season to taste with salt and pepper.

3 Just before serving, toss the salad in the dressing and divide it among four serving plates. Arrange the drained goat's cheese balls or cubes over the leaves, sprinkle over the remaining chopped nuts and serve.

Cook's tip A grilled (broiled) slice from a goat's cheese log can replace the cheese balls or cubes if you prefer.

Per portion Energy 225Kcal/931kJ; Protein 11g; Carbohydrate 1.4g, of which sugars 1.3g; Fat 19.5g, of which saturates 8.7g; Cholesterol 41mg; Calcium 138mg; Fibre 1.2g; Sodium 325mg

Pears with Cashel Blue cream and walnuts

The success of this dish depends on the quality of the pears, which must be very succulent, and, of course, the cheese. Cashel Blue, made from cow's milk in County Tipperary, is one of Ireland's great artisan food success stories and is widely available.

Serves 6

- 115g/4oz fresh cream cheese
- 75g/3oz Cashel Blue cheese
- 30–45ml/2–3 tbsp single (light) cream
- 115g/4oz/1 cup roughly chopped walnuts
- 6 ripe pears
- 15ml/1 tbsp lemon juice
- mixed salad leaves, such as frisée, oakleaf lettuce and radicchio
- 6 cherry tomatoes
- sea salt and ground black pepper
- walnut halves and sprigs of fresh flat leaf parsley, to garnish

For the dressing

- juice of 1 lemon
- a little finely grated lemon rind
- pinch of caster (superfine) sugar
- 60ml/4 tbsp olive oil

1 Mash the cream cheese and Cashel Blue cheese together in a mixing bowl with a good grinding of black pepper, then blend in the cream to make a smooth mixture. Add 25g/1oz/¼ cup chopped walnuts and mix to distribute evenly. Cover and chill until required.

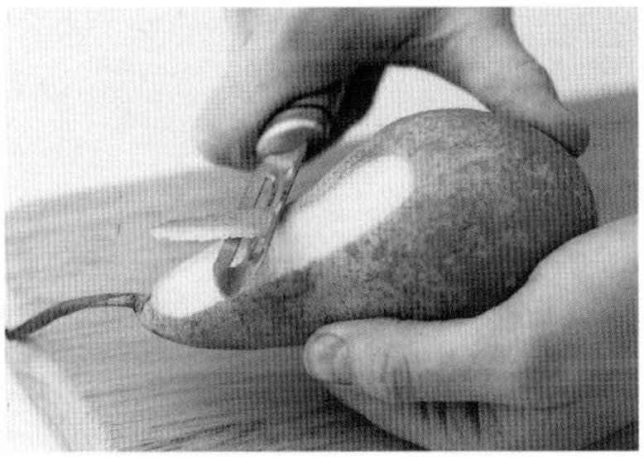

2 Peel and halve the pears and scoop out the core. Put them into a bowl of water with the 15ml/1 tbsp lemon juice to prevent them from browning.To make the dressing: whisk the lemon juice, lemon rind, caster sugar and olive oil together and season to taste.

3 Arrange a bed of salad leaves on six plates – shallow soup plates are ideal – add a tomato to each and sprinkle over the remaining chopped walnuts.

4 Drain the pears well and pat dry with kitchen paper, then turn them in the prepared dressing and arrange, hollow side up, on the salad leaves. Divide the Cashel Blue mixture between the six halved pears, and spoon the dressing over the top. Garnish each pear with a walnut half and a sprig of flat leaf parsley before serving.

Variation Crozier Blue or other mature blue cheese can be used instead.

Per portion Energy 331Kcal/1373kJ; Protein 6.7g; Carbohydrate 16.3g, of which sugars 16.1g; Fat 27g, of which saturates 9.8g; Cholesterol 30mg; Calcium 120mg; Fibre 4.1g; Sodium 219mg

Cheese and Guinness fondue

This simple dish can be made with any melting cheese – richly flavoured farmhouse cheeses are the most interesting. It can be used as a hot dip for drinks parties, or as a light meal for a smaller number, perhaps served with crusty bread cubes and followed by a green salad.

Serves 8

300ml/½ pint/1¼ cups stout, such as Guinness

5ml/1 tsp lemon juice

15ml/1 tbsp cornflour (cornstarch)

450g/1lb Irish "melting" cheese(s), grated or finely diced

salt and ground black pepper

selection of crudités, such as celery, cauliflower and broccoli florets, carrot sticks, button mushrooms, and chunks of sweet (bell) pepper, to serve

1 Heat the stout and lemon juice gently in a heavy pan, until it is just reaching boiling point.

2 Mix the cornflour and cheese. Add to the pan gradually, over a gentle heat, stirring until the cheese has melted. Season to taste and cook gently until the fondue thickens. Transfer to a fondue pot and place on a burner at the table.

3 To serve, spear the crudités with a fork and dip into the fondue.

Cook's tips

- The fondue will thicken as it cools, so it is necessary to keep it warm over a flame, or serve it in a preheated electric slow cooker.
- Choose cheeses such as farmhouse cheddar and other semi-hard melting cheeses such as Gabriel and Desmond and Ardrahan, a vegetarian washed-rind cheese from west Cork.

Per portion Energy 250Kcal/1036kJ; Protein 14.5g; Carbohydrate 1.8g, of which sugars 0.6g; Fat 18.4g, of which saturates 12.2g; Cholesterol 55mg; Calcium 417mg; Fibre 0g; Sodium 410mg

Fishcakes

A well-made fishcake is always a treat and they can be made with salmon or any fresh or smoked white fish. This dish makes a little fish go a long way, but don't stretch it beyond equal quantities of fish and potato. Parsley sauce is the traditional accompaniment.

Serves 4

- 450g/1lb fresh salmon or smoked white fish
- wedge of lemon
- small bay leaf and a few fresh parsley stalks
- 25g/1oz/2 tbsp butter
- 1 onion, finely chopped
- 450g/1lb potatoes, cooked and mashed
- 30ml/2 tbsp chopped fresh parsley
- pinhead oatmeal, to coat
- butter and oil, for frying
- ground black pepper

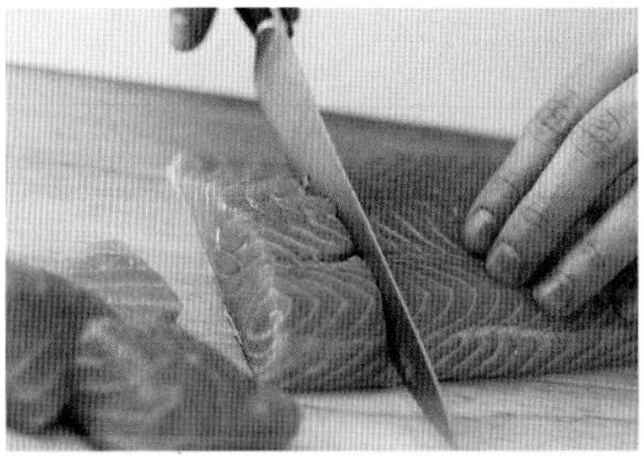

1 Rinse the fish and cut it into medium-size pieces. Put it into a pan with the lemon, bay leaf and parsley stalks and enough cold water to cover. Bring slowly to the boil, then reduce the heat and simmer gently for 5–7 minutes. Remove the fish and drain well.

2 When cool enough to handle, flake the flesh and discard the skin and bones. Melt the butter in a large pan, add the onion and cook gently for a few minutes until softened but not coloured. Add the flaked fish, potato and parsley. Season to taste with pepper.

3 Turn the mixture on to a work surface generously covered with pinhead oatmeal. Divide in half, and then quarter each piece. Form into eight flat cakes and coat them with the oatmeal.

4 Heat a little butter and an equal quantity of oil in a heavy frying pan, add the fishcakes (in batches, if necessary) and fry until golden on both sides. Drain and serve immediately.

Per portion Energy 380Kcal/1584kJ; Protein 25.3g; Carbohydrate 20.5g, of which sugars 3.3g; Fat 22.4g, of which saturates 8.6g; Cholesterol 83mg; Calcium 49mg; Fibre 1.8g; Sodium 138mg

Smoked Wicklow trout with cucumber

Rainbow trout is farmed in the Wicklow Hills and the smoked trout fillets are widely available in vacuum packs. They need no further cooking or preparation except for any accompanying salad or sauce, making them an excellent fresh convenience food and a deservedly popular cold first course or light meal. Allow one or two fillets per person.

Serves 4

- 1 small cucumber
- 4–8 smoked trout fillets
- sprigs of dill, to garnish
- brown bread and butter, to serve

For the dressing

- 90ml/6 tbsp extra virgin olive oil
- 30ml/2 tbsp white wine vinegar
- 15ml/1 tbsp chopped fresh dill
- sea salt and ground black pepper

1 To make the dressing, whisk the oil and vinegar together vigorously, or shake in a screw-top jar, then blend in the dill and seasoning to taste.

2 Peel the cucumber, if you prefer, and slice it thinly. Arrange with the trout fillets on four serving plates.

3 Sprinkle the fish with the dressing, and garnish with sprigs of dill. Serve with brown bread and butter.

Above *The clear waters of the Glendasin river flowing through Glendalough, County Wicklow.*

Per portion Energy 467Kcal/1943kJ; Protein 55g; Carbohydrate 0.7g, of which sugars 0.6g; Fat 27g, of which saturates 4.7g; Cholesterol 226mg; Calcium 92mg; Fibre 0.3g; Sodium 206mg

Smoked salmon with warm potato cakes

Although the ingredients are timeless, this combination makes an excellent modern dish, which is deservedly popular as a first course or as a substantial canapé to serve with drinks. It also makes a perfect brunch dish, served with lightly scrambled eggs and freshly squeezed orange juice. Choose wild fish if possible.

Serves 6

450g/1lb potatoes, cooked and mashed

75g/3oz/⅔ cup plain (all-purpose) flour

2 eggs, beaten

2 spring onions (scallions), chopped

a little freshly grated nutmeg

50g/2oz/¼ cup butter, melted

150ml/¼ pint/⅔ cup sour cream

12 slices of smoked salmon

salt and ground black pepper

chopped fresh chives, to garnish

1 Put the potatoes, flour, eggs and spring onions into a large bowl. Season with salt, pepper and a little nutmeg, and add half the butter. Mix thoroughly and shape into 12 small potato cakes.

◀ **2** Heat the remaining butter in a non-stick pan and cook the potato cakes until browned on both sides.

3 To serve, mix the sour cream with some salt and pepper. Fold a piece of smoked salmon and place on top of each potato cake. Top with the cream and chives and serve immediately.

Cook's tip If it is more convenient, you can make the potato cakes in advance and keep them overnight in the refrigerator. When required, warm them through in a hot oven 15 minutes before serving and assembling.

Variation Top the potato cakes with smoked mackerel and a squeeze of lemon juice, if you like.

Per portion Energy 326Kcal/1365kJ; Protein 21.9g; Carbohydrate 22.9g, of which sugars 2.3g; Fat 17g, of which saturates 8.6g; Cholesterol 119mg; Calcium 70mg; Fibre 1.2g; Sodium 1315mg

Three-fish terrine

This attractive striped terrine uses haddock, salmon and turbot – all native fish to Irish seas and rivers. Serve with a small salad, freshly made brown bread or Melba toast and butter.

Serves 8–10

- 450g/1lb spinach
- 350–450g/12oz–1lb haddock, cod or other white fish, skinned and chopped
- 3 eggs
- 115g/4oz/2 cups fresh breadcrumbs
- 300ml/½ pint/1¼ cups fromage blanc
- a little freshly grated nutmeg
- 350–450g/12oz–1lb fresh salmon fillet
- 350–450g/12oz–1lb fresh turbot fillet, or other flat fish
- oil, for greasing
- salt and ground black pepper
- lemon wedges and sprigs of fresh dill or fennel, to garnish

1 Preheat the oven to 160°C/325°F/ Gas 3. Remove the stalks from the spinach and cook the leaves briskly in a pan without any added water, shaking the pan occasionally, until the spinach is just tender. Drain and squeeze out the excess water.

2 Put the spinach into a food processor or blender with the haddock or other white fish, eggs, breadcrumbs, fromage blanc, salt, pepper and nutmeg to taste. Process until smooth.

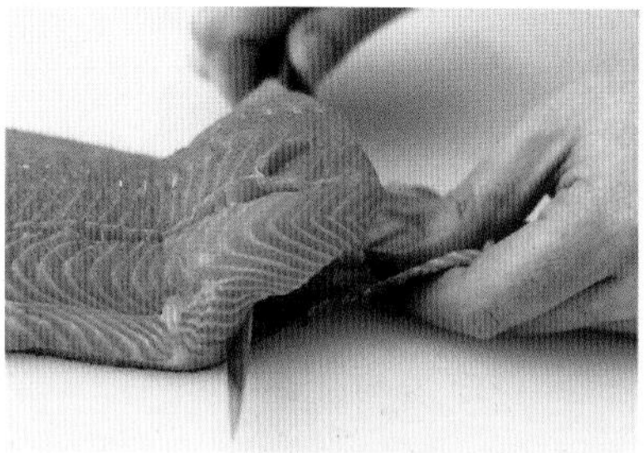

3 Skin and bone the salmon fillet and cut it into long thin strips. Repeat with the turbot.

4 Oil a 900g/2lb loaf tin (pan) or terrine and line the base with a piece of oiled baking parchment or foil, cut to fit. Make layers from the spinach mixture and the strips of salmon and turbot, starting and finishing with the spinach.

5 Press down carefully and cover with lightly oiled baking parchment. Prick a few holes in it, then put the terrine into a roasting pan and pour enough boiling water around it to come two-thirds of the way up the sides.

6 Bake in the preheated oven for 1–1½ hours, or until risen, firm and set. Leave to cool, then chill well before serving.

7 To serve, ease a sharp knife down the sides to loosen the terrine and turn the terrine on to a flat serving dish. Using a sharp knife, cut the terrine into slices and serve garnished with lemon wedges and fresh dill or fennel.

Cook's tip If you cannot find fromage blanc, substitute it with low-fat soft cream cheese.

Below *Boats moored on the tranquil waters of the Kenmare River, Ring of Kerry, County Kerry.*

Per portion Energy 290Kcal/1216kJ; Protein 32.5g; Carbohydrate 13.7g, of which sugars 2.8g; Fat 12.1g, of which saturates 3.9g; Cholesterol 112mg; Calcium 203mg; Fibre 1.5g; Sodium 306mg

Garlic-stuffed mussels

Mussels are a speciality of Wexford, on the south-east corner of Ireland, but they're also plentiful all around the coast and safe to gather from the rocks anywhere down the west coast if the water is clean. Wild herbs, including garlic, have been used in Ireland for hundreds of years, so this way of cooking mussels is more Irish than it might sound.

Serves 4–6

- 2kg/4½lb fresh mussels
- 175g/6oz/¾ cup butter
- 4–6 garlic cloves
- 50g/2oz/1 cup fresh white breadcrumbs
- 15ml/1 tbsp chopped fresh parsley
- juice of 1 lemon
- brown bread, to serve

1 Wash the mussels in cold water. Remove the beards and discard any with broken shells, or those that don't close when tapped.

2 Put the mussels into a shallow, heavy pan, without adding any liquid. Cover tightly and cook over a high heat for a few minutes, until all the mussels have opened. Discard any that fail to open.

3 Remove the top shell from each mussel and arrange the bottom shells with the mussels in a shallow flameproof dish.

4 Melt the butter in a small pan, add the crushed garlic, breadcrumbs, parsley and lemon juice. Mix well and sprinkle this mixture over the mussels.

5 Cook under a hot grill (broiler) until golden brown. Serve very hot, with freshly baked brown bread.

***Above** Cockles, mussels and shellfish are a popular catch all over Ireland.*

Per portion Energy 500Kcal/2082kJ; Protein 27.7g; Carbohydrate 10g, of which sugars 0.6g; Fat 39.2g, of which saturates 23.3g; Cholesterol 153mg; Calcium 319mg; Fibre 0.3g; Sodium 675mg

Oysters on the half-shell

The best native Irish oysters come from the Galway area on the west coast and, every September, festivals are held in Galway and Clarenbridge to celebrate the beginning of the new season. Dulse or dillisk, an edible seaweed, is an ideal garnish. Enjoy the oysters with freshly made brown soda bread and butter, and a glass of Guinness.

Serves 2–4

- 24 Galway oysters, in the shell
- crushed ice and dulse or dillisk (soaked if dried), to garnish
- soda bread and butter, and lemon wedges, to serve

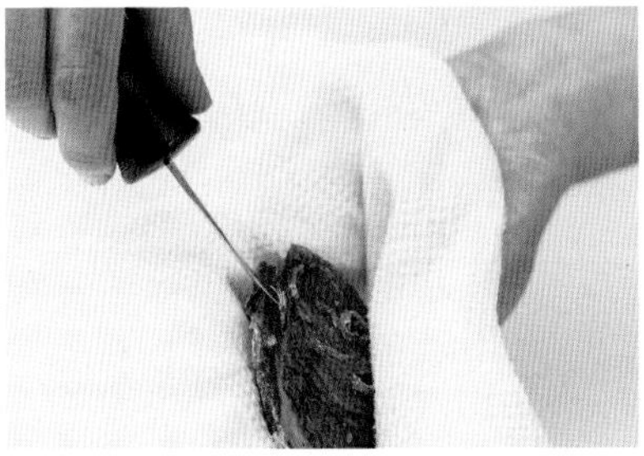

1 Use a blunt-ended oyster knife to shuck the oysters: insert the end of the knife between the shells near the hinge and work it until you cut through the muscle that holds the shells together. Catch the oyster liquid in a bowl.

2 When the oysters are all open, discard the flat shells. Divide the oysters, in the deep halves, among four serving plates lined with crushed ice and soaked dulse.

3 Strain the reserved liquid over the oysters. Serve with the lemon wedges.

Cook's tips

• Although they were once plentiful, Galway oysters are now a delicacy and eaten raw – buy them with their shells tightly clamped together, showing that they are still alive. The edible seaweed, dulse, or dillisk as it is also known, is an appropriate garnish for oysters.

• If you want oysters for a cooked dish, look for the widely cultivated, larger Pacific oysters, which are available all year round, unlike the native oyster which is found only when there's an 'r' in the month. Native oysters are named after their place of origin, such as the Irish Galway and the English Whitstable.

Per portion Energy 78Kcal/330kJ; Protein 13g; Carbohydrate 3.3g, of which sugars 0g; Fat 1.6g, of which saturates 0.3g; Cholesterol 68mg; Calcium 168mg; Fibre 0g; Sodium 612mg

Duck liver pâté with redcurrant sauce

For this classic recipe, duck or chicken livers are interchangeable, depending on availability. Redcurrant sauces are much favoured by Irish chefs, who appreciate the colour, lightness of texture and piquancy of the pretty little berries. This recipe is easy to prepare and keeps for about a week in the refrigerator if the butter seal is not broken.

Serves 4–6

- 1 onion, finely chopped
- 1 large garlic clove, crushed
- 115g/4oz/½ cup butter
- 225g/8oz duck livers
- 10–15ml/2–3 tsp chopped fresh mixed herbs, such as parsley, thyme or rosemary
- 15–30ml/1–2 tbsp brandy
- bay leaf (optional)
- 50–115g/2–4oz/¼ –½ cup clarified butter (see Cook's tip), or melted unsalted (sweet) butter
- salt and ground black pepper
- a sprig of flat leaf parsley, to garnish

For the redcurrant sauce

- 30ml/2 tbsp redcurrant jelly
- 15–30ml/1–2 tbsp port
- 30ml/2 tbsp redcurrants

For the Melba toast

- 8 slices white bread, crusts removed

Above *The attractive harbour and town of Dún Laoghaire, County Dublin.*

1 Cook the onion and garlic in 25g/1oz/2 tbsp of the butter in a pan over gentle heat, until just turning colour.

2 Trim the duck livers. Add to the pan with the herbs and cook together for about 3 minutes, or until the livers have browned on the outside but are still pink in the centre. Allow to cool.

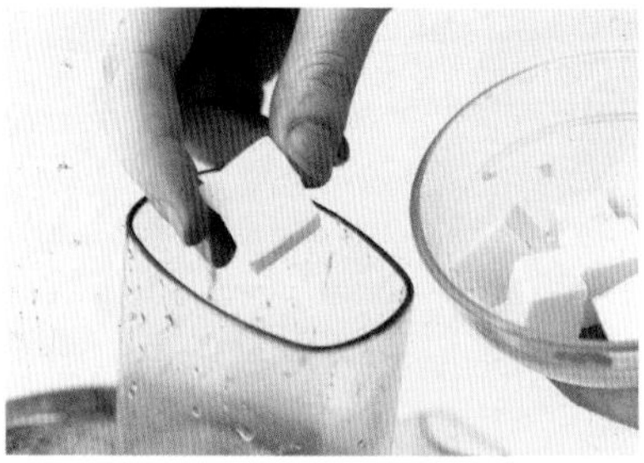

3 Dice the remaining butter, then process the liver mixture in a food processor, gradually working in the cubes of butter by dropping them down the chute on to the moving blades, to make a smooth purée.

4 Add the brandy, then check the seasoning and transfer to a 450–600ml/½–1 pint/scant 2 cups dish. Lay a bay leaf on top if you wish, then seal the pâté with clarified or unsalted butter. Cool, and then chill in the refrigerator until required.

5 To make the redcurrant sauce, put the redcurrant jelly, port and redcurrants into a small pan and bring gently to boiling point. Simmer to make a rich consistency. Leave to cool.

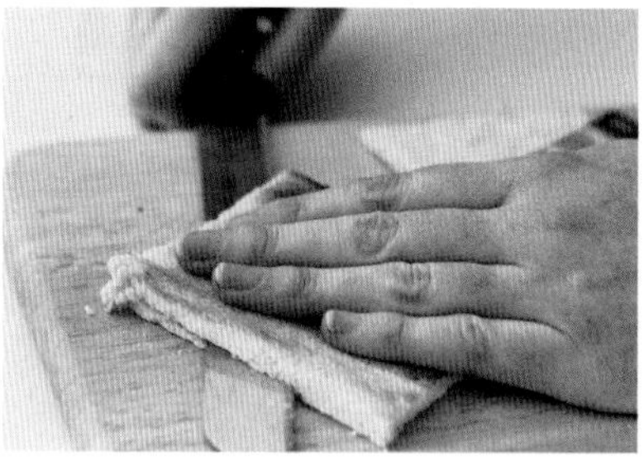

6 To make the Melba toast, toast the bread on both sides, then slice vertically to make 16 very thin slices. Place the untoasted side up on a grill (broiler) rack and grill until browned. (The toast can be stored in an airtight container for a few days, then warmed through to crisp up again just before serving.)

7 Serve the chilled pâté garnished with parsley and accompanied by Melba toast and the redcurrant sauce.

Cook's tip To make clarified butter, melt ordinary butter and pour off the clear liquid on top – this is the clarified butter. Discard any sediment left behind.

Per portion Energy 794Kcal/3312kJ; Protein 101.3g; Carbohydrate 11.3g, of which sugars 9.9g; Fat 36.8g, of which saturates 19g; Cholesterol 2213mg; Calcium 73mg; Fibre 1.3g; Sodium 608mg

Leek and bacon tart

This versatile tart soon becomes a favourite. While it makes a deliciously savoury first course, it is equally suitable served in more generous proportions with a mixed leaf salad as a light main course for lunch or supper.

Makes 6–8 individual tartlets or serves 8–10 as an appetizer

275g/10oz/2½ cups plain (all-purpose) flour

pinch of salt

175g/6oz/¾ cup butter

2 egg yolks

about 45ml/3 tbsp very cold water

lettuce leaves and tomato, to garnish

For the filling

225g/8oz streaky (fatty) bacon, diced

4 leeks, sliced

6 eggs

115g/4oz/½ cup cream cheese

15ml/1 tbsp mild mustard

pinch of cayenne pepper

salt and ground black pepper

1 Sieve the flour and salt into a bowl, and rub in the butter until it resembles fine breadcrumbs. Add the egg yolks and just enough water to combine the dough. Alternatively, you can use a food processor. Wrap the dough in clear film (plastic wrap) and place in the refrigerator for 30 minutes.

2 Meanwhile, preheat the oven to 200°C/400°F/Gas 6. Roll out the pastry thinly and use to line 6–8 tartlet cases or a 28cm/11in tart dish. Remove any air pockets and prick the base with a fork. Line the pastry loosely with baking parchment, weigh down with baking beans and bake the pastry shell blind for 15–20 minutes, or until golden.

3 To make the filling, cook the bacon in a hot pan until crisp. Add the leeks and continue to cook for 3–4 minutes until just softening. Remove from the heat. In a bowl, beat the eggs, cream cheese, mustard, cayenne pepper and seasoning together, then add the leeks and bacon.

4 Remove the paper and baking beans from the tartlet or tart case, pour in the filling and bake for 35–40 minutes.

5 To serve, plate the tartlets on to individual serving plates or cut the tart into narrow wedges and serve warm.

Per portion Energy 487Kcal/2026kJ; Protein 15.4g; Carbohydrate 28.2g, of which sugars 1.6g; Fat 35.7g, of which saturates 19.1g; Cholesterol 265mg; Calcium 107mg; Fibre 2.1g; Sodium 681mg

Bacon salad with farmhouse cheese dressing

This recipe combines complementary quality products: dry-cured bacon (which a number of companies are now making again) and one of Ireland's finest farmhouse cheeses, Cooleeney Camembert, from County Tipperary – also known for its apple production.

Serves 4

30ml/2 tbsp olive oil

50g/2oz diced streaky (fatty) bacon rashers (strips), preferably dry-cured, diced

1 eating apple, cored and chopped

2 small heads of cos or romaine lettuce

squeeze of lemon juice

salt and ground black pepper

warm soda bread, to serve

For the dressing

150ml/¼ pint/⅔ cup sour cream

15ml/1 tbsp cider

50g/2oz Cooleeney, or other Camembert-style cheese, chopped

a dash of cider vinegar

1 Heat 15ml/1 tbsp of the olive oil in a large frying pan and add the diced streaky bacon. Cook over a medium heat until crisp and golden. Add the chopped apple and cook gently for 1–2 minutes until golden brown and softened.

2 Tear the cos or romain lettuce carefully into bitesize pieces.

◀ **3** To make the dressing, heat the sour cream, cider, cheese and vinegar together in a small pan over a low heat until smooth and creamy. Dress the lettuce with some of the remaining oil and the lemon juice and season to taste, then divide among four plates. Place the warm apple and bacon on top, then drizzle over the dressing.

Per portion Energy 219Kcal/905kJ; Protein 6.7g; Carbohydrate 4g, of which sugars 4g; Fat 19.3g, of which saturates 9g; Cholesterol 41mg; Calcium 138mg; Fibre 0.6g; Sodium 300mg

Black pudding with potato and apple

Black pudding has come a long way from its once humble position in traditional Irish cooking. Made in West Cork and widely available, Clonakilty black pudding is especially popular, and features on many a contemporary restaurant menu.

Serves 4

- 4 large potatoes, peeled
- 45ml/3 tbsp olive oil
- 8 slices of black pudding (blood sausage), such as Clonakilty
- 115g/4oz cultivated mushrooms, such as oyster or shiitake
- 2 eating apples, peeled, cored and cut into wedges
- 15ml/1 tbsp sherry vinegar or wine vinegar
- 15g/1oz/2 tbsp butter
- salt and ground black pepper

1 Grate the potatoes, putting them into a bowl of water as you grate them, drain and squeeze out the excess moisture.

2 Heat 30ml/2 tbsp olive oil in a large non-stick frying pan, add the grated potatoes and seasoning. Press the potatoes into the pan with your hands.

3 Cook the potatoes until browned, then turn over and cook the other side. When cooked, slide on to a warm plate.

4 Heat the remaining oil and sauté the black pudding and mushrooms together for a few minutes. Remove from the pan and keep warm.

5 Add the apple wedges to the frying pan and gently sauté to colour them golden brown. Add the sherry or wine vinegar to the apples, and boil up the juices. Add the butter, stir with a wooden spatula until it has melted and season to taste with salt and ground black pepper.

6 Cut the potato cake into wedges and divide among four warmed plates. Arrange the black pudding and cooked mushrooms on the bed of potato cake, pour over the apples and the warm juices and serve immediately with a glass of Irish cider.

Per portion Energy 247Kcal/1034kJ; Protein 4.2g; Carbohydrate 28.8g, of which sugars 5.4g; Fat 13.6g, of which saturates 4g; Cholesterol 13mg; Calcium 16mg; Fibre 2.4g; Sodium 132mg

Lamb's kidneys with mustard sauce

This piquant recipe is simple and flexible, so the exact amounts of any one ingredient are unimportant. It makes a tasty first course but would be equally suitable as a supper dish for two, in which case rice makes a good accompaniment, followed by a green salad.

Serves 4

- 4–6 lamb's kidneys
- butter, for frying
- Dijon mustard or other mild mustard, to taste
- 250ml/8fl oz/1 cup white wine
- 5ml/1 tsp chopped fresh mixed herbs, such as rosemary, thyme, parsley and chives
- 1 small garlic clove, crushed
- about 30ml/2 tbsp single (light) cream
- salt and ground black pepper
- fresh parsley, to garnish

1 Skin the kidneys and slice them horizontally. Remove the cores with scissors, and then wash them thoroughly in plenty of cold water. Drain and dry off with kitchen paper.

◄ **2** Heat a little butter in a heavy frying pan and gently cook the kidneys in it until cooked as you like them, but be careful not to overcook. Remove the kidneys from the pan and keep warm. Add a spoonful of mustard to the pan with the wine, herbs and garlic. Simmer to reduce by about half, then add enough cream to make a smooth sauce.

3 Return the kidneys to their sauce and reheat gently, without cooking any further, or the kidneys will be tough. Serve garnished with parsley, and with rice or a green salad.

Cook's tip Look for kidneys that are firm, with a rich, even colour. Avoid those with dry spots or a dull surface.

Per portion Energy 138Kcal/578kJ; Protein 15.6g; Carbohydrate 0.6g, of which sugars 0.6g; Fat 3.8g, of which saturates 1.7g; Cholesterol 288mg; Calcium 20mg; Fibre 0g; Sodium 140mg

Fish and shellfish

As an island nation, the Irish prize fish and shellfish as specialities, and these foods are much appreciated by residents and visitors alike. Dublin Bay prawns (jumbo shrimp), Galway oysters, wild salmon from the great fishing rivers and loughs, Wexford mussels, lobster and crab from all around the coast are among the many treats in store, presented in both traditional and creative modern dishes.

Black sole on the bone

In Ireland the fish known elsewhere as Dover sole is generally called black sole – and it is no relation to lemon sole, a softer and less expensive fish. Ask your fishmonger to remove the coarse black skin for you, but retain the white skin, as it adds flavour and keeps the cooked fish in shape. New potatoes are delicious with the sole, with a mixed leaf salad.

Serves 4

- 4 medium-size black sole
- 115g/4oz/¼ cup butter
- juice of ½ lemon
- ground black pepper
- finely chopped fresh parsley, to garnish
- lemon wedges, to serve

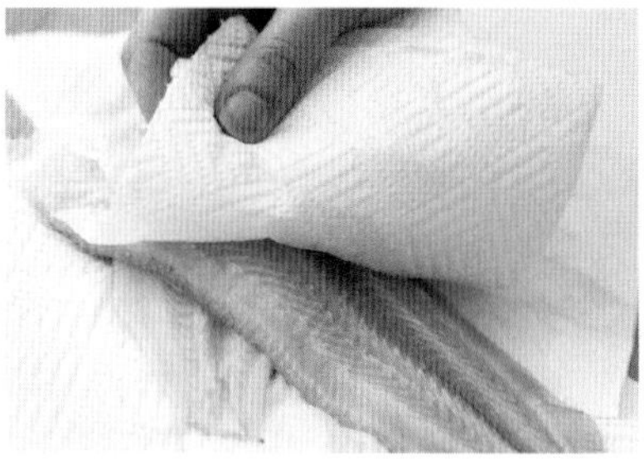

1 Wash the fish and dry thoroughly with kitchen paper. Heat the butter and oil in a heavy frying pan.

2 Season the fish on both sides with lemon juice and ground black pepper, then cook for 4 or 5 minutes flesh side down, depending on thickness; turn carefully with a fish slice or metal spatula and cook the second side until the flesh is opaque and it comes away easily from the bone when tested with the tip of a knife.

3 Carefully transfer the fish to warmed serving plates, pour over any pan juices, sprinkle with parsley and serve with lemon wedges.

Above *Moored up for the evening in Tralee Bay, County Kerry.*

Per portion Energy 109Kcal/463kJ; Protein 24.8g; Carbohydrate 0g, of which sugars 0g; Fat 1g, of which saturates 0.2g; Cholesterol 88mg; Calcium 26mg; Fibre 0g; Sodium 145mg

Ray with black butter

The butter in this classic dish is not really black but a deep nutty brown, and its flavour complements the sweetish flesh perfectly. Ray has soft ribs instead of bones, but the skin is very hard to remove from the raw fish, so make sure the fishmonger does this for you. Offer boiled new potatoes and a side salad to accompany the ray.

Serves 4

- 675g/1½lb ray wings, skinned
- half a small onion, sliced
- bay leaf
- a few parsley stalks
- 1 slice of lemon
- 75g/3oz/6 tbsp butter
- 50g/2oz capers
- 2.5ml/½ tsp white wine vinegar
- chopped fresh parsley, to garnish (optional)

1 Cut the ray wings into four serving pieces. Put 600ml/1 pint/2½ cups water into a wide pan with the onion, bay leaf, parsley stalks and lemon.

2 Bring to boiling point, then add the ray pieces and, when the water comes to the boil, reduce the heat to a gentle simmer. The cooking time will depend on the thickness of the ray, so cook very gently for about 15–20 minutes, or until the flesh lifts easily away from the cartilage.

3 Remove the fish as soon as it is tender, and transfer it to four warmed serving plates.

◀ **4** Meanwhile, melt the butter in a small pan over medium heat and cook until it turns a deep golden brown. Add the capers and white wine vinegar, and pour over the cooked ray.

5 Sprinkle the chopped parsley over the fish quickly, and serve straight away while it is sizzling hot.

Per portion Energy 253Kcal/1055kJ; Protein 25.8g; Carbohydrate 1.3g, of which sugars 1g; Fat 16.1g, of which saturates 9.8g; Cholesterol 40mg; Calcium 75mg; Fibre 0.2g; Sodium 317mg

Monkfish kebabs

Although it was until recently seen as little more than a cheap alternative to using Dublin Bay prawns for scampi, monkfish is now almost equally prized.

Serves 4

- 900g/2lb fresh monkfish tail, skinned
- 3 (bell) peppers, preferably red, green and yellow
- juice of 1 lemon
- 60ml/4 tbsp olive oil
- bay leaves, halved (optional)
- salt and ground black pepper
- rolls or pitta bread and lemon juice (optional), to serve

For the spicy barbecue sauce

- 15ml/1 tbsp olive oil
- 1 onion, finely chopped
- 1 garlic clove, finely chopped
- 300ml/½ pint/1¼ cups water
- 30ml/2 tbsp wine vinegar
- 30ml/2 tbsp soft brown sugar
- 10ml/2 tsp mild mustard
- grated rind and juice of ½ lemon
- pinch of dried thyme
- 30ml/2 tbsp Worcestershire sauce
- 60–75ml/4–5 tbsp tomato ketchup
- 30ml/2 tbsp tomato purée (paste) (optional)

1 Trim the skinned monkfish and cut it into bitesize cubes. Cut each pepper into quarters, and then seed and halve each quarter.

2 Combine the lemon juice and oil in a bowl and add seasoning. Turn the fish and pepper pieces in the mixture and leave to marinate for 20 minutes (this will add flavour and offset the natural dryness of the fish). Soak four wooden skewers in cold water for 30 minutes. This prevents them from burning during cooking.

3 To make the spicy barbecue sauce, heat the oil in a pan and fry the onion and garlic until soft but not browned. Add all the remaining ingredients, bring to the boil and simmer for 15 minutes to make a fairly chunky sauce.

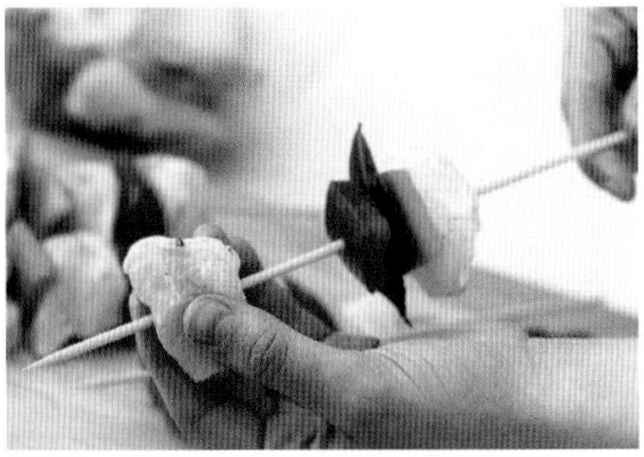

4 Preheat a very hot grill (broiler) or barbecue, and oil the grill rack. Thread pieces of fish and pepper alternately, with the occasional half bay leaf, if you like. Cook for about 10 minutes, turning and basting frequently.

5 Serve in rolls or pitta bread, with the sauce, or simply with a squeeze of fresh lemon juice.

Per portion Energy 377Kcal/1586kJ; Protein 37.4g; Carbohydrate 24.1g, of which sugars 23.1g; Fat 15.3g, of which saturates 2.4g; Cholesterol 32mg; Calcium 54mg; Fibre 2.8g; Sodium 382mg

Salmon with light hollandaise and asparagus

This summery dish is light and colourful. Irish asparagus makes the ideal accompaniment for salmon when it is in season – in early summer. Serve with boiled new potatoes.

Serves 4

- bunch of 20 asparagus spears, trimmed
- 4 salmon portions, such as fillets or steaks, about 200g/7oz each
- 15ml/1 tbsp olive oil
- juice of ½ lemon
- 25g/1oz/2 tbsp butter
- salt and ground black pepper

For the hollandaise sauce

- 45ml/3 tbsp white wine vinegar
- 6 peppercorns
- 1 bay leaf
- 3 egg yolks
- 175g/6oz/¾ cup butter, softened

1 Peel the lower stems of the asparagus. Stand in a deep pan; cook in salted boiling water for about 1 minute, or until just beginning to become tender, then remove from the pan and cool quickly under cold running water to prevent further cooking. Drain.

2 To make the hollandaise sauce: in a small pan, boil the vinegar and 15ml/1 tbsp water with the peppercorns and bay leaf until reduced to 15ml/1 tbsp. Leave to cool. Cream the egg yolks with 15g/½oz/1 tbsp butter and a pinch of salt. Strain the vinegar into the eggs and set the bowl over a pan of boiling water. Remove from the heat.

3 Whisk in the remaining butter, no more than 10g/¼oz/1½ tsp at a time, until the sauce is shiny and has the consistency of thick cream. Season with salt and pepper.

4 Heat a ridged griddle pan or grill (broiler) until very hot. Brush the salmon with olive oil, sprinkle with the lemon juice and season with salt and black pepper. Cook the fish on the griddle or under a grill for 3–5 minutes on each side, depending on the thickness of the fish. Avoid over-cooking; the fish should be seared on the outside, moist and succulent within.

5 Melt the butter in a separate large pan and gently reheat the asparagus in it for 1–2 minutes before serving with the fish and hollandaise sauce.

Cook's tip If the hollandaise sauce separates, remove it from the heat and beat in 15ml/1 tbsp cold water.

Variation Blender hollandaise: this version is an easier substitute (and, if it doesn't work – you can rescue it by heating it over hot water): put 3 egg yolks into a blender with 30ml/2 tbsp lemon juice and seasoning. Blend for a few seconds. Heat 115g/4oz/½ cup butter until very hot, and then run the blender at high speed and gradually add the butter in a thin stream. Blend for about 30 seconds until thick.

Per portion Energy 834Kcal/3449kJ; Protein 46.5g; Carbohydrate 2.8g, of which sugars 2.7g; Fat 7.7g, of which saturates 31.6g; Cholesterol 358mg; Calcium 102mg; Fibre 2.1g; Sodium 401mg

Whole salmon

Salmon is highly esteemed in Ireland and, while fish farming has made salmon more accessible, wild Atlantic salmon is more prized than ever. Serve with new potatoes and old-fashioned drawn butter sauce or hollandaise sauce.

Serves about 10

1 whole salmon or sea trout, cleaned and gutted

court-bouillon or salt water

fresh parsley sprigs and lemon wedges, to garnish

For the drawn butter

115g/4oz/½ cup butter

5–10ml/1–2 tsp lemon juice

a sprinkling of freshly grated nutmeg

1 Wash the fish well, but don't scale it, and leave the head and tail intact. Measure the salmon at its thickest point and allow a cooking time of 10 minutes per 2.5cm/1in of thickness.

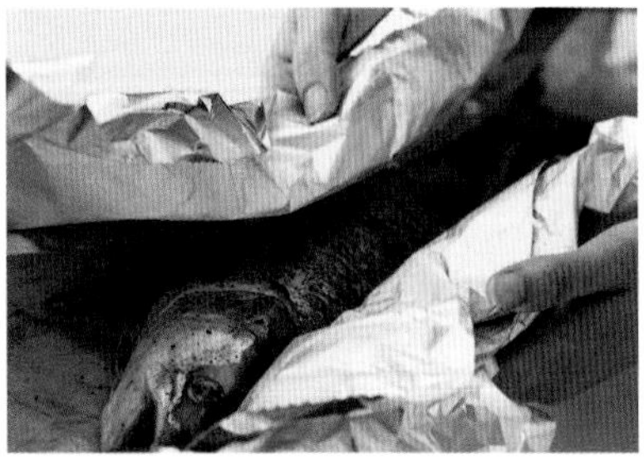

2 If using foil, wrap the salmon in a double layer, securing it at the ends.

3 Add just enough cold court-bouillon (15ml/1 tbsp court-bouillon powder to 600ml/1 pint/2½ cups water) or salted water to cover. If using a fish kettle, lay the salmon in the kettle, cover with just enough cold court-bouillon or salted water, place over a medium heat and gradually bring to simmering point. Do not allow it to boil, as it will harm the delicate flavour of the fish.

4 If using foil, bake at 180°C/350°F/Gas 4, allowing 10 minutes per lb/450g. If using the fish kettle, simmer gently for the time calculated. Test by lifting the flesh off the backbone at the thickest point – where the flesh meets the head – with the tip of a knife; when cooked, the flesh comes away easily.

5 While the fish is cooking, make the drawn butter: melt the butter in a small pan, season with lemon juice and a pinch of grated nutmeg.

6 Remove the salmon from the foil or lift the salmon out of the fish kettle, drain, then slide it on to a warmed serving dish. Garnish with plenty of fresh parsley and lemon wedges. The skin helps to keep the fish warm and moist, so peel it back only as far as necessary as you serve. Remove all the flesh from the top half first, then remove the backbone as neatly as you can before continuing with the bottom layer. Hand the sauce round separately.

Cook's tip Cooking from cold allows the fish to heat through gradually and there is no danger of the outer flesh being cooked before the inside is done. Use a fish kettle large enough to take the whole fish flat for poaching if at all possible. Salmon is very rich so allow portions of 115–150g/4–5oz per person; quite a small fish, 3–3.2kg/6½–7lb, will serve about 10 people.

Variation To serve cold, remove the fish from the heat just before it comes to the boil and cover with a lid. The salmon will cook in the liquor as it cools. When just cold, remove from the cooking liquor and drain on a rack. Line a serving dish with lettuce, watercress, cucumber and lemon wedges. Slide the salmon on to the dish. Peel off the skin, but leave the head and tail intact. Garnish and serve with mayonnaise.

Per portion Energy 385.6Kcal/1601.8kJ; Protein 33.67g; Carbohydrate 0.07g, of which sugars 0.07g; Fat 27.85g, of which saturates 9.19g; Cholesterol 108mg; Calcium 36.1mg; Fibre 0g; Sodium 144mg

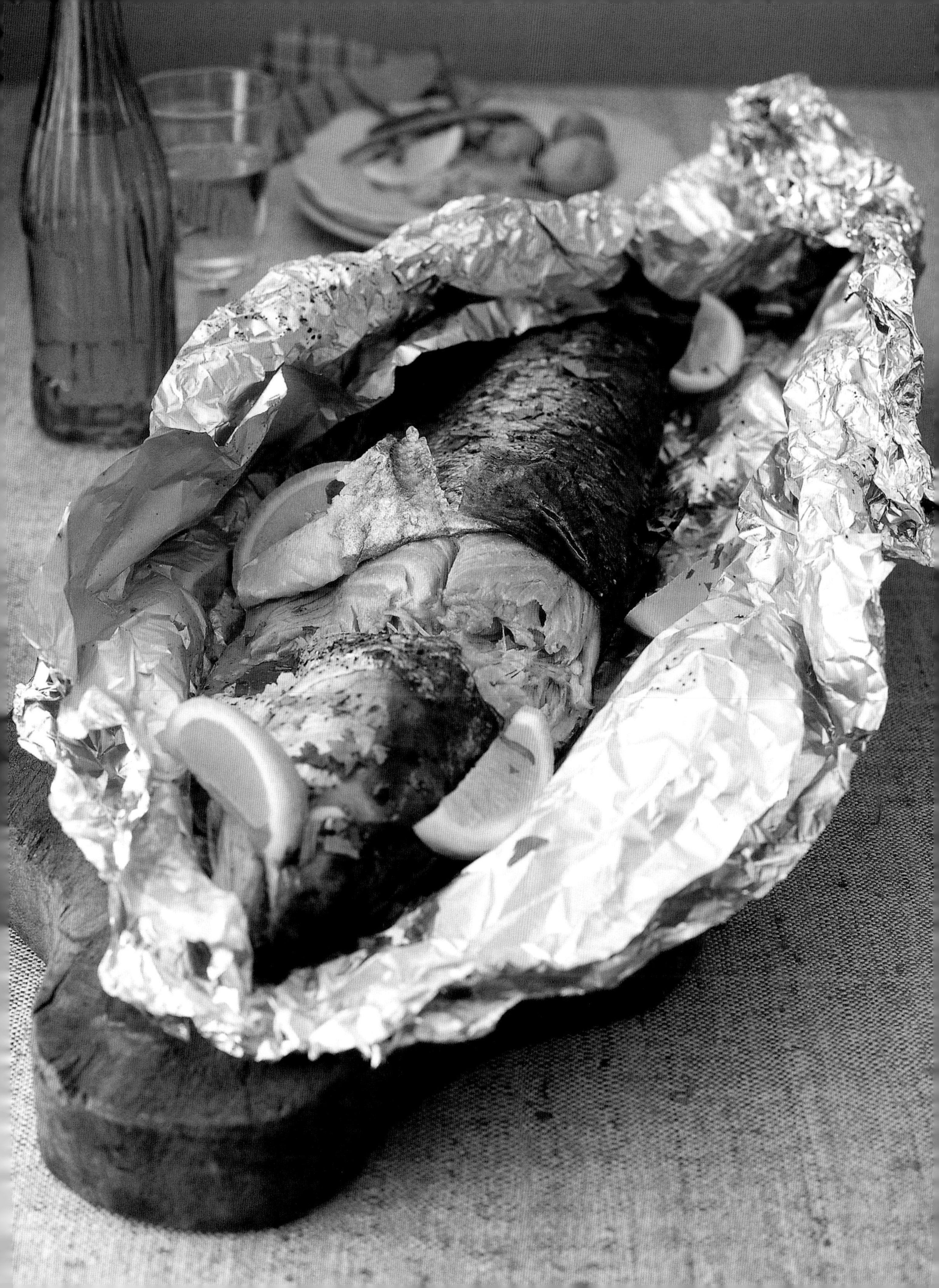

Stuffed white fish wrapped in bacon

Caught mainly off the east coast of Ireland, and available all year round, plentiful but rather bland fish such as whiting and lemon sole, plaice and flounder, are good for this recipe. Serve with boiled new potatoes and a green vegetable.

Serves 4

4 good-size or 8 small fish fillets, such as whiting, trimmed

4 streaky (fatty) bacon rashers (strips)

For the stuffing

50g/2oz/¼ cup butter

1 onion, finely chopped

50g/2oz/1 cup fine fresh brown breadcrumbs

5ml/1 tsp finely chopped fresh parsley

a good pinch of mixed dried herbs

sea salt and ground black pepper

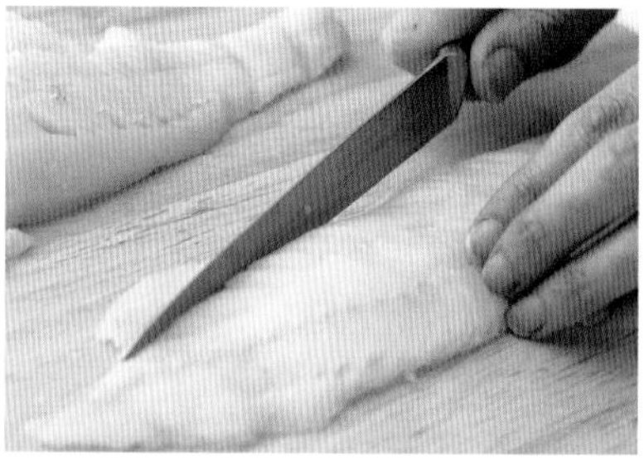

1 Preheat the oven to 190°C/375°F/ Gas 5. Trim the fish fillets. If they are fairly big, cut them in half lengthways; leave small ones whole. Remove the rind and any gristle from the streaky bacon rashers.

2 To make the stuffing, melt the butter in a small pan, add the onion and cook gently until softened but not browned. Add the breadcrumbs, parsley and herbs. Season to taste.

3 Divide the stuffing between the fillets, roll them up and wrap a bacon rasher around each one.

4 Secure the rolls with wooden cocktail sticks (toothpicks) and lay them in a single layer in the base of a shallow buttered baking dish. Cover with foil and bake in the preheated oven for 15 minutes, removing the cover for the last 5 minutes. Serve with potatoes and green beans or broccoli.

Per portion Energy 344Kcal/1436kJ; Protein 38.1g; Carbohydrate 12.5g, of which sugars 2.4g; Fat 15.9g, of which saturates 8.2g; Cholesterol 120mg; Calcium 44mg; Fibre 0.8g; Sodium 662mg

Poached turbot with saffron sauce

The saffron sauce complements the firm white flesh of the turbot well. Turbot is a treat by any standards and this is a rich elegant dish, most suitable for entertaining. Offer rice, or new boiled potatoes, and mangetouts or peas with the turbot.

Serves 4

- pinch of saffron threads
- 50ml/2fl oz/¼ cup single (light) cream
- 1 shallot, finely chopped
- 175g/6oz/¾ cup cold unsalted (sweet) butter, cut into small cubes
- 175ml/6fl oz/¾ cup dry sherry
- 475ml/16fl oz/2 cups fish stock
- 4 medium turbot fillets, about 150–175g/5–6oz each, skinned
- flat leaf parsley leaves, to garnish

Cook's tip White fish such as plaice fillets can also be used in this recipe.

1 Put the saffron threads into the single cream and allow them to infuse (steep) for 10 minutes. Cook the chopped shallot very gently in a large heavy-based frying pan with 15g/½oz/1 tbsp of the butter until it is soft.

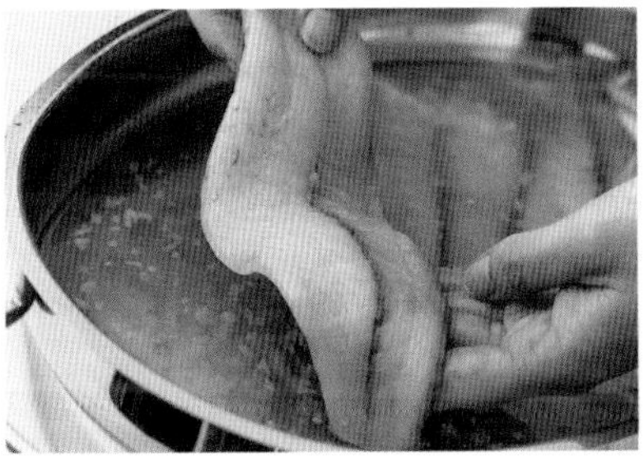

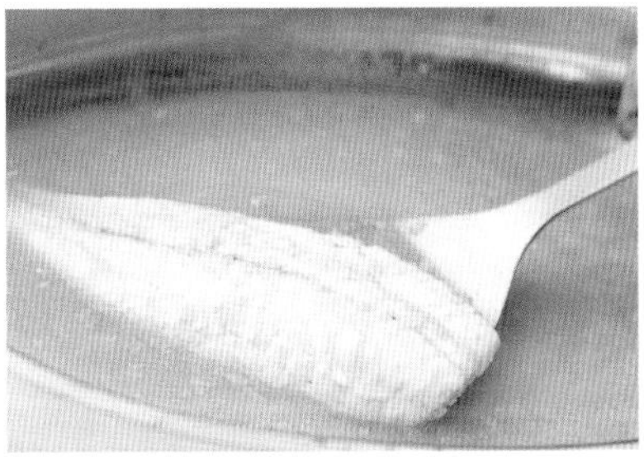

2 Put the cooked shallot, with the dry sherry and fish stock, into a fish kettle or other large pan. Lay the turbot fillets in the pan, without overlapping them, and bring gently to the boil. Reduce the heat immediately and simmer gently for about 5 minutes, depending on the thickness of the fillets.

3 When cooked, remove the fillets from the poaching liquid with a slotted fish slice or metal spatula and lay them on a heated dish. Cover and keep warm.

4 To make the sauce: bring the poaching liquor to the boil and boil fast to reduce it to 60ml/4 tbsp.

5 Add the cream and saffron and bring back to the boil. Remove from the heat, add the butter, whisking constantly until a smooth sauce has formed.

6 Pour the sauce on to warmed serving plates, lay the turbot on top and sprinkle with parsley leaves to serve.

Per portion Energy 544Kcal/2256kJ; Protein 27.4g; Carbohydrate 1.4g, of which sugars 1.4g; Fat 42.4g, of which saturates 25.4g; Cholesterol 100mg; Calcium 97mg; Fibre 0.1g; Sodium 376mg

Seafood pie

A well-made fish pie is absolutely delicious, and is particularly good made with a mixture of fresh and smoked fish – ideal winter fare when the fishing fleets are hampered by gales and fresh fish is in short supply. Cooked shellfish, such as mussels, can be included too.

Serves 4–5

- 450g/1lb haddock or cod fillet
- 225g/8oz smoked haddock or cod
- 150ml/¼ pint/⅔ cup milk
- 150ml/¼ pint/⅔ cup water
- 1 slice of lemon
- 1 small bay leaf
- a few fresh parsley stalks

For the sauce

- 25g/1oz/2 tbsp butter
- 25g/1oz/¼ cup plain (all-purpose) flour
- 5ml/1 tbsp lemon juice, or to taste
- 45ml/3 tbsp chopped fresh parsley
- ground black pepper

For the topping

- 450g/1lb potatoes, boiled and mashed
- 25g/1oz/2 tbsp butter

Below *Sunset over the Blasket Islands, Inishtooskert, County Kerry.*

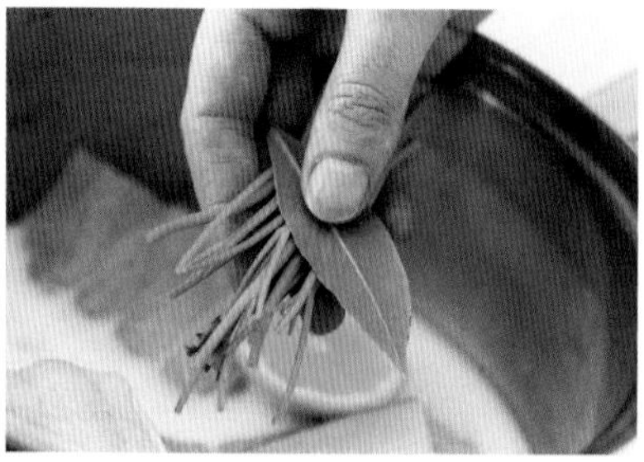

1 Preheat the oven to 190°C/375°F/Gas 5. Rinse the fish, cut it into manageable pieces and put into a pan with the milk, water, lemon, bay leaf and parsley stalks. Bring slowly to the boil, then simmer gently for 15 minutes until tender.

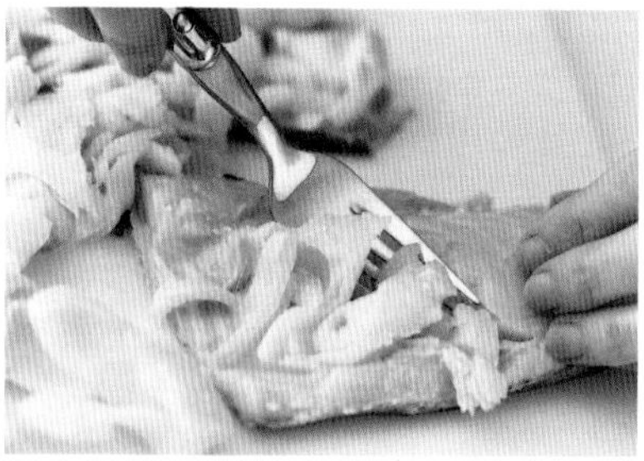

2 Strain and reserve 300ml/½ pint/1¼ cups of the cooking liquor. Leave the fish until cool, then flake the flesh and discard the skin and bones. Set aside.

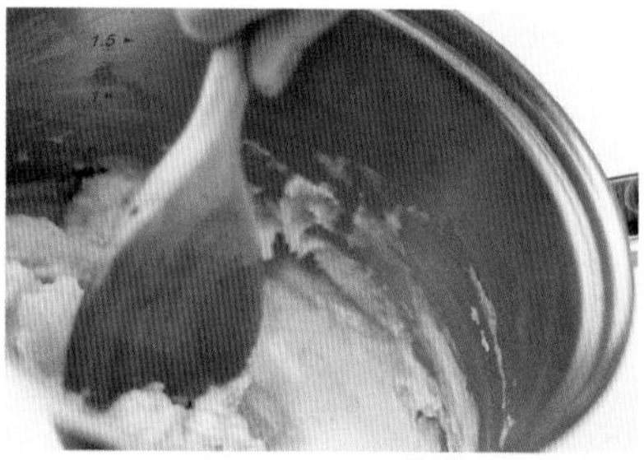

3 To make the sauce, melt the butter in a heavy pan, add the flour and cook for 1–2 minutes over low heat stirring constantly. Then gradually add the reserved cooking liquor, stirring well to make a smooth sauce.

4 Simmer the sauce gently for 1–2 minutes, then remove from the heat and stir in the flaked fish, chopped parsley and lemon juice. Season to taste with ground black pepper.

5 Turn into a buttered 1.75 litre/3 pint/7½ cup pie dish or shallow casserole, cover with the mashed potato for the topping and dot with the butter.

6 Cook in the oven for about 20 minutes, or until thoroughly heated through. The top should be golden brown and crunchy. Divide the pie among 4–5 warmed plates and serve with a lightly cooked green vegetable, such as fresh broccoli spears.

Per portion Energy 336Kcal/1413kJ; Protein 35.1g; Carbohydrate 24.3g, of which sugars 0.9g; Fat 11.6g, of which saturates 6.7g; Cholesterol 87mg; Calcium 45mg; Fibre 1.7g; Sodium 587mg

Haddock in cider sauce

Haddock, both smoked and unsmoked, is a popular fish in Ireland and it finds its way into dishes that are the backbone of the Irish repertoire, such as chowders. Cider, which is made in Ireland and often used in cooking, complements the haddock well. Small, new, boiled potatoes, matchstick carrots and peas or mangetouts are perfect accompaniments.

Serves 4

- 675g/1½lb haddock fillet
- 1 medium onion, thinly sliced
- 1 bay leaf
- 2 sprigs fresh parsley
- 10ml/2 tsp lemon juice
- 450ml/¾ pint/2 cups dry (hard) cider
- 25g/1oz/¼ cup cornflour (cornstarch)
- 30ml/2 tbsp single (light) cream
- salt and ground black pepper

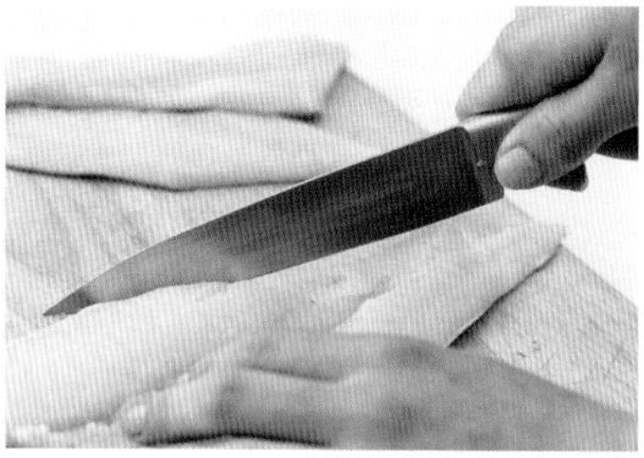

1 Cut the haddock fillet into four equal portions and place in a pan big enough to hold them neatly in a single layer. Add the onion, bay leaf, parsley, lemon juice and season with salt.

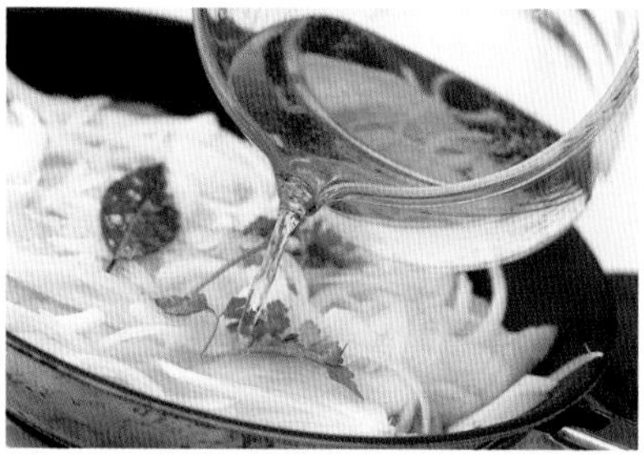

2 Pour in most of the cider, reserving 30ml/2 tbsp for the sauce. Cover and bring to the boil, reduce the heat and simmer for 10 minutes, or until the fish is just cooked.

3 Strain 300ml/½ pint/1¼ cups of the fish liquor into a measuring jug (cup). In a small pan, mix the cornflour with the reserved cider, then gradually whisk in the fish liquor and bring to the boil, whisking constantly for about 2 minutes, until it is smooth and thickened. Add more of the cooking liquor, if necessary, to make a pouring sauce. Remove the pan from the heat, stir in the single cream and season to taste with salt and freshly ground black pepper.

4 To serve, remove any skin from the fish, arrange on individual hot serving plates with the onion over the vegetables and pour the sauce over.

Per portion Energy 227Kcal/964kJ; Protein 32.8g; Carbohydrate 11.8g, of which sugars 5.2g; Fat 2.6g, of which saturates 1.1g; Cholesterol 65mg; Calcium 50mg; Fibre 0.5g; Sodium 128mg

Herring fillets in oatmeal with apples

The herring has been a cheap and plentiful source of food in Ireland for many generations. Traditionally most were dried, salted or smoked for winter use, but, although kippers are still very popular, herrings are now more likely to be eaten fresh. This dish is traditional in Scotland as well as Ireland and is one of the most delicious ways of cooking herring.

Serves 4

8 herring fillets

seasoned flour, for coating

1 egg, beaten

115g/4oz/1 cup fine pinhead oatmeal or oatflakes

oil, for frying

2 eating apples

25g/1oz/2 tbsp butter

1 Wash the fish and pat dry with kitchen paper. Check that all bones have been removed.

2 Toss the herring fillets in the seasoned flour, and then dip them in the beaten egg and coat them evenly with the oatmeal or oatflakes.

3 Heat a little oil in a heavy frying pan and fry the fillets, a few at a time, until golden brown. Drain on kitchen paper and keep warm.

4 Core the apples, but do not peel. Slice them quite thinly. In another pan, melt the butter and fry the apple slices gently until just softened, then serve the herring fillets garnished with the apple slices.

Variations

• Mackerel fillets can be cooked in the same way.

• A fruit sauce – apple, gooseberry or rhubarb – could be served instead of the sliced apples. Cook 225g/8oz of your preferred fruit with 90ml/6 tbsp cold water until just softened. Purée and serve with the fish.

Per portion Energy 420Kcal/1754kJ; Protein 26.5g; Carbohydrate 24.3g, of which sugars 3.4g; Fat 24.8g, of which saturates 7.6g; Cholesterol 120mg; Calcium 97mg; Fibre 2.6g; Sodium 209mg

Mackerel with rhubarb sauce

Mackerel are available in Ireland for most of the year, but they are really at their best in early summer, just when rhubarb is growing strongly – a happy coincidence, as the tartness of rhubarb offsets the richness of the oily fish to perfection.

Serves 4

- 4 whole mackerel, cleaned
- 25g/1oz/2 tbsp butter
- 1 onion, finely chopped
- 90ml/6 tbsp fresh white breadcrumbs
- 15ml/1 tbsp chopped fresh parsley
- finely grated rind of 1 lemon
- freshly grated nutmeg
- 1 egg, lightly beaten
- melted butter or olive oil, for brushing
- sea salt and ground black pepper

For the sauce

- 225g/8oz rhubarb (trimmed weight), cut into 1cm/½in lengths
- 25–50g/1–2oz/2–4 tbsp caster (superfine) sugar
- 25g/1oz/2 tbsp butter
- 15ml/1 tbsp chopped fresh tarragon (optional)

1 Ask the fishmonger to bone the mackerel, or do it yourself: open out the body of the cleaned fish, turn flesh side down on a board and run your thumb firmly down the backbone – when you turn the fish over, the bones should lift out in one complete section.

2 Melt the butter in a pan and cook the onion gently for 5–10 minutes, until softened but not browned. Add the breadcrumbs, parsley, lemon rind, salt, pepper and grated nutmeg. Mix well, and then add the beaten egg to bind.

3 Divide the mixture among the four fish, wrap the fish over and secure with cocktail sticks (toothpicks). Brush with melted butter or olive oil. Preheat the grill (broiler) and cook under a medium heat for about 8 minutes on each side.

4 Meanwhile, make the sauce: put the rhubarb into a pan with 75ml/2½fl oz/⅓ cup water, 25g/1oz/2 tbsp of the sugar and the butter. Cook over a gentle heat until the rhubarb is tender. Taste for sweetness and add extra sugar if necessary, bearing in mind that the sauce needs to be quite sharp.

5 Serve the stuffed mackerel with the hot sauce garnished with the tarragon.

Per portion Energy 728Kcal/3034kJ; Protein 48.2g; Carbohydrate 27.5g, of which sugars 9.8g; Fat 48g, of which saturates 14.3g; Cholesterol 193mg; Calcium 129mg; Fibre 1.8g; Sodium 398mg

Dublin Bay prawns in garlic butter

Although they are caught in the Irish Sea, Dublin Bay prawns are in fact the ubiquitous "scampi". This all-time favourite is equally popular as a first or main course. Serve with lemon wedges, rice and a side salad.

Serves 4

- 32–36 large live Dublin Bay prawns (jumbo shrimp)
- 225g/8oz/1 cup butter
- 15ml/1 tbsp olive oil
- 4 or 5 garlic cloves, crushed
- 15ml/1 tbsp lemon juice
- sea salt and ground black pepper

1 Drop the live Dublin Bay prawns into a large pan of briskly boiling salted water. Bring rapidly back to the boil, cover with a lid and simmer for a few minutes; the time required depends on their size and will be very short for small ones – do not overcook. They are ready when the underside of the shell has lost its translucency and becomes an opaque whitish colour.

2 Drain, refresh under cold water, and leave in a colander until cool. Twist off the heads and the long claws, then peel the shell off the tails and remove the meat. If the claws are big it is worthwhile extracting any meat you can from them with a lobster pick.

3 Make a shallow cut along the back of each prawn. Remove the trail (the dark vein) that runs along the back.

4 Heat a large heavy pan over medium heat, add the butter and oil and the garlic. When the butter is foaming, sprinkle the prawns with a little salt and a good grinding of pepper, and add them to the pan. Cook for about 2 minutes until the garlic is cooked and the prawns thoroughly heated through.

5 Add lemon juice to taste, and adjust the seasoning, and then turn the prawns and their buttery juices on to warmed plates and serve immediately.

Cook's tips

- Dublin Bay prawns can weigh up to 225g/8oz each, although the average weight is 45g/1¾oz. You'll need 8–9 per person for a main course.
- These crustaceans are also known as Norway lobsters and langoustine.

Variation This recipe works very well with scallops (puréed Jerusalem artichokes are a good accompaniment), small queen scallops, or with a firm-fleshed fish such as monkfish.

Per portion Energy 498Kcal/2054kJ; Protein 13g; Carbohydrate 0.4g, of which sugars 0.4g; Fat 49.4g, of which saturates 29.8g; Cholesterol 260mg; Calcium 67mg; Fibre 0g; Sodium 478mg

Dublin Lawyer

This traditional dish used to be made with raw lobster, but it is now more usually lightly boiled first. The origins of the name are uncertain, but it is generally thought to refer to the fact that lawyers are more likely than most to be able to afford this luxurious dish.

Serves 2

- 1 large, (over 900g/2lb) lightly cooked lobster (see Cook's tip)
- 175g/6oz/¾ cup butter
- 75ml/2½fl oz/⅓ cup Irish whiskey
- 150ml/¼ pint/⅔ cup double (heavy) cream
- sea salt and ground black pepper

1 Tear off the claws from the cooked lobster. Split the body in half lengthways, with a sharp knife, just slightly to the right of the centre line to avoid cutting into the digestive tract. Remove the grey matter from the head of the shell and discard. Remove the digestive tract right down the length of the body and discard. Lift the flesh from the tail – it usually comes out in one piece. Set the shells aside for serving and keep them warm. ▶

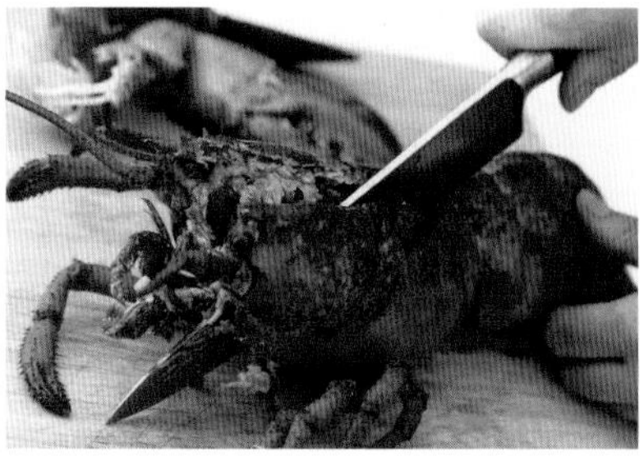

2 Tear the two joints in the claw to separate them and, using a small knife, scoop out the flesh. With the back of a heavy knife, hit the claw near the pincers, rotating the claw and hitting until the claw opens. Remove the flesh and cut into bitesize pieces.

3 Melt the butter in a pan over a low heat. Add the lobster pieces and turn in the butter to warm through. Warm the whiskey in a separate pan and pour it over the lobster. Carefully set it alight. Add the cream and heat gently without allowing the sauce to boil, then season to taste. Turn the hot mixture into the warm shells and serve immediately.

Cook's tip To cook, weigh the live lobster and put it into a pan of boiling salted water. Bring back to the boil and cook for 12 minutes per 450g/1lb for small lobsters, a little less if 900g/2lb or over. Remove the cooked lobster from the water and leave to cool.

Per portion Energy 1273Kcal/5259kJ; Protein 37.8g; Carbohydrate 1.8g, of which sugars 1.8g; Fat 114.9g, of which saturates 71.1g; Cholesterol 469mg; Calcium 152mg; Fibre 0g; Sodium 1.08g

Crab bake

Plentiful all around the Irish coast, crabs are popular on bar menus, especially fresh crab open sandwiches. Cork Dry Gin, which is made in Midleton, County Cork, brings an extra dimension to this delicious dish. Serve hot with rice, or fresh crusty bread, and a side salad.

Serves 4 as a first course

- 225g/8oz cooked white crab meat
- juice of ½ lemon
- 15ml/1 tbsp chopped fresh herbs, such as parsley, chives and fennel
- 20ml/4 tsp Cork Dry Gin
- 5ml/1 tsp smooth Dijon mustard
- 5ml/1 tsp wholegrain Dijon mustard
- 60ml/4 tbsp grated hard cheese, such as Dubliner
- ground black pepper

For the béchamel sauce

- 1 small onion
- 3 cloves
- 300ml/½ pint/1¼ cups milk
- ½ bay leaf
- 25g/1oz/2 tbsp butter
- 25g/1oz/¼ cup plain (all-purpose) flour

1 First make an infusion for the béchamel sauce: stud the onion with the cloves, and then put it into a small pan with the milk and bay leaf. Bring slowly to the boil, then allow to infuse (steep) for 15 minutes, and strain.

2 Preheat the oven to 180°C/350°F/Gas 4 and butter four gratin dishes. Toss the crab meat in the lemon juice. Divide it among the dishes and add a pinch of herbs to each. Sprinkle each dish with 5ml/1 tsp gin and pepper.

3 Melt the butter for the sauce in a pan, stir in the flour and cook over a low heat for 1–2 minutes. Gradually add the infused milk, stirring constantly to make a smooth sauce. Simmer over a low heat for 1–2 minutes.

4 Blend the béchamel sauce with the two mustards and use to cover the crab. Sprinkle the cheese on top, and bake for 20–25 minutes, or until hot and bubbling. Serve immediately.

Cook's tip The recipe can also be divided between two larger dishes to serve two as a main course.

Per portion Energy 224Kcal/936kJ; Protein 17.4g; Carbohydrate 9.6g, of which sugars 4.5g; Fat 11.9g, of which saturates 7.4g; Cholesterol 73mg; Calcium 282mg; Fibre 0.4g; Sodium 489mg

Meat

While Ireland's "soft" climate and rich green pastures make perfect grazing for sheep and cattle, meats that now take pride of place in every Irish meal were once seen as a treat for feast days. The pig was probably the first Irish domestic animal and – although beef is probably now the nation's favourite meat and mutton or lamb feature in the national dish, Irish stew – pork and bacon are the main ingredients in many traditional dishes.

Bacon chops with apple and cider sauce

Either thick bacon or pork chops could be used in this recipe, which brings traditional ingredients together in an attractive modern Irish dish. Serve with lots of creamy mashed potatoes and steamed buttered cabbage.

Serves 4

15ml/1 tbsp oil

4 bacon chops

1 or 2 cooking apples

knob (pat) of butter

1 or 2 garlic cloves, finely chopped

5ml/1 tsp sugar

150ml/¼ pint/⅔ cup dry (hard) cider

5ml/1 tsp cider vinegar

15ml/1 tbsp wholegrain mustard

10ml/2 tsp chopped fresh thyme

salt and ground black pepper

sprigs of thyme, to garnish

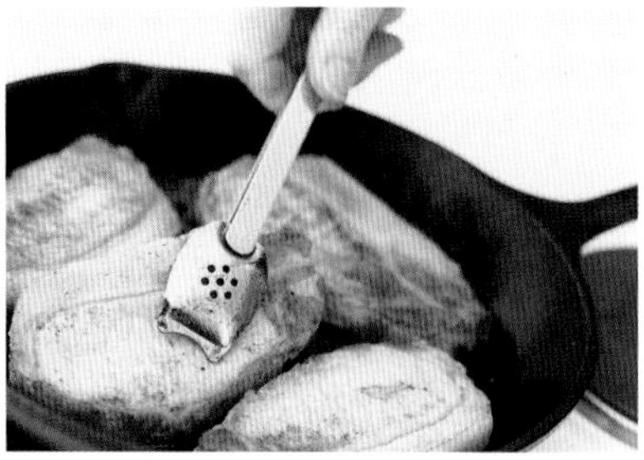

1 Heat the oil in a large heavy frying pan, over a medium heat, and cook the chops for 10–15 minutes, browning well on both sides.

2 Peel, core and slice the apples. Remove the chops from the pan and keep warm. Add the butter and apples to the pan and cook until the juices begin to brown.

3 Add the finely chopped garlic and sugar, and cook for 1 minute, then stir in the cider, cider vinegar, mustard and chopped thyme. Boil for a few minutes until reduced to a saucy consistency.

4 Season to taste and place the chops on warmed serving plates. Garnish with the thyme sprigs and serve.

Per portion Energy 285Kcal/1190kJ; Protein 26.4g; Carbohydrate 6.5g, of which sugars 6.5g; Fat 16.1g, of which saturates 5.4g; Cholesterol 40mg; Calcium 17mg; Fibre 0.8g; Sodium 1.34g

Bacon with cabbage and parsley sauce

This recipe is a modern rendition of a great old favourite and brings together a number of the most typical of Irish ingredients – perfect for the climate. Traditional accompaniments include boiled or mashed potatoes and/or mashed swede, also known as turnip in Ireland.

Serves 6

- 1.3kg/3lb loin of bacon
- 1 carrot, chopped
- 2 celery sticks, chopped
- 2 leeks, chopped
- 5ml/1 tsp peppercorns
- 15ml/1 tbsp Irish mustard
- 15ml/1 tbsp oven-dried breadcrumbs
- 7.5ml/1½ tsp light muscovado (brown) sugar
- 25g/1oz/2 tbsp butter
- 900g/2lb green cabbage, sliced

For the parsley sauce

- 50g/2oz/¼ cup butter
- 25g/1oz/¼ cup plain (all-purpose) flour
- 300ml/½ pint/1¼ cups half cooking liquid and half single (light) cream
- bunch of parsley, leaves chopped
- salt and ground black pepper

1 Place the bacon joint in a large pan. Add the vegetables to the pan, with the peppercorns. Cover with cold water and bring to the boil. Simmer gently for about 20 minutes per 450g/1lb. Preheat the oven to 200°C/400°F/Gas 6.

2 Remove the joint from the pan, reserving the cooking liquid. Remove the rind, and score the fat. Place the joint in a roasting pan. Mix the mustard, breadcrumbs, sugar and 15g/½oz/1 tbsp butter; spread this mixture over the joint. Place in the oven for 15–20 minutes.

3 To make the parsley sauce, melt the butter in a small pan, then add the flour and cook for 1–2 minutes, stirring constantly. Whisk in the cooking liquid and cream. Bring to the boil. Reduce the heat and simmer for 3–4 minutes, then stir in the chopped fresh parsley. Season to taste with salt and pepper. The sauce should have the consistency of thin cream. Keep warm.

4 In another pan cook the cabbage with a little of the cooking liquid from the bacon. Drain well, season to taste and toss in the remaining butter.

5 To serve, slice the bacon and serve on a bed of cabbage, with a little of the parsley sauce.

Variation Limerick ham: ham smoked over oak chippings and juniper berries was a famous speciality of Limerick in the 18th century, and ham – the name refers only to the leg, all the rest is called bacon – is still one of Ireland's most highly regarded foods. Smoked ham can be cooked as above, adding a few crushed juniper berries to the cooking pot with the peppercorns, if you like.

Per portion Energy 689Kcal/2857kJ; Protein 40.4g; Carbohydrate 16.3g, of which sugars 10.6g; Fat 51.5g, of which saturates 23.1g; Cholesterol 155mg; Calcium 139mg; Fibre 5g; Sodium 3.46g

Dublin coddle

This utterly Irish dish combines bacon and sausages, two foods known since the earliest Irish literature, and is said to have been Dean Swift's favourite meal. Leeks and oatmeal were originally used but potatoes and onion are popular nowadays.

Makes 4 large or 8 small portions

8 x 8mm/⅓in thick ham or dry-cured bacon slices

8 best-quality lean pork sausages

4 large onions, thinly sliced

900g/2lb potatoes, peeled and sliced

90ml/6 tbsp chopped fresh parsley

salt and ground black pepper

1 Cut the ham or bacon into large chunks and cook with the sausages in 1.2 litres/2 pints/5 cups boiling water for 5 minutes. Drain, but reserve the cooking liquor.

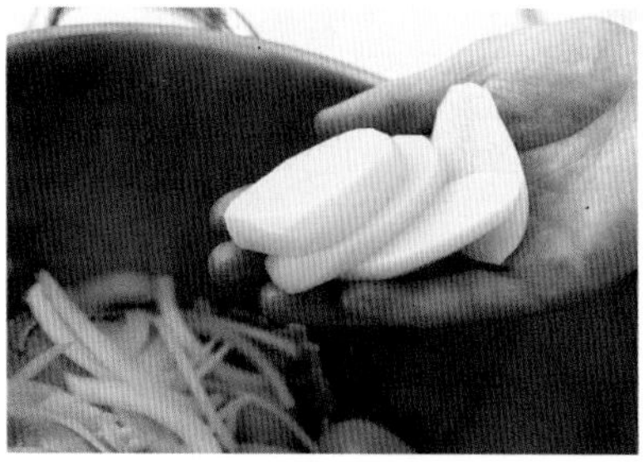

2 Put the meat into a pan or ovenproof dish with the onions, potatoes and the parsley. Season, and add just enough of the reserved cooking liquor to cover. Cover with a tight-fitting lid; lay a piece of buttered foil or baking parchment on top before putting on the lid.

3 Simmer gently over a low heat for about 1 hour, or until the liquid is reduced by half and all the ingredients are cooked but not mushy. Serve hot with the vegetables on top with the traditional accompaniments of fresh soda bread and a glass of stout.

Per portion Energy 432Kcal/1809kJ; Protein 20.6g; Carbohydrate 52g, of which sugars 10.2g; Fat 17.2g, of which saturates 6.1g; Cholesterol 45mg; Calcium 83mg; Fibre 5.7g; Sodium 1.27g

Ham with mustard sauce and crispy cabbage

This is an updated version of the traditional boiled bacon and cabbage, in which the meat – either gammon or any cut of boiling bacon – is cooked in milk. This helps to counteract the saltiness and imparts a delicious and unusual flavour.

Serves 4–6

- 1.3kg/3lb piece of gammon or boiling bacon
- 30ml/2 tbsp oil
- 2 large onions, sliced
- 1 bay leaf
- 750ml/1¼ pints/3 cups milk, plus extra if necessary
- 15ml/1 tbsp cornflour (cornstarch), dissolved in 15ml/1 tbsp milk
- 45ml/3 tbsp wholegrain mustard
- 15–30ml/2–3 tbsp single (light) cream (optional)
- 1 head of cabbage, such as Savoy, trimmed, ribs removed and leaves finely sliced
- ground black pepper

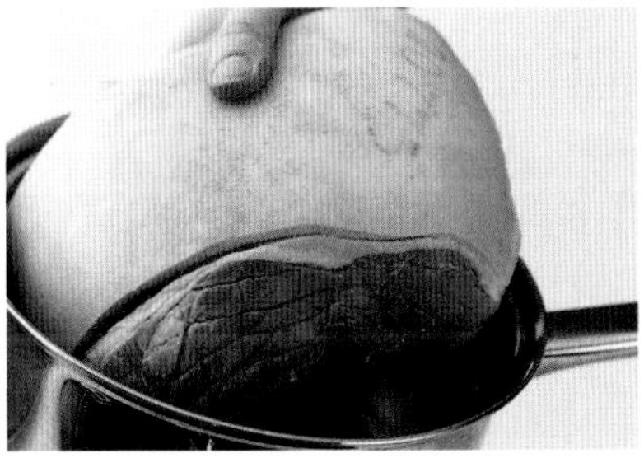

1 Soak the bacon joint in cold water overnight. To cook, heat 15ml/1 tbsp oil in a large pan, add the onions and cook gently for a few minutes.

2 Place the joint on the bed of onions. Add the bay leaf and milk, and season with pepper. Bring to the boil, cover with a tight-fitting lid and cook over a gentle heat for about 1½ hours. When the meat is cooked, the skin will peel off easily.

3 Remove the meat from the pan and keep warm. Strain the cooking liquid. Reserve 300ml/½ pint/1¼ cups for the sauce and put the remainder aside for soup. Add the cornflour mixture to the reserved liquid and bring up to the boil, stirring constantly. As it begins to thicken, stir in the wholegrain mustard and cream, if using.

4 Rinse the cabbage in cold running water and drain well. Heat the remaining oil in a wok or large frying pan and stir-fry the cabbage for 2–3 minutes until cooked but still crunchy. Slice the ham and serve on warmed serving plates with the mustard sauce and crisply cooked cabbage.

Per portion Energy 541Kcal/2253kJ; Protein 58.4g; Carbohydrate 7.4g, of which sugars 5g; Fat 30.8g, of which saturates 9.4g; Cholesterol 77mg; Calcium 76mg; Fibre 2.1g; Sodium 2.87g

Roast loin of pork with apple and spinach

This is an updated variation on the traditional pork and apple theme – the three main ingredients have been in common use in Irish kitchens for centuries.

Serves 6–8

- 1.6–1.8kg/3½–4lb loin of pork, boned and skinned
- 1 onion, sliced
- juice of 1 orange
- 15ml/1 tbsp wholegrain mustard
- 30ml/2 tbsp demerara (raw) sugar
- salt and ground black pepper

For the stuffing

- 50g/2oz/¼ cup dried apricots, chopped
- 50g/2oz spinach, blanched and chopped
- 50g/2oz Irish farmhouse Cheddar cheese, grated
- 1 cooking apple, peeled and grated
- grated rind of ½ orange

1 To make the stuffing, put all the stuffing ingredients into a bowl and mix well together. Preheat the oven to 180°C/350°F/Gas 4.

2 Place the loin of pork, fat side down, on a board and place the stuffing down the centre. Roll the meat up and tie with cotton string. Season and put it into a roasting pan with the onion and 60ml/4 tbsp water. Cook uncovered for about 35 minutes per 450g/1lb.

3 About 40 minutes before the end of the estimated cooking time, pour off the cooking liquid into a small pan and discard the onion. Add the orange juice to the cooking liquid.

4 Spread the joint with mustard and sprinkle with the sugar. Return it to the oven and increase to 200°C/400°F/ Gas 6 for 15 minutes or until crisp.

5 Meanwhile, boil up the juices and reduce to make a thin sauce. Serve with the sliced meat.

Per portion Energy 330Kcal/1385kJ; Protein 49.4g; Carbohydrate 6.9g, of which sugars 6.3g; Fat 11.6g, of which saturates 4.9g; Cholesterol 145mg; Calcium 105mg; Fibre 1.2g; Sodium 227mg

Stuffed pork steak

Pork steak is the Irish name for the cut known as pork fillet or tenderloin or boneless fillet. It is lean, tender and expensive, so it is usually served stuffed.

Serves 6

- 2 evenly sized pork steaks, about 400g/14oz each
- 115g/4oz/2 cups fresh white breadcrumbs
- small bunch of parsley and thyme, leaves chopped
- 1 onion, chopped
- 25g/1oz/2 tbsp butter, melted
- 1 egg, lightly beaten
- finely grated rind and juice of 1 small orange
- softened butter, for the steaks
- 15ml/1 tbsp plain (all-purpose) flour (optional)
- salt and ground black pepper

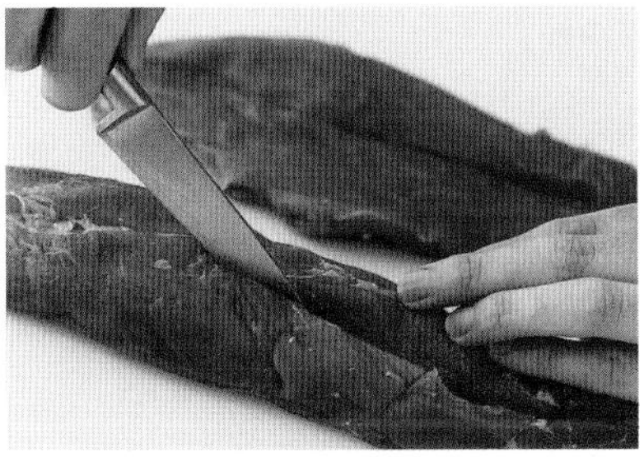

1 Preheat the oven to 180°C/350°F/Gas 4. Slit the pork steaks along the length with a sharp knife; do not cut right through. Hold out each of the flaps this has created and slit them lengthways in the same way, without cutting right through. Flatten out gently.

2 Put the breadcrumbs, herbs, onion, butter, egg, orange rind and salt and pepper in a bowl. Mix together with a fork, including as much of the orange juice as is required to bind the stuffing. Set aside any leftover juice.

3 To cook the pork steaks individually, divide the stuffing mixture in half and lay it down the centre of each steak; fold the flaps up towards the middle and secure with cotton string or skewers to make a roll. Alternatively, turn all the stuffing on to one of the steaks, spread evenly, and then cover with the second steak. Secure with string or skewers.

4 Rub the pork steaks with a little softened butter. Season with salt and pepper and put into a shallow dish or roasting pan with 300ml/½ pint/ 1¼ cups water to prevent the meat drying out during cooking.

5 Cover with a lid or foil and cook in the preheated oven for 1 hour, turning and basting halfway through the cooking time. Remove the steaks and keep warm while you make a gravy by reducing or thickening the juices with a little flour in the roasting pan. Add the reserved orange juice to the gravy, heat through and serve with the steaks.

Cook's tip Be careful to use cotton string to secure the stuffing, as synthetic twine will melt in the oven.

Per portion Energy 279Kcal/1173kJ; Protein 32g; Carbohydrate 16.1g, of which sugars 1.4g; Fat 10.1g, of which saturates 4.3g; Cholesterol 125mg; Calcium 44mg; Fibre 0.6g; Sodium 276mg

Spiced pork roast with apple and thyme cream sauce

Belly of pork (sometimes called "lap" of pork) makes a tasty and tender roasting joint. In this unusual dish, the pork is boned and skinned for stuffing and rolling. Serve with mashed potato, carrots and sprouting broccoli.

Serves 6

- 1 medium onion, finely chopped
- 3 garlic cloves, crushed
- 75g/3oz/6 tbsp butter
- bunch of mixed fresh herbs, leaves finely chopped
- 225g/8oz/4 cups fine fresh breadcrumbs
- 1 egg, beaten
- 1 piece of pork belly, about 1.3kg/3lb
- 15ml/1 tbsp oil
- salt and ground black pepper

For the spicy paste

- 25g/1oz/2 tbsp butter, melted
- 30ml/2 tbsp chutney
- 15ml/1 tbsp lemon juice
- 2 garlic cloves, crushed
- 30ml/2 tbsp mild Irish mustard, with Guinness or whiskey, if available

For the sauce

- 2 large cooking apples, peeled, cored and chopped
- 1 medium onion, chopped
- 2 garlic cloves, crushed
- 1 or 2 thyme sprigs
- 150ml/¼ pint/⅔ cup medium cider
- about 150ml/¼ pint/⅔ cup chicken stock
- 300ml/½ pint/1¼ cups single (light) cream

1 Cook the onion and garlic in the butter until soft, then add the herbs and breadcrumbs. Cool a little before mixing in the egg, and season well with salt and ground pepper. Preheat the oven to 150°C/300°F/Gas 2.

2 Meanwhile, trim off any fat from the meat and prick the centre with a fork; combine all the spicy paste ingredients together and brush the meat with this. Spread the stuffing over the meat, then roll it up and tie it with cotton string.

3 Brown the meat in the oil in a hot roasting pan and cook for 3 hours. Halfway through cooking remove the joint from the oven and brush liberally with the spicy paste; turn over, return to the oven, and continue cooking.

4 To make the thyme cream sauce, put the cooking apples, onion and garlic in a large pan and add the thyme sprigs, cider and stock. Bring to the boil and simmer gently for 15 minutes, then discard the thyme. Add the cream. Process the mixture in a blender, strain and season to taste with salt and black pepper. If the sauce seems too thick, adjust the texture with extra stock.

5 Serve the sliced meat on heated plates with the sauce.

Left *Apple trees in blossom on a fruit farm in County Armagh.*

Per portion Energy 814Kcal/3409kJ; Protein 73.2g; Carbohydrate 41.9g, of which sugars 12.6g; Fat 39.8g, of which saturates 20.2g; Cholesterol 264mg; Calcium 145mg; Fibre 2.4g; Sodium 581mg

Irish stew

Ireland's national dish was traditionally made with mature mutton, but lamb is now usual. There are long-standing arguments about the correct ingredients for an authentic Irish stew apart from the meat (which may or may not be cooked on the bone), and whether or not carrots are permitted. This is a modern variation using lamb chops.

Serves 4

1.3kg/3lb best end of neck of mutton or lamb chops

900g/2lb potatoes

small bunch each of parsley and thyme, chopped

450g/1lb onions, sliced

salt and ground black pepper

1 Trim all the fat, bone and gristle from the meat, and cut it into fairly large pieces. See Variations if using chops. Slice one-third of the potatoes and cut the rest into large chunks.

2 Arrange the potatoes in a casserole, and then add a sprinkling of herbs, then half the meat and finally half the onion, seasoning each layer. Repeat the layers, finishing with the potatoes. ▶

3 Pour over 450ml/¾ pint/scant 2 cups water, and cover tightly; add a sheet of foil before putting on the lid if it is not a very close-fitting one. Simmer the stew very gently for about 2 hours, or cook in the oven at 120°C/250°F/Gas ½, if you prefer. Shake the casserole from time to time to prevent sticking.

4 Check the liquid level occasionally during the cooking time and add extra water if necessary; there should be enough cooking liquor to have made a gravy, thickened by the sliced potatoes.

Variations

- Trimmed lamb or mutton chops can be arranged around the edge of the pan, with the sliced onions and chopped potatoes, herbs and seasonings in the middle. Add the water and cook as above.
- Hogget – lamb over a year old – is available in the spring and early summer.

Per portion Energy 869Kcal/3627kJ; Protein 69.1g; Carbohydrate 47.6g, of which sugars 7.7g; Fat 45.9g, of which saturates 20.8g; Cholesterol 244mg; Calcium 53mg; Fibre 4.5g; Sodium 218mg

Lamb and carrot casserole with barley

Barley and carrots make natural partners for lamb and mutton. In this convenient casserole the barley ekes out the meat and adds to the flavour and texture as well as thickening the sauce. The dish is comfort food at its best. Serve with boiled or baked potatoes and a green vegetable, such as spring cabbage.

Serves 6

675g/1½lb stewing lamb

15ml/1 tbsp oil

2 onions, sliced

675g/1½lb carrots, thickly sliced

4–6 celery sticks, sliced

45ml/3 tbsp pearl barley, rinsed

stock or water

salt and ground black pepper

chopped fresh parsley, to garnish

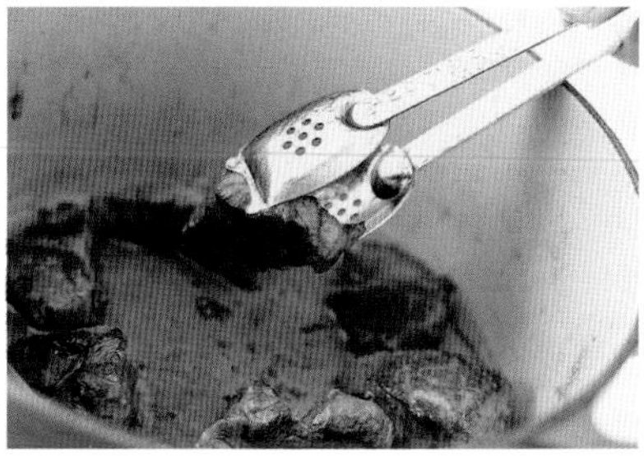

1 Trim the lamb and cut it into bitesize pieces. Heat the oil in a flameproof casserole and brown the lamb.

2 Add the vegetables to the casserole and fry them briefly with the meat. Add the barley and enough stock or water to cover, and season to taste.

3 Cover the casserole and simmer gently or cook in a slow oven, 150°C/300°F/Gas 2 for 1–1½ hours until the meat is tender. Add extra stock or water during cooking if necessary. Serve garnished with the chopped fresh parsley.

Right *A flock of sheep grazing in summertime, Owenmore Valley, Dingle, County Kerry.*

Per portion Energy 304Kcal/1263kJ; Protein 23.2g; Carbohydrate 13g, of which sugars 11.3g; Fat 18g, of which saturates 7.5g; Cholesterol 84mg; Calcium 53mg; Fibre 3.6g; Sodium 110mg

Dingle pies

These pies are traditional in Dingle for special occasions, notably Lammas Day, 1 August, which marked the first day of the harvest. There are numerous recipes for mutton pies in the Dingle area. This version contains more vegetables than the traditional recipe.

Makes 6 small pies

450g/1lb boneless mutton or lamb

1 large onion, diced

2 carrots, diced

1 potato, diced

2 celery sticks, diced

1 egg, beaten

salt and ground black pepper

For the shortcrust pastry

500g/1 ¼lb/5 cups plain (all-purpose) flour

250g/9oz/generous 1 cup butter, or half butter and half white vegetable fat (shortening)

120ml/4fl oz/½ cup very cold water

1 To make the pastry, sieve the flour into a large bowl and add the butter. Rub the butter into the flour with the fingertips or a pastry blender, lifting the mixture as much as possible to aerate. Add the chilled water. Mix with a knife or fork until the mixture clings together. Turn it on to a floured worktop and knead lightly once or twice until smooth. Wrap in baking parchment or foil and leave in the refrigerator to relax for 20 minutes before using.

2 Trim any fat or gristle from the meat and cut it up into very small pieces. Place in a large bowl and add the diced onion, carrots, potato and celery. Mix well and season with salt and freshly ground black pepper.

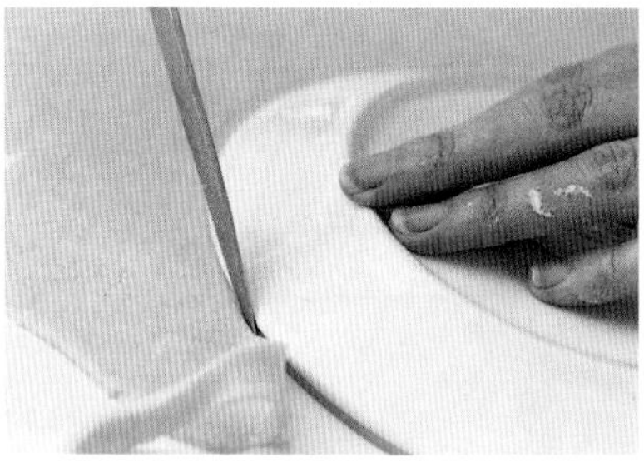

3 Preheat the oven to 180°C/350°F/Gas 4. Cut a third off the ball of pastry and reserve to make the lids of the pies. Roll out the rest and, using a small plate as a guide and re-rolling the pastry as necessary, cut out six circles. Divide the meat and vegetable mixture between the circles, piling it in the middle of each.

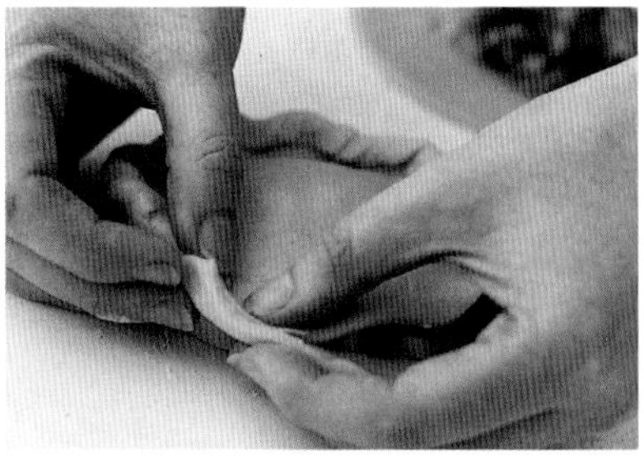

4 Roll out the remaining pastry and cut out six smaller circles, about 10cm/4in across. Lay these on top. Dampen the edges of the pastry bases, bring the pastry up around the meat, pleat it to fit the lid and pinch the edges together.

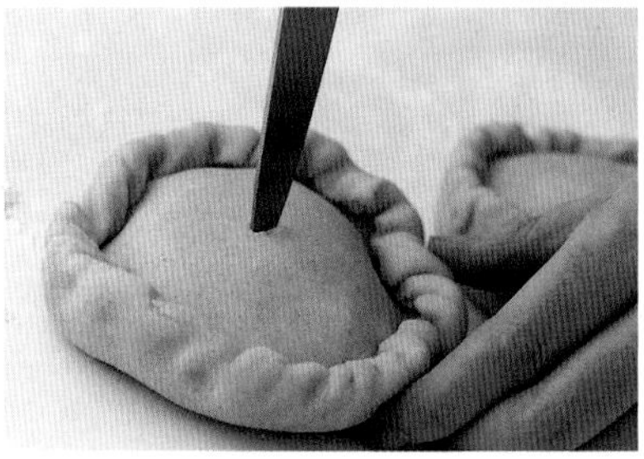

5 Make a small hole in the top of each pie to let out the steam, brush them with beaten egg and slide the pies on to baking sheets. Bake in the preheated oven for an hour. Serve hot or cold.

Variations

- If there is any lamb gravy left over from a roast, mix a little in with the raw ingredients: it makes the pies juicier.
- Pies are commonly baked in the oven, and regular shortcrust pastry is usual, although some restaurants make the pies in individual dishes topped with puff pastry.

Left *The picturesque town of Dingle and the Irish coastline, County Kerry.*

Per pie Energy 784Kcal/3275kJ; Protein 25.1g; Carbohydrate 74.6g, of which sugars 5.2g; Fat 44.9g, of which saturates 26.1g; Cholesterol 178mg; Calcium 155mg; Fibre 4g; Sodium 345mg

Rack of lamb with herb crust

This dish is very popular in Irish restaurants and for special occasions at home. Serve with creamy potato gratin, baby carrots and a green vegetable such as mangetouts or green beans. Offer mint jelly separately.

Serves 6–8

2 racks of lamb (fair end), chined and trimmed by the butcher

salt, ground black pepper and a pinch of cayenne pepper

For the herb crust

115g/4oz/½ cup butter

10ml/2 tsp mustard powder

175g/6oz/3 cups fresh breadcrumbs

2 garlic cloves, finely chopped

30ml/2 tbsp chopped fresh parsley

5ml/1 tsp very finely chopped fresh rosemary

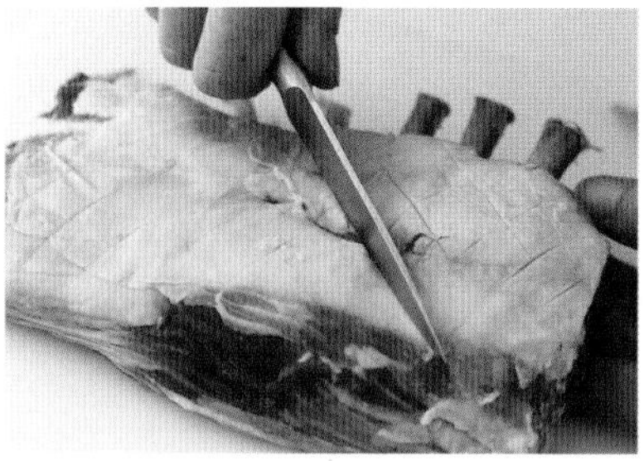

1 Preheat the oven to 200°C/400°F/Gas 6. Remove any meat and fat from the top 4–5cm/1½–2in of the bones and scrape the bones clean, then wrap the bones in foil to prevent burning. Remove almost all the fat from the lamb and score the thin layer remaining to make a lattice pattern; this will help to hold the herb crust in place later.

2 Season the lamb with salt, pepper and cayenne pepper, and cook the racks in the preheated oven for 20 minutes. Remove from the oven and allow to cool to room temperature.

3 Next make the herb crust: when the lamb is cold, blend 75g/3oz/6 tbsp of the butter with the mustard to make a smooth paste, and spread it over the fatty sides of the lamb.

4 Mix the breadcrumbs, garlic, parsley and rosemary together in a bowl. Melt the remaining butter, add it to the bowl and combine well. Divide the herb mixture between the two racks, laying it on top of the butter paste and pressing it well on to the lamb. Set aside and keep at room temperature until ready to finish cooking.

5 When ready to cook the meat, preheat the oven to 200°C/400°F/Gas 6, and roast for a final 20 minutes. To serve, remove the foil from the bones; finish them with paper cutlet frills, if you wish. Carve into cutlets, allowing 2 or 3 per person, and replace any of the crust that falls off.

Cook's tip This modern dish is convenient for entertaining as it is made in two stages, allowing the main preparation to be done ahead.

Per portion Energy 455Kcal/1899kJ; Protein 26.4g; Carbohydrate 22.7g, of which sugars 0.9g; Fat 29.4g, of which saturates 16.1g; Cholesterol 130mg; Calcium 51mg; Fibre 0.7g; Sodium 438mg

Pan-fried Gaelic steaks

A good steak is always popular in Ireland and top quality raw materials plus timing are the keys to success. Choose small, thick steaks rather than large, thin ones if you can. Traditional accompaniments include potato chips, fried onions, mushrooms and peas.

Serves 4

4 x 225–350g/8–12oz sirloin steaks, at room temperature

5ml/1 tsp oil

15g/½oz/1 tbsp butter

50ml/2fl oz/¼ cup Irish whiskey

300ml/½ pint/1¼ cups double (heavy) cream

salt and ground black pepper

1 Dry the steaks with kitchen paper and season with pepper. Heat a cast-iron frying pan, or other heavy pan, over high heat. When it is very hot, add the oil and butter. Add the steaks to the foaming butter, one at a time, to seal the meat quickly. Lower the heat to moderate. Allowing 3–4 minutes for rare, 4–5 minutes for medium or 5–6 minutes for well-done steaks, leave undisturbed for half of the specified cooking time; very thick steaks will take longer than thin ones. Turn only once.

2 To test if the timing is right, press down gently in the middle of the steak: soft meat will be rare; when there is some resistance but the meat underneath the outside crust feels soft, it is medium; if it is firm to the touch, the steak is well done.

3 When the steaks are cooked to your liking, transfer them to warmed plates and keep warm. Pour off the fat from the pan and discard. Add the whiskey and stir around to scrape off all the sediment from the base of the pan.

4 Allow the liquid to reduce a little, then add the cream and simmer over low heat for a few minutes, until the cream thickens. Season to taste, pour the sauce around or over the steaks, as preferred, and serve immediately.

Right *Beef cattle grazing in Mournes, Trassy Road, Slieve Bearnagh, Co. Down.*

Per portion Energy 738Kcal/3062kJ; Protein 54.1g; Carbohydrate 1.3g, of which sugars 1.3g; Fat 54.2g, of which saturates 31.6g; Cholesterol 226mg; Calcium 49mg; Fibre 0g; Sodium 197mg

Spiced beef

This is quite a traditional dish, although it is a modern version of the old recipe, as it omits the initial pickling stage and takes only three or four days to cure in comparison with ten days for the older method. Serve on thinly sliced brown bread, with chutney.

Serves 8

- 15ml/1 tbsp coarsely ground black pepper
- 10ml/2 tsp ground ginger
- 15ml/1 tbsp juniper berries, crushed
- 15ml/1 tbsp coriander seeds, crushed
- 5ml/1 tsp ground cloves
- 15ml/1 tbsp ground allspice
- 45ml/3 tbsp soft dark brown sugar
- 2 bay leaves, crushed
- 1 small onion, finely chopped
- 1.8kg/4lb corned beef, silverside or tail end
- 300ml/½ pint/1¼ cups Guinness
- fruit chutney and bread, to serve

1 First, spice the beef: blend the pepper, spices and sugar thoroughly, then mix in the bay leaves and onion. Rub the mixture into the meat, then put it into a suitable lidded container and refrigerate for 3–4 days, turning and rubbing with the mixture daily.

2 Put the meat into a pan and barely cover with cold water. Place a tight lid on the pan and bring to the boil. Reduce the heat and cook very gently for about 3½ hours. For the last hour add the Guinness to the cooking liquid.

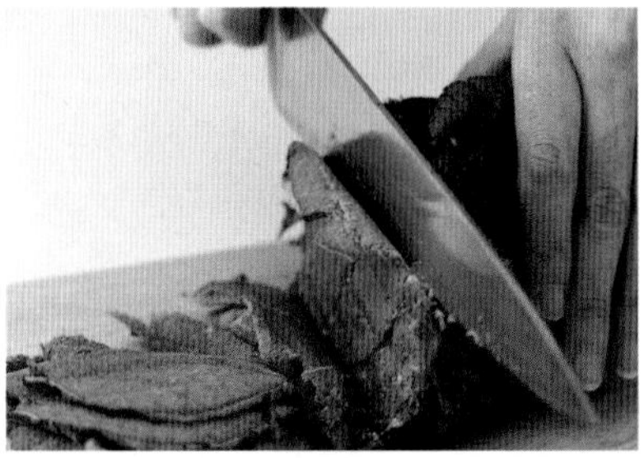

3 When the joint is cooked, leave it to cool in the liquid. Wrap in foil and keep in the refrigerator until required, then slice to serve. It will keep for about 1 week.

Variation Spiced beef is excellent as finger food for parties, sliced thinly and served with sour cream lightly flavoured with horseradish and black pepper.

Per portion Energy 309Kcal/1301kJ; Protein 53.6g; Carbohydrate 2g, of which sugars 2g; Fat 9.7g, of which saturates 3.6g; Cholesterol 137mg; Calcium 15mg; Fibre 0g; Sodium 140mg

Beef and Guinness casserole

Stout and beef make natural partners and occur frequently in Irish cooking. This richly flavoured version of a popular dish is suitable for any occasion, including informal entertaining. Serve with creamy well-buttered mashed potatoes.

Serves 4

30ml/2 tbsp olive oil

900g/2lb stewing beef (such as rib steak or shoulder), cut into thin slices

1 onion, chopped

2 leeks, sliced

2 carrots, sliced

2 celery sticks, sliced

2 garlic cloves, finely chopped

300ml/½ pint/1¼ cups well-reduced beef stock

150ml/¼ pint/⅔ cup Guinness

50g/2oz/¼ cup butter

75g/3oz streaky (fatty) bacon, trimmed and diced

115g/4oz wild or cultivated mushrooms, quartered or sliced

50g/2oz shallots or small onions, left whole

25g/1oz/¼ cup plain (all-purpose) flour

salt and ground black pepper

1 Heat the oil in a pan and brown the meat. Transfer to a casserole. Sauté the vegetables for 5 minutes in the pan.

2 Add the vegetables to the meat, and add the garlic. Add the stock and the Guinness. Season. Cover the casserole and bring to the boil, then reduce the heat and simmer for about 1½ hours.

3 Remove the meat from the casserole and strain the cooking liquid and reserve. Discard the vegetables.

4 Clean the casserole and sauté the bacon, mushrooms and shallots or onions in the butter for 5–10 minutes. When the vegetables are tender, sprinkle in the flour and cook, stirring, over a low heat for 2–3 minutes, then slowly blend in the reserved cooking liquid. Return the meat to the casserole, and reheat. Serve with mashed potatoes.

Per portion Energy 670Kcal/2786kJ; Protein 57.5g; Carbohydrate 14g, of which sugars 7.3g; Fat 42g, of which saturates 17.5g; Cholesterol 169mg; Calcium 71mg; Fibre 3.7g; Sodium 478mg

Corned beef with dumplings and cabbage

Once the traditional favourite for Easter, corned beef now tends to be associated with St Patrick's Day. If lightly cured, the meat may need to be soaked before cooking, but check with the butcher when buying; if in doubt, soak in cold water overnight.

Serves 6

- 1.3kg/3lb corned silverside or brisket
- 1 onion
- 4 cloves
- 2 bay leaves
- 8–10 whole black peppercorns
- 1 small cabbage

For the dumplings

- 1 small onion, finely chopped
- small bunch of parsley, chopped
- 115g/4oz/1 cup self-raising (self-rising) flour
- 50g/2oz shredded beef suet (chilled, grated shortening) or similar
- salt and ground black pepper

1 Soak the meat in cold water, if necessary, for several hours or overnight. When ready to cook, drain the meat and put it into a large heavy pan or flameproof casserole. Cover with fresh cold water.

2 Stick the cloves into the onion and add it to the pan with the bay leaves and peppercorns. Bring slowly to the boil, cover and simmer for 2 hours, or until the meat is tender.

3 Meanwhile, make the dumplings: mix the onion and parsley with the flour, suet and seasoning, and then add just enough water to make a soft, but not too sticky, dough. Dust your hands with a little flour and shape the dough into 12 small dumplings.

4 When the meat is cooked, remove it from the pan and keep warm. Bring the cooking liquid to a brisk boil, put in the dumplings and bring back to the boil. Cover tightly and cook the dumplings briskly for 15 minutes.

5 Meanwhile, slice the cabbage leaves finely and cook lightly in a little of the beef stock (keep the remaining stock for making soup). Serve the beef sliced with the dumplings and shredded cabbage. Boiled potatoes and parsley sauce are traditional accompaniments.

Per portion Energy 451Kcal/1895kJ; Protein 54.6g; Carbohydrate 21g, of which sugars 4.5g; Fat 17.4g, of which saturates 7.7g; Cholesterol 139mg; Calcium 86mg; Fibre 2.4g; Sodium 142mg

Turf-smoked beef with potato pancakes

This unusual recipe was inspired by a dish created for a modern Irish cookery competition by a chef based in the west of Ireland, where turf (peat) is an integral part of the way of life. Chargrilled beef fillet is a delicious alternative to the turf-smoked original.

Serves 4

500g/1¼lb trimmed beef fillet

salt and ground black pepper

oil, for chargrilling

herb sprigs, to garnish

broccoli florets, white turnip and courgettes, to serve

For the potato pancakes

250g/9oz potatoes, cooked

50g/2oz/½ cup plain (all-purpose) flour

1 egg

freshly grated nutmeg

oil, for frying

For the sauce

4 shallots, finely diced

200ml/7fl oz/scant 1 cup chicken stock

120ml/4fl oz/½ cup white wine

200ml/7fl oz/scant 1 cup double (heavy) cream

15ml/1 tbsp chopped fresh herbs, such as flat leaf parsley, tarragon, chervil and basil

lemon juice, to taste

1 To make the potato pancakes, blend the potatoes with the flour and egg to make a thick purée. Add nutmeg and seasoning to taste.

2 Heat and lightly oil a heavy pan, then use the potato purée to make eight small pancakes, cooking on both sides until golden brown. Keep warm.

3 To make the sauce, put the shallots, stock, wine and half the cream into a pan and cook over a medium heat until reduced by two-thirds. Purée the mixture and strain it, then mix in enough herbs to turn the sauce green.

4 Season the beef with salt and freshly ground black pepper. In a heavy, preheated pan, seal the meat on all sides over medium heat.

5 Place the meat in a smoker for about 10 minutes until it is cooked medium-rare. Alternatively, to chargrill the meat if you don't have a smoker, preheat a dry cast-iron ridged pan until very hot. Brush the meat with a little oil and cook for 3–5 minutes, turning once. Keep warm.

6 When ready to serve, whip the remaining cream and fold it into the sauce, adjusting the flavour with salt, black pepper and lemon juice if required. Divide the sauce between four warm plates. Cut the beef fillet into eight slices and place two slices on top of the sauce on each plate. Arrange potato pancakes around the meat. Garnish with sprigs of herbs and serve with the broccoli florets, white turnip and courgettes.

Per portion Energy 683Kcal/2834kJ; Protein 32.9g; Carbohydrate 23g, of which sugars 3g; Fat 49.5g, of which saturates 27.5g; Cholesterol 219mg; Calcium 82mg; Fibre 1.9g; Sodium 166mg

Poultry and game

Every Irish countrywoman used to keep poultry – which provided an independent source of income as well as supplying eggs and the family table – and goose, turkey and chicken have long been associated with feasting, such as eating goose on Michaelmas Day on 29 September. Wild game, both furred and feathered, has always been plentiful in Ireland and, in addition to supplies of farmed produce such as venison, wild game is still available in season.

Mustard baked chicken

In this Irish recipe, a mild, aromatic wholegrain mustard makes a tasty way of cooking chicken. Speciality mustards are made by several companies in Ireland, although the mustard seeds are imported. Serve with new potatoes and peas or mangetouts.

Serves 4–6

- 8–12 chicken joints, or 1 medium chicken, about 1kg/2¼lb, jointed
- juice of ½ lemon
- 15–30ml/2–3 tbsp whiskey mustard
- 10ml/2 tsp chopped fresh tarragon
- sea salt and ground black pepper

Variation A whole chicken can also be baked this way. Allow about 1½ hours in an oven preset to 180°C/350°F/ Gas 4. When cooked, the juices will run clear without any trace of blood.

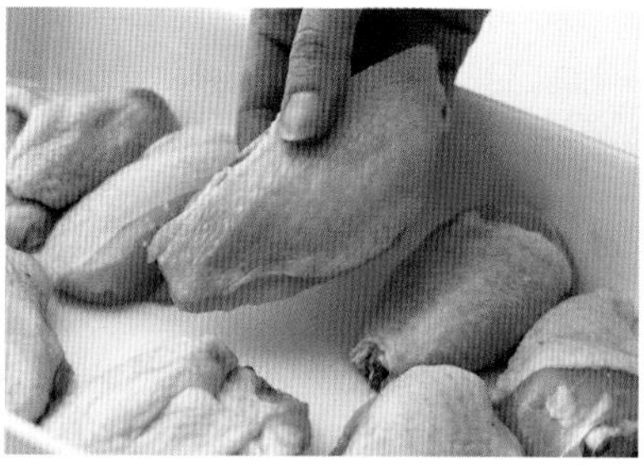

1 Preheat the oven to 190°C/375°F/ Gas 5. Put the chicken joints into a large shallow baking dish in a single layer and sprinkle the lemon juice over the chicken to flavour the skin. Season well with sea salt and black pepper.

2 Spread the mustard over the joints and sprinkle with the chopped tarragon. Bake in the preheated oven for 20–30 minutes or until thoroughly cooked, depending on the size of the chicken pieces. Serve immediately.

Per portion Energy 426Kcal/1768kJ; Protein 40.3g; Carbohydrate 0g, of which sugars 0g; Fat 29.3g, of which saturates 8.1g; Cholesterol 215mg; Calcium 13mg; Fibre 0g; Sodium 146mg

Hen in a pot with parsley sauce

Every country family used to keep hens, and the older ones were destined for the table. Although harder to find nowadays, a boiling fowl will feed a family well. A large chicken could replace the boiling fowl. Serve with potatoes boiled in their jackets, and cabbage.

Serves 6

- 1.6–1.8kg/3½–4lb boiling fowl
- ½ lemon, sliced
- small bunch of parsley and thyme
- 675g/1½lb carrots, cut into large chunks
- 12 shallots or small onions, left whole

For the sauce

- 50g/2oz/¼ cup butter
- 50g/2oz/½ cup plain (all-purpose) flour
- 15ml/1 tbsp lemon juice
- 60ml/4 tbsp finely chopped fresh parsley
- 150ml/¼ pint/⅔ cup milk
- salt and ground pepper
- fresh parsley sprigs, to garnish

1 Put the fowl into a large pan with enough water to cover. Add the sliced lemon and parsley and thyme, and season well with salt and pepper. Cover the pan and bring to the boil, then reduce the heat and simmer over a gentle heat for 2½ hours, turning several times during cooking.

2 Add the carrots and whole onions to the pot and cook for another 30–40 minutes, or until the fowl and the vegetables are tender.

3 Using a slotted spoon, lift the fowl on to a warmed serving dish, arrange the vegetables around it and keep warm. Remove the herbs and lemon slices from the cooking liquor and discard.

4 Bring the liquor back to the boil and boil it, uncovered, to reduce the liquid by about a third. Strain and leave to settle for 1–2 minutes, then skim the fat off the surface.

5 Melt the butter in a pan, add the flour and cook, stirring, for 1 minute. Gradually stir in the stock (there should be about 600ml/1 pint/2½ cups) and bring to the boil. Add the lemon juice, parsley and the milk. Adjust the seasoning and simmer the sauce for another 1–2 minutes.

6 To serve, pour a little of the sauce over the fowl and the carrots and onions, then garnish with a few sprigs of fresh parsley and take to the table for carving. Pour the rest of the sauce into a heated sauceboat and hand round separately.

Per portion Energy 509Kcal/2114kJ; Protein 36.2g; Carbohydrate 20.1g, of which sugars 12.2g; Fat 31.9g, of which saturates 11.4g; Cholesterol 195mg; Calcium 109mg; Fibre 4g; Sodium 214mg

Traditional roast chicken with herb stuffing

There's nothing to beat a traditional roast chicken when a free-range bird and fresh herbs are used. Traditional accompaniments include roast potatoes, sausages and bacon rolls, bread sauce and a fruit sauce or jelly, such as cranberry sauce or elderberry jelly.

Serves 6

- 1 large chicken, about 1.8kg/4lb, with giblets and neck if possible
- 1 small onion, sliced
- 1 small carrot, sliced
- small bunch of parsley and thyme
- 15g/½oz/1 tbsp butter
- 30ml/2 tbsp chicken fat or oil
- 6 rashers (strips) of streaky (fatty) bacon
- salt and ground black pepper

For the stuffing

- 1 onion, finely chopped
- 50g/2oz/¼ cup butter
- 150g/5oz/2½ cups fresh white breadcrumbs
- 15ml/1 tbsp fresh chopped parsley
- 15ml/1 tbsp fresh chopped mixed herbs, such as thyme, marjoram and chives
- finely grated rind and juice of ½ lemon
- 1 small egg, lightly beaten (optional)
- 15ml/1 tbsp plain (all-purpose) flour

1 Remove the giblets from the chicken; also remove the piece of fat which is found just inside the vent and put this fat into a roasting pan – it can be rendered down and used when cooking the roast potatoes. Wipe out the inside of the bird thoroughly. Separate the liver from the rest of the giblets, chop it and set it aside to use in the gravy.

2 Put the giblets and the neck into a pan with the sliced onion and sliced carrot, the bunch of parsley and thyme and a good sprinkling of salt and pepper. Add enough water cold water to cover generously, bring to the boil and leave to simmer gently for about 1 hour. Strain the chicken stock and discard the giblets. Preheat the oven to 200°C/400°F/Gas 6.

3 Meanwhile, make the herb stuffing: cook the chopped onion in the butter in a large pan over a low heat without colouring for a few minutes until it is just beginning to soften. Remove from the heat, and add the breadcrumbs, fresh herbs and chopped lemon rind. Mix thoroughly. Mix in the lemon juice, beaten egg, if using, and a good seasoning of salt and pepper. (The egg will bind the stuffing and make it firmer when cooked, but it can be omitted if you prefer a lighter, more crumbly texture.)

4 Spoon the stuffing into the neck cavity of the chicken, without packing it in too tightly, and secure the opening with a small skewer. Spread the breast with the butter, then put the chicken fat or oil into a roasting pan and lay the bird in it. Season and lay the bacon rashers over the top of the bird to protect it in the oven.

5 Weigh the stuffed chicken and work out the cooking time at 20 minutes per 450g/1lb and 20 minutes over, then put into the preheated oven. After 20 minutes, reduce the temperature to 180°C/350°F/Gas 4 for another 45–60 minutes, or until cooked. Test by inserting a sharp knife between the body and thigh: if the juices run clear with no hint of blood, it is cooked.

6 Transfer the cooked chicken to a serving dish and allow it to rest for 10 minutes in a warm place while you make the gravy.

7 To make the gravy, pour off the excess fat from the roasting pan, then add the finely chopped liver and stir over low heat for 1 minute, or until it has turned light brown. Sprinkle in just enough flour to absorb the remaining chicken fat and cook gently, stirring to blend, for 1 or 2 minutes. Gradually add some of the giblet stock, scraping the pan to dissolve the residues and stirring well to make a smooth gravy. Bring to the boil, stirring, gradually adding more stock until the consistency is as you like it. Adjust the seasoning, and then pour into a heated sauceboat to hand round separately.

8 Carve the chicken. Serve on heated plates with the herb stuffing and gravy.

Per portion Energy 562Kcal/2342kJ; Protein 40.9g; Carbohydrate 23.2g, of which sugars 2.7g; Fat 34.5g, of which saturates 11.9g; Cholesterol 216mg; Calcium 72mg; Fibre 1.5g; Sodium 381mg

Roast mallard

Shooting is an important Irish country pursuit in winter and wildfowl, such as mallard, teal and widgeon are in good supply from game stores during the late autumn and early winter. Serve with game chips, apple sauce or rowan jelly, and puréed Jerusalem artichokes.

Serves 2–3

1 oven-ready mallard

1 small onion studded with cloves

a few apple slices

25g/1oz/2 tbsp butter, softened

salt and ground black pepper

5 streaky (fatty) bacon rashers (strips)

1 Thoroughly wash the bird inside and out under cold running water and wipe dry on kitchen paper.

2 Weigh the mallard and calculate the cooking time at 15 minutes per 450g/1lb for rare meat, 20 minutes per 450g/1lb if you prefer the meat well done. Preheat the oven to 200°C/400°F/Gas 6.

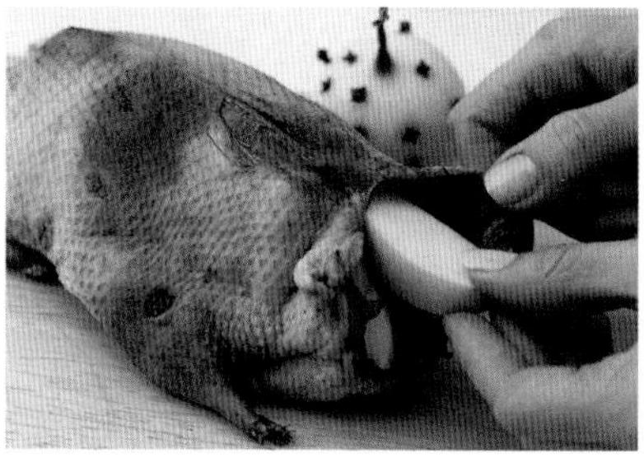

3 Put the clove-studded onion and a few apple slices inside the bird. Spread the butter all over the skin, and season.

4 Cover with the bacon and put the duck into a roasting pan with 30ml/2 tbsp water and roast in the preheated oven for the time estimated, removing the rashers for the last 10 minutes to allow the skin to brown.

5 To serve, carve the meat and arrange on heated plates, leaving the legs whole.

Cook's tips

- Wild fowl from coastal areas can have a fishy flavour. To offset this, put the oven-ready bird into a pan of cold, salted water and bring to the boil; leave to simmer for 15–20 minutes, then remove the bird and wash and dry both inside and out before proceeding.
- Wildfowl are often served rare; the meat is lean and will be dry unless slowly cooked to retain moisture.

Per portion Energy 486Kcal/2028kJ; Protein 49.6g; Carbohydrate 0.1g, of which sugars 0.1g; Fat 32g, of which saturates 14.1g; Cholesterol 278mg; Calcium 28mg; Fibre 0g; Sodium 1.08g

Roast farmyard duck with apples and cider

Sharp fruit flavours offset the richness of duck: orange is the classic, but cooking apples from Armagh are used here with Clonmel cider. Serve with a selection of vegetables, including roast potatoes and, perhaps, some red cabbage.

Serves 4

- 2kg/4½lb oven-ready duck or duckling
- 300ml/½ pint/1¼ cups Clonmel or other dry (hard) cider
- 60ml/4 tbsp double (heavy) cream
- sea salt and ground black pepper

For the stuffing

- 75g/3oz/6 tbsp butter
- 115g/4oz/2 cups fresh white breadcrumbs
- 450g/1lb cooking apples, peeled, cored and diced
- 15ml/1 tbsp sugar, or to taste
- freshly grated nutmeg

1 Preheat the oven to 200°C/400°F/Gas 6. To make the stuffing, melt the butter in a pan and fry the breadcrumbs until golden brown. Add the apples to the breadcrumbs with salt, pepper, the sugar and a pinch of nutmeg. Mix well.

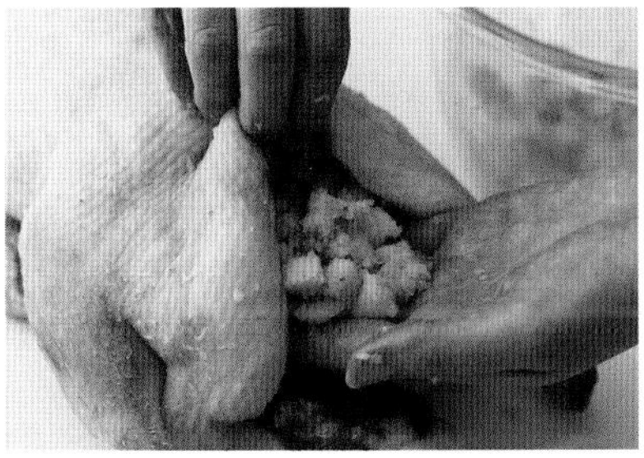

2 Wipe the duck out with a clean, damp cloth, and remove any obvious excess fat (including the flaps just inside the vent). Rub the skin with salt. Stuff the duck with the prepared mixture, then secure the vent with a small skewer.

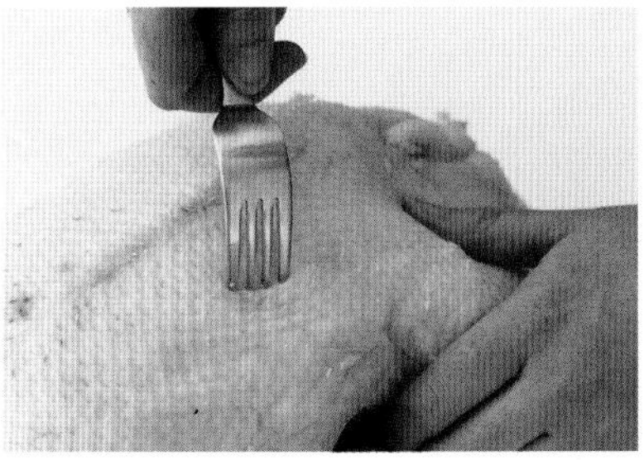

3 Weigh the stuffed duck and calculate the cooking time, allowing 20 minutes per 450g/1lb. Prick the skin all over with a fork to allow the fat to run out during the cooking time, then lay it on top of a wire rack in a roasting pan, sprinkle with freshly ground black pepper and put it into the preheated oven to roast.

4 About 20 minutes before the end of the estimated cooking time, remove the duck from the oven and pour off all the fat that has accumulated under the rack (reserve it for frying). Slide the duck off the rack into the roasting pan and pour the cider over it. Return to the oven and finish cooking, basting occasionally.

5 When the duck is cooked, remove it from the pan and keep warm while you make the sauce. Set the roasting pan over a medium heat and boil the cider to reduce it by half. Stir in the cream, heat through and season. Meanwhile, remove the stuffing from the duck. Carve the duck into slices or quarter it using poultry shears. Serve with a portion of stuffing and the cider sauce.

Per portion Energy 572Kcal/2397kJ; Protein 31.5g; Carbohydrate 34.6g, of which sugars 13.1g; Fat 33.1g, of which saturates 17.8g; Cholesterol 211mg; Calcium 74mg; Fibre 2.4g; Sodium 498mg

Quail with apples

Nowadays, quail often appear on restaurant menus in Ireland, and they are increasingly used by domestic cooks too. As they are very tiny, the cooking time is short and it is necessary to allow one for each person as a first course and two for a main course.

Serves 2 as a main course or 4 as a first course

4 oven-ready quail

120ml/4fl oz/½ cup olive oil

2 firm eating apples

115g/4oz/½ cup butter

4 slices white bread

salt and ground black pepper

1 Preheat the oven to 220°C/425°F/ Gas 7. Core the apples and slice them thickly (leave the peel on if it is pretty and not too tough).

2 Brush the quail with half the olive oil and roast them in a pan in the oven for 10 minutes, or until brown and tender.

3 Meanwhile, heat half the butter in a frying pan and sauté the apple slices for about 3 minutes until they are golden but not mushy. Season with pepper, cover and keep warm until required.

4 Remove the crusts from the bread. Heat the remaining olive oil and the butter in a frying pan and fry the bread on both sides until brown and crisp.

5 Lay the fried bread on heated plates and place the quail on top. Arrange the fried apple slices around them, and serve immediately.

Per portion Energy 814Kcal/3389kJ; Protein 53.3g; Carbohydrate 33.3g, of which sugars 10.5g; Fat 43.6g, of which saturates 23.4g; Cholesterol 69mg; Calcium 169mg; Fibre 2.4g; Sodium 644mg

Pigeons in stout

The pigeons on sale in Ireland are wild, available all year round, inexpensive and usually sold in breast portions, as the edible meat is mainly on the breast. The flesh is dark and, like most small birds, dry, so casseroling them in stout is an ideal cooking method.

Serves 6

- 175g/6oz thick streaky (fatty) bacon
- 2 medium onions, finely chopped
- 2 or 3 garlic cloves, crushed
- seasoned flour, for coating
- 50g/2oz/¼ cup butter
- 15ml/1 tbsp olive oil
- 6 pigeon breasts
- 30ml/2 tbsp Irish whiskey (optional)
- 600ml/1 pint/2½ cups chicken stock
- 300ml/½ pint/1¼ cups stout
- 175g/6oz button (white) mushrooms
- beurre manié, if needed (see Cook's tip)
- 15–30ml/1–2 tbsp rowan jelly
- sea salt and ground black pepper

Cook's tip To make beurre manié mix together 15g/½oz/1 tbsp of butter with 15ml/1 tbsp flour. Add small pieces of the mixture to the boiling gravy or sauce and stir until thickened.

1 Preheat the oven to 150°C/300°F/Gas 2. Trim the streaky bacon and cut it into strips. Cook gently in a large, flameproof casserole until the fat runs out, then add the two chopped onions and crushed garlic and continue cooking until they are soft. Remove from the casserole and set aside.

2 Coat the breast portions thickly with seasoned flour. Add the butter and oil to the pan, heat until the butter is foaming, then add the meat and brown well on all sides. Pour in the Irish whiskey, if using. Carefully set it alight and shake the pan until the flames go out – this improves the flavour.

3 Stir in the stock, stout and the mushrooms, and bring slowly to the boil. Cover closely and cook in the preheated oven for 1½–2 hours, or until the pigeons are tender.

4 Remove from the oven and lift the pigeons on to a serving dish. Thicken the gravy, if necessary, by adding small pieces of beurre manié, stirring until the sauce thickens. Stir in rowan jelly to taste and adjust the seasoning. Serve the pigeons with the gravy while hot.

Per portion Energy 436Kcal/1817kJ; Protein 38.7g; Carbohydrate 6.7g, of which sugars 5.3g; Fat 27.2g, of which saturates 6.2g; Cholesterol 33mg; Calcium 48mg; Fibre 1.7g; Sodium 639mg

Pheasant with oatmeal stuffing

Fresh pheasant tastes bland, like chicken – in cold weather it may need a week hanging in a cool place to acquire a gamey flavour. Like most game, pheasant tends to be dry, so offset dryness by laying slices of fatty unsalted bacon over the breast.

Serves 4–6

- 2 oven-ready pheasants
- 6 unsmoked streaky (fatty) bacon rashers (strips)
- 50g/2oz/¼ cup softened butter
- 15g/½oz/2 tbsp seasoned flour
- 450ml/¾ pint/scant 2 cups chicken stock
- salt and ground black pepper
- watercress or rocket, to garnish

For the stuffing

- 1 small onion, finely chopped
- pheasant livers, finely chopped
- 115g/4oz/1 cup pinhead oatmeal
- 50g/2oz/¼ cup butter, melted

1 To prepare the stuffing, put the onion and the pheasant livers into a mixing bowl with the oatmeal and butter. Mix thoroughly and season well with salt and pepper. Add a little cold water to moisten slightly.

2 Preheat the oven to 200°C/400°F/Gas 6. Wipe the birds inside and out and divide the stuffing between the two birds, spooning in loosely to allow the stuffing to expand during cooking.

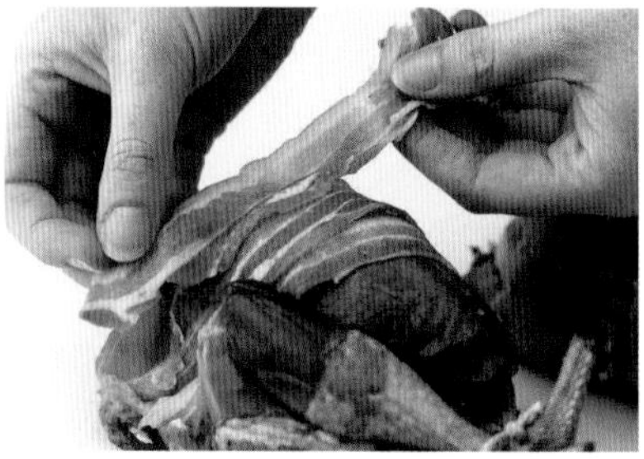

3 Use cotton string to truss them for cooking, and lay the bacon rashers over the breasts. Spread half the softened butter over the birds and lay them in a roasting pan with the remaining butter.

4 Cook in the oven for 45–50 minutes, basting often. Ten minutes before the end of the cooking time, remove the rashers, baste the birds and then dredge them with seasoned flour. Baste again and return to the oven to brown.

5 When cooked, remove the trussing strings and put the pheasants on to a heated serving dish. Keep warm, uncovered, while you make the gravy.

6 Pour all but 30ml/2 tbsp of the fat out of the roasting pan and sprinkle in the remaining flour, stirring well to blend and dislodge any sediment on the bottom of the pan. Gradually blend in the stock, season and bring to the boil. Simmer for a few minutes, stirring, then pour into a heated sauceboat.

7 To serve, garnish the pheasant breasts with the bacon pieces and watercress or rocket. Hand the gravy round separately.

Cook's tip Traditional accompaniments include game chips, breadcrumbs and redcurrant sauce or bread sauce.

Per portion Energy 847Kcal/3529kJ; Protein 69.7g; Carbohydrate 25.2g, of which sugars 1.1g; Fat 52.5g, of which saturates 23.1g; Cholesterol 598mg; Calcium 92mg; Fibre 2.3g; Sodium 697mg

Michaelmas goose with apple stuffing

This delicious recipe includes apples, at their best in autumn and a refreshing foil to the richness of the goose and the traditional black pudding. Serve the goose with roast potatoes, seasonal vegetables and apple sauce or bramble jelly.

Serves 6–8

1 goose, 4.5kg/10lb, with giblets

1 onion, sliced

2 carrots, sliced

2 celery sticks, sliced

a small bunch of parsley and thyme

450g/1lb black pudding (blood sausage), crumbled or chopped

2 large cooking apples, peeled, cored and finely chopped

1 large garlic clove, crushed

250ml/8fl oz/1 cup dry (hard) cider

15ml/1 tbsp plain (all-purpose) flour

salt and ground black pepper

watercress or parsley, to garnish

1 Remove the goose liver from the giblets and put the remainder into a pan with the onion, carrots, celery and herbs. Cover with cold water, season and simmer for 30–45 minutes to make a stock for the gravy. Preheat the oven to 200°C/400°F/Gas 6.

2 Meanwhile, chop the liver finely and mix it with the black pudding, garlic and apples. Add salt and ground pepper, and then sprinkle in 75ml/ 2½fl oz/⅓ cup cider to bind.

3 Wipe out the goose and stuff it with this mixture, being careful not to pack it too tightly. Prick the skin all over with a fork, sprinkle generously with salt and pepper and rub in well.

4 Weigh the stuffed goose and calculate the cooking time at 15 minutes per 450g/1lb and 15 minutes over. Put the goose on a rack in a large roasting pan, cover with foil and put it into the preheated oven.

5 After 1 hour, remove the goose from the oven and carefully pour off the hot fat that has accumulated in the bottom of the pan; reserve this fat for cooking. Pour the remaining dry cider over the goose and return to the oven.

6 Half an hour before the end of the estimated cooking time, remove the foil and carefully baste the goose with the juices.

7 Return to the oven, uncovered, and allow the bird to brown, basting occasionally. When cooked, transfer the goose to a heated serving dish and put it in a warm place to rest.

8 Meanwhile, make the gravy. Pour off any excess fat from the roasting pan, leaving 30ml/2 tbsp, then sprinkle in enough plain flour to absorb it. Cook over a medium heat for a minute, scraping the pan to loosen the sediment. Strain the giblet stock and stir in enough to make the gravy. Bring it to the boil and simmer for a few minutes, stirring constantly. Add any juices that have accumulated under the cooked goose, season to taste and pour the gravy into a heated sauceboat.

9 Garnish the goose with the parsley or watercress. Carve into slices at the table and serve with the gravy, roast potatoes and some seasonal vegetables.

Per portion Energy 795Kcal/3297kJ; Protein 32.8g; Carbohydrate 17.1g, of which sugars 2.3g; Fat 65.4g, of which saturates 20.6g; Cholesterol 171mg; Calcium 109mg; Fibre 0.4g; Sodium 800mg

Game pie

This country dish is adaptable and could be made with whatever game birds are available. Serve the pie with seasonal vegetables: potatoes boiled in their skins, puréed Jerusalem artichokes and winter greens, such as purple sprouting broccoli or Brussels sprouts.

Serves 8–10

- 4 pheasant and/or pigeon skinless breast portions
- 225g/8oz lean stewing steak
- 115g/4oz streaky (fatty) bacon, trimmed
- butter, for frying
- 2 medium onions, finely chopped
- 1 large garlic clove, crushed
- 15ml/1 tbsp plain (all-purpose) flour
- about 300ml/½ pint/¼ cup pigeon or pheasant stock
- 15ml/1 tbsp tomato purée (paste) (optional)
- 15ml/1 tbsp chopped fresh parsley
- a little grated lemon rind
- 15ml/1 tbsp rowan or redcurrant jelly
- 50–115g/2–4oz button (white) mushrooms, halved or quartered if large
- a small pinch of freshly grated nutmeg or ground cloves (optional)
- milk or beaten egg, to glaze
- sea salt and ground black pepper

For the rough-puff pastry

- 225g/8oz/2 cups plain (all-purpose) flour
- 2.5ml/½ tsp salt
- 5ml/1 tsp lemon juice
- 115g/4oz/½ cup butter, in walnut-sized pieces

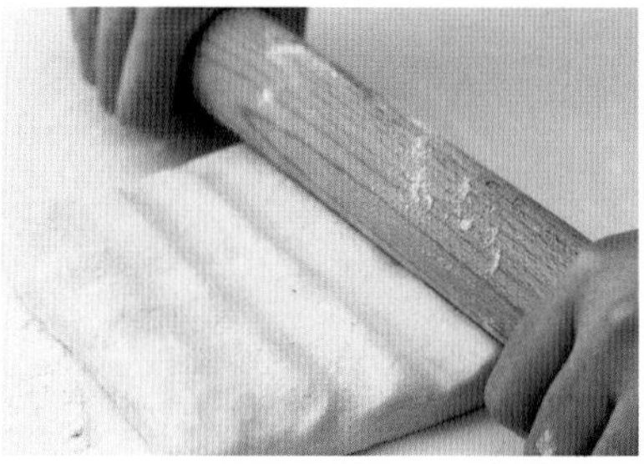

1 To make the rough-puff pastry, sieve the flour and salt into a large mixing bowl. Add the lemon juice and the butter pieces and just enough cold water to bind the ingredients together. Turn the mixture on to a floured board and roll the pastry into a long strip. Fold it into three and press the edges together. Half-turn the pastry, rib it with the rolling pin to equalize the air in it and roll it into a strip once again. Repeat this folding and rolling process three more times.

2 Slice the pheasant or pigeon breasts from the bone and cut the meat into fairly thin strips. Trim away any fat from the stewing steak and slice it in the same manner. Cut the streaky (fatty) bacon into thin strips, and then cook it very gently in a heavy frying pan until the fat runs. Add some butter and brown the sliced pigeon or pheasant and stewing steak in it, a little at a time.

3 Remove the meats from the pan and set aside. Cook the onions and garlic in the fat for 2–3 minutes over a medium heat. Remove and set aside with the meats, then stir the flour into the remaining fat. Cook for 1–2 minutes, and then gradually stir in enough stock to make a fairly thin gravy. Add the tomato purée, if using, parsley, lemon rind and rowan or redcurrant jelly and the mushrooms. Season to taste and add the nutmeg or cloves, if you like.

4 Return the browned meats, chopped onion and garlic to the pan containing the gravy, and mix well before turning into a deep 1.75 litre/3 pint/7½ cup pie dish. Leave to cool. Meanwhile, preheat the oven to 220°C/425°F/Gas 7.

5 Roll the prepared pastry out to make a circle 2.5cm/1in larger all round than the pie dish, and cut out to make a lid for the pie. Wet the rim of the pie dish and line with the remaining pastry strip. Dampen the strip and cover with the lid, pressing down well to seal.

6 Trim away any excess pastry and knock up the edges with a knife. Make a hole in the centre for the steam to escape and use any pastry trimmings to decorate the top. Glaze the top of the pie with milk or beaten egg. Bake in the oven for about 20 minutes, until the pastry is well-risen, then reduce the oven to 150°C/300°F/Gas 2 for another 1½ hours, until cooked. Protect the pastry from over-browning if necessary by covering it with a double layer of wet baking parchment. Serve.

Cook's tip Frozen puff pastry could replace the home-made rough-puff pastry, if you prefer.

Per portion Energy 448Kcal/1871kJ; Protein 28.3g; Carbohydrate 29.5g, of which sugars 5.3g; Fat 24.9g, of which saturates 9.5g; Cholesterol 55mg; Calcium 67mg; Fibre 1.5g; Sodium 393mg

Braised rabbit

Rabbit now features frequently on restaurant menus. It is delicious served with potatoes boiled in their skins and a lightly cooked green vegetable.

Serves 4–6

- 1 rabbit, prepared and jointed by the butcher
- 30ml/2 tbsp seasoned flour
- 30ml/2 tbsp olive oil or vegetable oil
- 25g/1oz/2 tbsp butter
- 115g/4oz streaky (fatty) bacon
- 1 onion, roughly chopped
- 2 or 3 carrots, sliced
- 1 or 2 celery sticks, trimmed and sliced
- 300ml/½ pint/1¼ cups chicken stock
- 300ml/½ pint/1¼ cups dry (hard) cider or stout
- a small bunch of parsley leaves, chopped
- salt and ground black pepper

1 Soak the joints in cold salted water for at least two hours, then pat them dry with kitchen paper and toss them in seasoned flour. Preheat the oven to 200°C/400°F/Gas 6.

2 Heat the oil and butter together in a heavy flameproof casserole. Shake off (and reserve) any excess flour from the rabbit joints and brown them on all sides. Lift out and set aside.

3 Add the bacon to the casserole and cook for a few minutes, then remove and set aside with the rabbit. Add the vegetables to the casserole and cook gently until just colouring, then sprinkle over any remaining seasoned flour to absorb the fats in the casserole. Stir over a low heat for 1 minute, to cook the flour. Add the stock and cider or stout, stirring, to make a smooth sauce.

4 Return the rabbit and bacon to the casserole, and add half of the chopped parsley and a light seasoning of salt and pepper. Mix gently together, then cover with a lid and put into the preheated oven. Cook for 15–20 minutes, then reduce the temperature to 150°C/300°F/Gas 2 for about 1½ hours, or until the rabbit is tender. Add the remaining parsley and serve.

Cook's tip Buy rabbit whole or jointed, from butchers and good supermarkets.

Per portion Energy 368Kcal/1535kJ; Protein 32.9g; Carbohydrate 10.5g, of which sugars 5.8g; Fat 19.7g, of which saturates 8g; Cholesterol 133mg; Calcium 88mg; Fibre 1.4g; Sodium 567mg

Home-made venison sausages

Venison sausages have an excellent flavour, a much lower fat content than most sausages and they're easy to make. The only tricky bit, obtaining and filling sausage skins, is omitted.

Makes 1.4kg/3lb

900g/2lb finely minced (ground) venison

450g/1lb finely minced (ground) belly of pork

15ml/1 tbsp salt

10ml/2 tsp ground black pepper

1 garlic clove, crushed

5ml/1 tsp dried thyme

1 egg, beaten

plain (all-purpose) flour, for dusting

oil, for frying

mashed potatoes, fried onions, grilled (broiled) or fried field (portobello) mushrooms and grilled tomatoes, to serve

1 Combine all the ingredients, except the flour and oil, in a bowl. Take a small piece of the mixture and fry it in a little oil in a heavy frying pan, then taste to check the seasoning for the batch. Adjust if necessary.

2 Form the mixture into chipolata-size sausages using floured hands.

3 Heat the oil in a large, heavy frying pan and shallow-fry the sausages for 10 minutes or until they are golden brown and cooked right through.

4 Serve the sausages with creamy mashed potatoes, fried onions, and grilled mushrooms and tomatoes.

Cook's tip Venison sausages also freeze well if stored in an airtight container.

Right *A large herd of fallow deer grazing in the evening sun at Phoenix Park, Dublin.*

Per portion Energy 2715Kcal/11322kJ; Protein 274.9g; Carbohydrate 0g, of which sugars 0g; Fat 185.1g, of which saturates 67.7g; Cholesterol 964mg; Calcium 110mg; Fibre 0g; Sodium 894mg

Casseroled venison with stout

Venison, both wild and (more usually) farmed, is widely available in Ireland. It is popular on restaurant menus and, increasingly, available for home cooks from butchers and the better supermarkets. Serve with boiled or baked potatoes and red cabbage.

Serves 6

- 900g/2lb stewing venison, such as shoulder
- 45ml/3 tbsp seasoned flour
- 30ml/2 tbsp olive oil
- 2 or 3 large onions, sliced
- 5 or 6 juniper berries, crushed
- 3 allspice berries
- rind of ½ lemon or orange
- 25g/1oz/2 tbsp butter
- about 300ml/½ pint/1¼ cups chicken or beef stock
- 150ml/¼ pint/⅔ cup red wine vinegar or cider vinegar
- 300ml/½ pint/1¼ cups stout or red wine
- salt and ground black pepper

1 Preheat the oven to 180°C/350°F/Gas 4. Cut the meat into 5cm/2in cubes. Toss the meat in the seasoned flour. Shake off and reserve the excess flour.

2 Heat the oil in a heavy frying pan and fry the meat in it until well browned all over. Lift out the pieces with a slotted spoon and put them into a casserole. Add the onions to the casserole with the juniper berries and allspice, a little salt and black pepper and the lemon or orange rind.

3 Melt the butter in the pan in which the meat was browned, add the reserved flour, and stir and cook for 1 minute. Mix the stock, vinegar and stout or red wine together and gradually add to the pan, stirring until it boils and thickens.

4 Pour the sauce over the meat in the casserole, cover closely and cook in the oven for 1 hour. Reduce the temperature to 150°C/300°F/Gas 2 and cook for a further 2 hours, or until the venison is tender. Check the casserole occasionally and add a little extra stock or water if required. Serve piping hot.

Cook's tip Venison is not difficult to cook but, like other game, it is lean, so marinating, basting and braising all help to offset any tendency to dryness.

Per portion Energy 294Kcal/1233kJ; Protein 34.7g; Carbohydrate 9.3g, of which sugars 4.9g; Fat 10.6g, of which saturates 3.9g; Cholesterol 84mg; Calcium 37mg; Fibre 1.3g; Sodium 114mg

Roast loin of boar with poitín-soaked prunes

Farmed "wild" boar is produced in Northern Ireland and is popular in restaurants throughout the country. Whiskey can replace the poitín. Suggested accompaniments include black pudding mash and cooked cabbage with some apple sauce.

Serves 4–6

- 8 pitted prunes
- 1 glass poitín or Irish whiskey
- 675g/1½lb boned loin of boar, any excess fat removed
- salt and ground black pepper

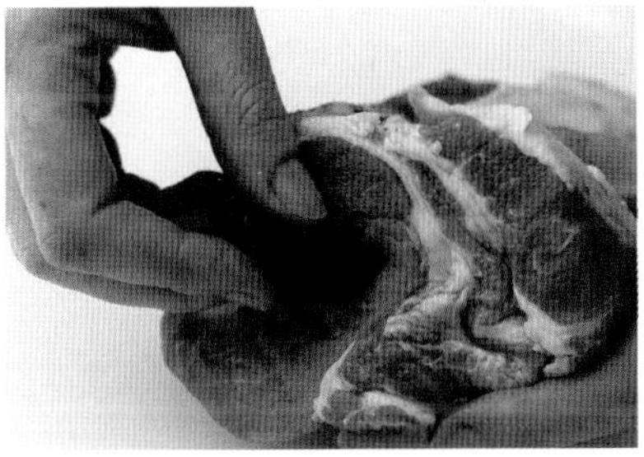

1 Soak the prunes overnight in enough poitín or whiskey to cover.

Cook's tip To prepare the mash add 225g/8oz cooked black pudding to 1kg/2¼lb cooked mash potatoes. Mash well with cream and butter to taste. Stir in 15ml/1 tbsp mustard and season.

2 Use a skewer to make a circular incision along the loin of boar and stuff with the prunes. Place a large square of foil on a flat surface. On top of the foil place a large square of clear film (plastic wrap). Place the loin on one end of the clear film and roll up tightly. Refrigerate for 2 hours.

3 Preheat the oven to 200°C/400°F/Gas 6. Remove the foil and clear film and cut the loin into tournedos (steaks). Preheat a heavy pan and sear the meat on both sides until brown. Season. Transfer to a roasting pan and cook in the oven for 7–10 minutes. Leave to rest before serving on heated plates.

Per portion Energy 290Kcal/1214kJ; Protein 36.6g; Carbohydrate 6.8g, of which sugars 6.8g; Fat 6.8g, of which saturates 2.4g; Cholesterol 106mg; Calcium 19mg; Fibre 1.2g; Sodium 120mg

Salads and vegetable dishes

The wide range of vegetables enjoyed in Ireland today is a modern trend – most gardeners just grew simple vegetables like potatoes and cabbage until relatively recently. Now, however, Irish farmers, gardeners and cooks are making up for lost time and making the most of a surge of interest in vegetables, both traditional and more exotic.

Globe artichoke salad

Globe artichokes are grown widely in Irish gardens, especially in the warm climate of West Cork, where they are valued as highly for their architectural qualities in the garden as for the table. This salad makes a versatile first course, and is equally good served hot or cold.

Serves 4

- 4 artichokes
- juice of 1 lemon
- 900ml/1½ pints/3¾ cups home-made vegetable stock and water mixed
- 2 garlic cloves, chopped
- 1 small bunch parsley
- 6 whole peppercorns
- 15ml/1 tbsp olive oil, plus extra for drizzling

1 To prepare the artichokes: trim the stalks of the artichokes close to the base, cut the very tips off the leaves and then divide them into quarters. Remove the inedible hairy choke (the central part), carefully scraping the hairs away from the heart at the base of the artichoke.

2 Squeeze a little of the lemon juice over the cut surfaces of the artichokes to prevent discoloration.

3 Put the artichokes into a pan and cover with the stock and water, garlic, parsley, peppercorns and olive oil. Cover with a lid and cook gently for 1 hour, or until the artichokes are tender. They are ready when the leaves will come away easily when pulled.

4 Remove the artichokes with a slotted spoon and keep them warm if serving hot. Boil the cooking liquor hard without the lid, to reduce by half, and then strain.

5 To serve, arrange the artichokes in small serving dishes and pour over the reduced juices. Drizzle over a little extra olive oil and lemon juice. Provide finger bowls and a large bowl for the leaves. To eat, pull a leaf away from the artichoke and scrape the fleshy part at the base with your teeth. Discard the remainder of the leaves and then eat the heart at the base.

Variation The fleshy bases of the leaves and the artichoke heart or "fond" can be nibbled warm or cold with a dip such as hollandaise sauce or a vinaigrette. Serve with finger bowls and a large dish for the debris.

Per portion Energy 59Kcal/245kJ; Protein 0.7g; Carbohydrate 7.8g, of which sugars 7.3g; Fat 3.1g, of which saturates 0.5g; Cholesterol 0mg; Calcium 25mg; Fibre 2.4g; Sodium 61mg

Beetroot with lemon dressing

Beetroot is often grown in the large kitchen gardens attached to Irish country houses, where it also features on menus in summer. It is widely enjoyed and often used fresh rather than in the pickled form more familiar in other northern European countries.

Serves 4

450g/1lb evenly-sized raw beetroot (beets)

grated rind and juice of ½ lemon

about 150ml/¼ pint/⅔ cup extra virgin olive oil (or a mixture of olive and sunflower oil, blended to taste)

sea salt and ground black pepper

chopped fresh chives, to garnish (optional)

Cook's tip To avoid the beetroots "bleeding" during cooking, twist off the tops rather than cutting them with a knife.

1 Twist off the tops from the beetroot (see Cook's tip), and cook in a large pan of salted boiling water for about 30 minutes, or until the beetroot is tender. Pinch the skin between two fingers: when cooked, the skin will come away easily. Drain the beetroot and allow it to cool.

2 Peel when cool and slice into wedges into a bowl. Add the lemon rind and juice, and the oil; season to taste. Mix gently in the dressing and serve.

Variation Serve as a side dish or a first course, adding a sprinkling of chopped chives, if you like.

Per portion Energy 265Kcal/1097kJ; Protein 1.9g; Carbohydrate 8.6g, of which sugars 7.9g; Fat 25.1g, of which saturates 3.6g; Cholesterol 0mg; Calcium 23mg; Fibre 2.2g; Sodium 74mg

Warm potato salad with bacon dressing

This tasty summer salad becomes a favourite with all who try it. Use real new-season potatoes rather than all-year "baby" potatoes, if possible, and also dry-cured bacon. Using superior ingredients makes this a special dish and it's ideal for a barbecue or party.

Serves 4–6

- 900g/2lb small new potatoes
- sprig of mint
- 15–30ml/1–2 tbsp olive oil
- 1 onion, chopped
- 175g/6oz streaky (fatty) or back (lean) bacon, diced
- 2 garlic cloves, crushed
- 30ml/2 tbsp chopped parsley
- 1 small bunch chives, chopped
- 15ml/1 tbsp wine vinegar, or cider vinegar
- 15ml/1 tbsp Irish wholegrain mustard
- salt and ground black pepper

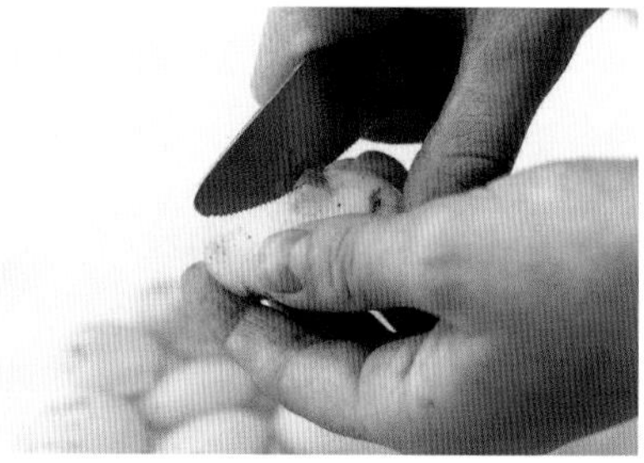

1 Scrape or rub off the skins from the new potatoes, and cook in salted water with the mint for about 10 minutes, or until just tender. Drain and allow to cool a little, then turn into a salad bowl.

2 Heat the oil in a frying pan, then add the onion and cook gently until just softening. Add the diced bacon to the pan and cook for 3–5 minutes, until beginning to crisp up.

3 Add the garlic and cook for another minute or so, and then add the chopped herbs, the vinegar, mustard and seasoning to taste, remembering that the bacon may be salty.

4 Pour the dressing over the potatoes. Toss gently to mix, and serve warm.

Variation Finely chopped spring onions (scallions) can replace the chopped chives and/or chopped parsley, if you like.

Per portion Energy 264Kcal/1112kJ; Protein 13.3g; Carbohydrate 39.9g, of which sugars 5.6g; Fat 6.8g, of which saturates 1.7g; Cholesterol 14mg; Calcium 76mg; Fibre 4g; Sodium 625mg

Griddle potatoes

This attractive dish has traditionally been cooked with leftover cooked potatoes that have been boiled in their skins. It makes a tasty accompaniment to grilled meat or fish or would be served as a light meal with glasses of milk or buttermilk.

Serves 4–6

2 onions, peeled and chopped

450–675g/1lb–1½lb whole cooked potatoes, boiled in their skins

a mixture of butter and oil, for shallow frying

salt and ground black pepper

1 Put the onions in a large pan and scald them briefly in boiling water. Refresh under cold water and drain well. Peel and slice the potatoes.

2 Put a mixture of butter and oil into a large, heavy frying pan and heat well.

3 When the fat is hot, fry the onion until tender. Add the potato slices and brown them together, turning the potato slices to brown as evenly as possible on both sides. Transfer to a warmed serving dish and season with salt and pepper. Serve very hot.

Per portion Energy 163Kcal/681kJ; Protein 3.4g; Carbohydrate 26.4g, of which sugars 5g; Fat 5.5g, of which saturates 3.3g; Cholesterol 13mg; Calcium 26mg; Fibre 2.6g; Sodium 49mg

Champ

This traditional dish of mashed potatoes flavoured with onion or herbs is especially associated with Northern Ireland. Flavourings for champ include a wide range of greens – freshly chopped chives or parsley, onions or scallions and even green peas. It is delicious served in the traditional way or as a side dish or base for grilled meat or sausages.

Serves 2–3 as a main dish

- 675g/1½lb potatoes
- 1 bunch spring onions (scallions), chopped
- about 300ml/½ pint/1¼ cups milk
- salt and ground black pepper
- butter, to serve

1 Peel and boil the potatoes in salted water until tender. Drain and return to the pan.

2 Boil the spring onions for 5 minutes in the milk. (Alternatively, bring the milk to boiling point on its own, if you prefer the spring onions raw.)

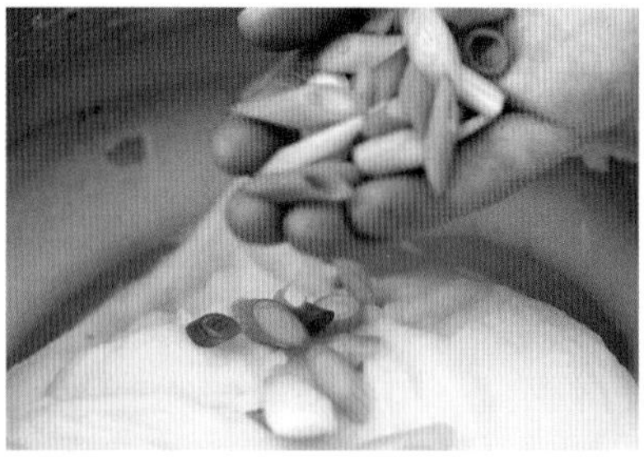

3 Cover the potatoes with a clean cloth and dry them at the side of the stove for a few minutes before mashing well. Beat in the boiling milk and spring onions. Working over the heat so that the champ is kept very hot, beat until the consistency is like well-creamed potatoes. Add more milk if necessary.

4 Season well with pepper and salt. To serve, divide the champ between heated bowls and make a well in the centre of each. Add a knob (pat) of butter. Dip the champ into the melting butter in the middle as you eat.

Per portion Energy 334Kcal/1415kJ; Protein 13.2g; Carbohydrate 66.6g, of which sugars 10.5g; Fat 3.5g, of which saturates 1.7g; Cholesterol 9mg; Calcium 217mg; Fibre 5.2g; Sodium 92mg

Colcannon

This traditional Irish dish is especially associated with Hallowe'en, when it is likely to be made with curly kale and would have a ring hidden in it – predicting marriage during the coming year for the person who found it. However, it is also served throughout the winter, and green cabbage is more often used.

Serves 3–4 as a main dish, 6–8 as an accompaniment

- 450g/1lb potatoes, peeled and boiled
- 450g/1lb curly kale or cabbage, cooked
- milk, if necessary
- 50g/2oz/2 tbsp butter, plus extra for serving
- 1 large onion, finely chopped
- salt and ground black pepper

1 Mash the potatoes. Chop the kale or cabbage, add it to the potatoes and mix. Stir in a little milk if the mash is too stiff.

2 Melt a little butter in a frying pan over a medium heat and add the onion. Cook until softened. Remove and mix well with the potato and kale or cabbage.

3 Add the remainder of the butter to the hot pan. When very hot, turn the potato mixture on to the pan and spread it out. Fry until brown, then cut it roughly into pieces and continue frying until they are crisp and brown.

4 Serve in bowls or as a side dish, with plenty of butter.

Right *A rustic temple in a walled garden, Glin Castle, County Limerick.*

Per portion Energy 306Kcal/1281kJ; Protein 5.4g; Carbohydrate 40.6g, of which sugars 13.6g; Fat 14.6g, of which saturates 8.8g; Cholesterol 36mg; Calcium 104mg; Fibre 5.9g; Sodium 127mg

Crispy cabbage

Second only to the potato, cabbage is the most widely grown and commonly eaten vegetable in Ireland. This quick side dish makes a crunchy base for slices of boiled ham or bacon. Savoy cabbage is especially pretty cooked this way, as it keeps its colour beautifully.

Serves 4–6

1 medium green or small white cabbage

30–45ml/2–3 tbsp oil

salt and ground black pepper

Variation For cabbage with a bacon dressing, fry 225g/8oz diced streaky (fatty) bacon in a pan. Set aside while cooking the cabbage. Remove the cabbage from the pan and keep warm with the bacon. Boil 15ml/1 tbsp wine or cider vinegar with the juices remaining in the pan.

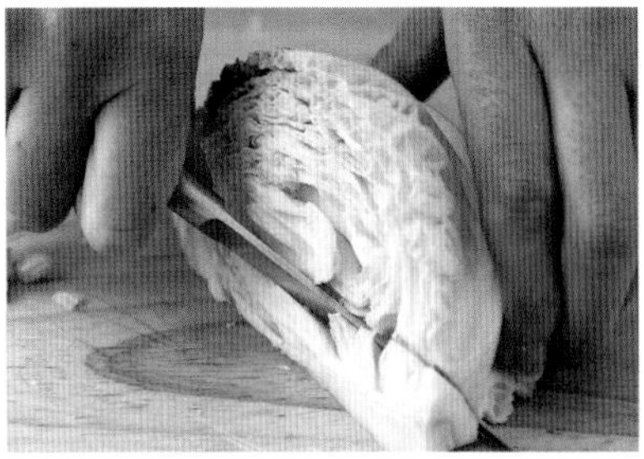

1 Remove any coarse outside leaves from the cabbage and also the central rib from the larger remaining leaves. Shred the leaves finely. Wash well under cold running water and shake well and blot on kitchen paper to dry.

2 Heat a wok or wide-based flameproof casserole over a fairly high heat. Heat the oil and add the cabbage. Stir-fry for 2–3 minutes, or until it is just cooked but still crunchy. Season and serve immediately.

Per portion Energy 54Kcal/224kJ; Protein 1.9g; Carbohydrate 4.6g, of which sugars 4.5g; Fat 3.2g, of which saturates 0.5g; Cholesterol 0mg; Calcium 59mg; Fibre 2.7g; Sodium 6mg

Braised Swiss chard

Swiss chard (also known as spinach beet) is less well known than spinach. It makes two tasty meals: on the first day, cook the leaves only; the next day cook the stalks in the same way as asparagus and serve with cream or a white sauce.

Serves 4

900g/2lb Swiss chard or spinach

15g/½oz/1 tbsp butter

a little freshly grated nutmeg

sea salt and ground black pepper

1 Remove the stalks from the Swiss chard or spinach (and reserve the chard stalks, if you like – see Cook's tip). Wash the leaves well and lift straight into a lightly greased heavy pan; the water clinging to the leaves will be all that is needed for cooking.

2 Cover with a tight-fitting lid and cook over medium heat for about 3–5 minutes, or until just tender, shaking the pan occasionally.

3 Drain well, and then add the butter and nutmeg, and season to taste. When the butter has melted, toss it into the Swiss chard and serve immediately.

Cook's tip To cook the stalks of Swiss chard, trim the bases, wash them well and tie in bundles like asparagus. Add to a pan of boiling water, with a squeeze of lemon juice added, and cook for about 20 minutes, or until tender but still slightly crisp. Drain and serve the chard stalks with a white sauce or simply pour over 30ml/2 tbsp fresh single (light) cream, heat through gently, season and serve.

Right *Swiss chard can have very brightly coloured leaves and stems.*

Per portion Energy 84Kcal/347kJ; Protein 6.3g; Carbohydrate 3.6g, of which sugars 3.4g; Fat 4.9g, of which saturates 2.2g; Cholesterol 8mg; Calcium 383mg; Fibre 4.7g; Sodium 338mg

Dry-panned mushrooms

Dry-panning is a traditional way of cooking mushrooms – the juices run out when the mushrooms are heated, and the resulting flavour is intense. These field mushrooms can be served as a snack or a light meal – on well-buttered hot toast or on potato cakes. They are delicious as part of a traditional Irish breakfast or to accompany steaks or any grilled meat.

Serves 4

8–12 flat field (portobello) mushrooms (about 5–7.5cm/2–3in diameter)

25–50g/1–2oz/2–4 tbsp butter

salt

◀ **1** Heat a frying pan without oil or butter, until very hot. Peel the mushrooms, if necessary, and remove the stalks.

2 Place them in the hot frying pan, with the gills on top. Add a small piece of butter, the size of a hazelnut, to each one with a pinch of salt.

3 Cook over a medium heat until the butter begins to boil and the mushrooms are juicy and tender. Divide among four serving plates and serve immediately on hot buttered toast.

Cook's tip Wild field mushrooms are at their best in late summer and early autumn, but cultivated "field" or "breakfast" mushrooms are also widely available in Irish stores all year round.

***Above** A traditional Irish brightly painted shop façade.*

Per portion Energy 76Kcal/315kJ; Protein 4.1g; Carbohydrate 1g, of which sugars 0.5g; Fat 6.3g, of which saturates 3.5g; Cholesterol 13mg; Calcium 15mg; Fibre 2.5g; Sodium 49mg

Carrot and parsnip purée

The most widely used of Irish root vegetables, carrots mix well with all the others. They are tasty roasted in chunks, either alone or as a mixed side dish with swede and parsnip, or with a pot-roast. Carrot and parsnips work especially well together and are often found in a soup, or in this popular side dish.

Serves 6–8

350g/12oz carrots

450g/1lb parsnips

pinch of freshly grated nutmeg or ground mace

15g/½oz/1 tbsp butter

about 15ml/1 tbsp single (light) cream, or top of the milk (optional)

1 small bunch parsley leaves, chopped (optional), plus extra to garnish

salt and ground black pepper

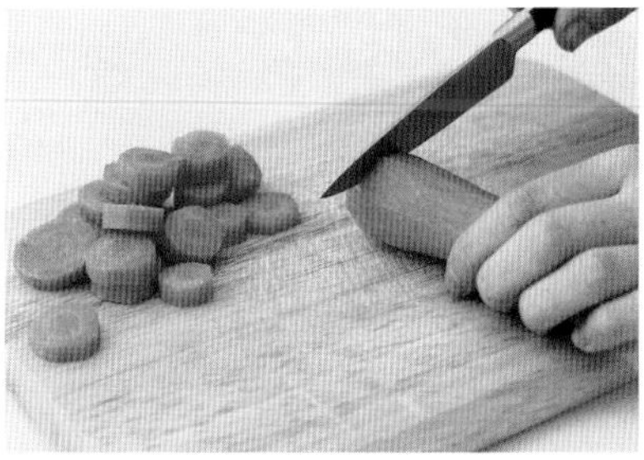

1 Peel the carrots and slice fairly thinly. Peel the parsnips and cut into bitesize chunks (they are softer and will cook more quickly than the carrots). Boil the two vegetables, separately, in salted water, until tender.

2 Drain them well and put them through a mouli-légumes (food mill) with the grated nutmeg or mace, a good seasoning of salt and ground black pepper and the butter. Purée together and taste for seasoning.

▶ **3** If you like, blend in some cream or top of the milk to taste, and add chopped parsley for extra flavour.

4 Transfer the carrot and parsnip purée to a warmed serving bowl, sprinkle with freshly chopped parsley to garnish and serve hot.

Cook's tip Any leftover purée can be thinned to taste with good quality chicken stock and heated to make a quick home-made soup.

Per portion Energy 92Kcal/385kJ; Protein 1.8g; Carbohydrate 14.1g, of which sugars 8.7g; Fat 3.5g, of which saturates 1.8g; Cholesterol 7mg; Calcium 48mg; Fibre 4.9g; Sodium 38mg

Leeks in cream sauce

This versatile vegetable makes a great winter standby and leeks find their way into many dishes, including casseroles and soups. Simple buttered leeks are underrated as a side dish, and this recipe makes a tasty accompaniment for plain food, such as chops or chicken, or it can be served as a light lunch or supper on its own.

Serves 4–6

4 large or 8 medium leeks

300ml/½ pint/1¼ cups milk

8 streaky (fatty) rashers (strips) of bacon, trimmed and sliced (optional)

1 egg, lightly beaten

150ml/¼ pint/⅔ cup single (light) cream

15ml/1 tbsp mild Irish mustard

75g/3oz/¾ cup grated cheese (optional)

salt and ground black pepper

1 Slice the leeks into fairly large chunks. Put them into a pan with the milk. Season and bring to the boil. Reduce the heat and simmer for 15–20 minutes, or until tender. Drain well and turn the leeks into a buttered shallow baking dish, reserving the cooking liquor.

2 Meanwhile, if using the bacon, put it into a frying pan and cook gently to allow the fat to run, then turn up the heat a little and cook for a few minutes until it crisps up. Remove from the pan with a slotted spoon and sprinkle the bacon over the leeks.

3 Rinse the pan used for the leeks. Blend the beaten egg, single cream and Irish mustard together and mix it with the reserved cooking liquor. Return to the pan and heat gently without boiling, allowing the sauce to thicken a little. Taste and adjust the seasoning with salt and freshly ground black pepper. Pour the sauce over the leeks and bacon.

4 Sprinkle with grated cheese, if using, and brown for a few minutes under a hot grill (broiler). (Alternatively, the leeks may served immediately without browning.) Serve with plain grilled (broiled) meat or poultry, if you like.

Variation The bacon may be grilled and served separately, if you prefer.

Per portion Energy 238Kcal/993kJ; Protein 18.6g; Carbohydrate 9g, of which sugars 7.9g; Fat 14.4g, of which saturates 7.3g; Cholesterol 90mg; Calcium 172mg; Fibre 3.5g; Sodium 830mg

Baked courgettes with farmhouse cheese

This easy dish makes a great accompaniment to a wide range of main courses, or it can be served with some fresh crusty bread as a light lunch or supper dish for one or two. A piquant hard cheese, such as Desmond or Gabriel, made in West Cork, will give the courgettes character, or you could use a mature farmhouse Cheddar.

Serves 4

4 courgettes (zucchini)

30ml/2 tbsp grated hard farmhouse cheese, such as Gabriel or Desmond

about 25g/1oz/2 tbsp butter

salt and ground black pepper

1 Preheat the oven to 180°C/350°F/ Gas 4. Slice the courgettes in half, lengthways. Butter a shallow baking dish and arrange the courgettes, cut side up, inside the dish.

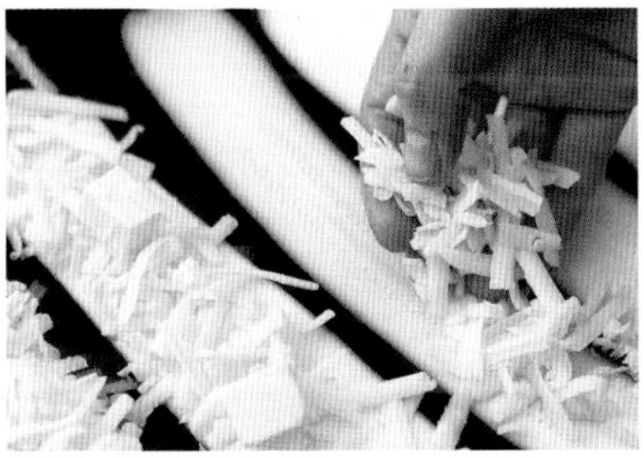

2 Sprinkle the cheese over the courgettes, and sprinkle over a few knobs (pats) of butter.

3 Bake in the preheated oven for about 20 minutes, or until the courgettes are tender and the cheese is bubbling and golden brown. Serve immediately.

Above *A rural cottage on the Iveragh peninsula, County Kerry.*

Per portion Energy 96Kcal/395kJ; Protein 3.8g; Carbohydrate 1.9g, of which sugars 1.8g; Fat 8g, of which saturates 5g; Cholesterol 21mg; Calcium 82mg; Fibre 0.9g; Sodium 93mg

Baked onions

One of Ireland's oldest and most widely used flavouring vegetables, the onion, also deserves to be used more as a vegetable in its own right. Onions become sweet and mildly flavoured when boiled or baked, and can be cooked very conveniently in the oven when baking potatoes or parsnips.

Serves 4

4 large even-sized onions

Cook's tip These onions are baked in their skins, but you could peel them, if preferred, before baking. The peeled onions are best baked in a covered casserole dish instead of a roasting pan.

◀ **1** Preheat the oven to 180°C/350°F/ Gas 4. Put a little cold water into a medium-size roasting pan, and arrange the unpeeled onions in it.

2 Bake in the preheated oven for about 1 hour, or until the onions feel soft when squeezed at the sides. Peel the skins and serve immediately.

Per portion Energy 90Kcal/375kJ; Protein 3g; Carbohydrate 19.8g, of which sugars 14g; Fat 0.5g, of which saturates 0g; Cholesterol 0mg; Calcium 63mg; Fibre 3.5g; Sodium 8mg

Roasted Jerusalem artichokes

Although not widely available in stores, Jerusalem artichokes grow easily in Ireland and conceal a deliciously sweet white flesh inside their knobbly brown exterior. While they are best known for soups, their natural sweetness enables them to glaze easily and they make a delicious side vegetable with many foods, but have a special affinity with game.

Serves 6

- 675g/1½lb Jerusalem artichokes
- 15ml/1 tbsp lemon juice or vinegar
- salt
- 50g/2oz/¼ cup unsalted (sweet) butter
- seasoned flour, for dusting

1 Peel the artichokes, dropping them straight into a bowl of water acidulated with lemon juice or vinegar to prevent browning. Cut up the artichokes so that the pieces are matched for size, otherwise they will cook unevenly.

2 Preheat the oven to 180°C/350°F/Gas 4. Bring a pan of salted water to the boil, drain the artichokes from the acidulated water and boil them for 5 minutes, or until just tender. Watch them carefully, as they break up easily.

◀ **3** Melt the butter in a roasting pan, coat the artichokes in the seasoned flour and roll them around in the butter in the pan.

4 Cook the butter and flour coated artichokes in the preheated oven for 20–30 minutes, or until golden brown. Serve immediately.

Variation Puréeing is a useful fall-back if the artichokes break up during cooking: simply blend or mash the drained boiled artichokes with salt and freshly ground black pepper to taste and a little single (light) cream, if you like. Puréed artichokes are especially good served with game, which tends to be dry.

Per portion Energy 101Kcal/419kJ; Protein 0.7g; Carbohydrate 8.9g, of which sugars 8.4g; Fat 7.2g, of which saturates 4.5g; Cholesterol 18mg; Calcium 30mg; Fibre 2.7g; Sodium 242mg

Desserts

Memorable Irish desserts and puddings tend to be in the comfort zone, homely dishes based on simple country ingredients like home-grown apples and pears, cottage garden summer fruits such as rhubarb, blackcurrants and strawberries – and wild berries, including blackberries and bilberries. Milk, buttermilk and cream play vital roles too in all sorts of puddings.

Christmas pudding

A simple boiled pudding was traditional in some areas of Ireland long before the present custom of serving a rich pudding at Christmas evolved. Serve with a traditional hot white sauce, flavoured with whiskey, brandy or rum.

Makes 2 puddings, each serving 6–8

- 275g/10oz/5 cups fresh breadcrumbs
- 225g/8oz/1 cup light muscovado (brown) sugar
- 225g/8oz/1 cup currants
- 275g/10oz/2 cups raisins
- 225g/8oz/1⅓ cups sultanas (golden raisins)
- 50g/2oz/⅓ cup chopped (candied) peel
- 115g/4oz/½ cup glacé (candied) cherries
- 225g/8oz suet (US chilled, grated shortening), or vegetarian equivalent
- 2.5ml/½ tsp salt
- 10–20ml/2–4 tsp mixed (apple pie) spice
- 1 carrot, peeled and coarsely grated
- 1 apple, peeled, cored and finely chopped
- grated rind and juice of 1 small orange
- 2 large (US extra large) eggs, lightly whisked
- 450ml/¾ pint/scant 2 cups stout

1 Mix the breadcrumbs, sugar, dried fruit and peel in a bowl. Shred and add the suet, salt, mixed spice, carrot, apple and orange rind. Mix well. Stir in the orange juice, eggs and stout. Leave overnight, stirring occasionally, if convenient.

2 Well grease and base line two 1.2 litre/2 pint/5 cup pudding bowls. Stir the mixture and turn into the bowls. Cover with buttered circles of baking parchment, then tie pudding cloths over the puddings, or tightly cover them with several layers of baking parchment and foil, tied well under the rim.

3 Steam for about 6–7 hours. Ensure the puddings do not go off the boil, and top up with more water as needed.

4 When cool, re-cover the puddings with paper or foil and store in a cool, dry place for at least a month. When required, steam for another 2–3 hours. Serve hot with a traditional white sauce.

Per portion Energy 7171Kcal/30,432kJ; Protein 38.8g; Carbohydrate 1596.3g, of which sugars 1479.8g; Fat 112.9g, of which saturates 58g; Cholesterol 321mg; Calcium 1071mg; Fibre 13.8g; Sodium 1965mg

Bread and butter pudding with whiskey sauce

Comfort food suits the Irish climate well, and versions of this dish feature as a speciality at many Irish restaurants. The whiskey sauce is heavenly, but the pudding can also be served with chilled cream or vanilla ice cream – the contrast between the hot and cold is delicious.

Serves 6

- 8 slices of white bread, buttered
- 115–150g/4–5oz/⅔–¾ cup sultanas (golden raisins), or mixed dried fruit
- 2.5ml/½ tsp grated nutmeg
- 150g/5oz/¾ cup caster (superfine) sugar
- 2 large (US extra large) eggs
- 300ml/½ pint/1¼ cups single (light) cream
- 450ml/¾ pint/scant 2 cups milk
- 5ml/1 tsp of vanilla essence (extract)
- light muscovado (brown) sugar, for sprinkling (optional)

For the whiskey sauce

- 150g/5oz/10 tbsp butter
- 115g/4oz/generous ½ cup caster (superfine) sugar
- 1 egg
- 45ml/3 tbsp Irish whiskey

1 Preheat the oven to 180°C/350°F/Gas 4. Remove the crusts from the bread and put four slices, buttered side down, in the base of an ovenproof dish. Sprinkle with the fruit, some of the nutmeg and 15ml/1 tbsp sugar.

2 Place the remaining four slices of bread on top, buttered side down, and sprinkle again with nutmeg and 15ml/1 tbsp sugar.

3 Beat the eggs lightly, add the cream, milk, vanilla essence and the remaining sugar, and mix well to make a custard. Pour this mixture over the bread, and sprinkle light muscovado sugar over the top, if you like to have a crispy crust. Bake in the preheated oven for 1 hour, or until all the liquid has been absorbed and the pudding is risen and brown.

4 Meanwhile, make the whiskey sauce: melt the butter in a heavy pan, add the caster sugar and dissolve over gentle heat. Remove from the heat and add the egg, whisking vigorously, and then add the whiskey. Serve the pudding on hot serving plates, with the whiskey sauce poured over the top.

Right *The entrance of The Old Jameson Whiskey Distillery in the capital city of Ireland, Dublin.*

Per portion Energy 757Kcal/3168kJ; Protein 11.7g; Carbohydrate 82g, of which sugars 65.2g; Fat 40.8g, of which saturates 24.3g; Cholesterol 207mg; Calcium 232mg; Fibre 0.9g; Sodium 472mg

Apple pie

Ireland's most popular dessert is on every informal menu in the country and, when well made, there is nothing to beat it. Bake in a traditional metal pie plate so that the pastry base will be perfectly cooked. Serve with chilled whipped cream, or vanilla ice cream.

Serves 6

- 225g/8oz/2 cups plain (all-purpose) flour
- 130g/4½oz/generous ½ cup butter, or mixed butter and white vegetable fat (shortening)
- 25g/1oz/2 tbsp caster (superfine) sugar
- 45ml/3 tbsp very cold milk or water

For the filling

- 675g/1½lb cooking apples
- 75g/3oz/½ cup sultanas (golden raisins) (optional)
- a little grated lemon rind (optional)
- 75g/3oz/6 tbsp caster (superfine) sugar
- a knob (pat) of butter or 15ml/1 tbsp of water
- a little milk, to glaze
- icing (confectioners') sugar and whipped cream, to serve

1 Sift the flour into a large mixing bowl, add the butter and cut it into small pieces. Rub the butter into the flour with the fingertips, or using a pastry (cookie) cutter, lifting the mixture as much as possible to aerate.

2 Mix the caster sugar with the chilled milk or water, add to the bowl and mix with a knife or fork until the mixture clings together. Turn on to a floured worktop and knead lightly once or twice until smooth.

3 Wrap in baking parchment or foil and leave in the refrigerator to relax for 20 minutes before using. Meanwhile, preheat the oven to 200°C/400°F/Gas 6.

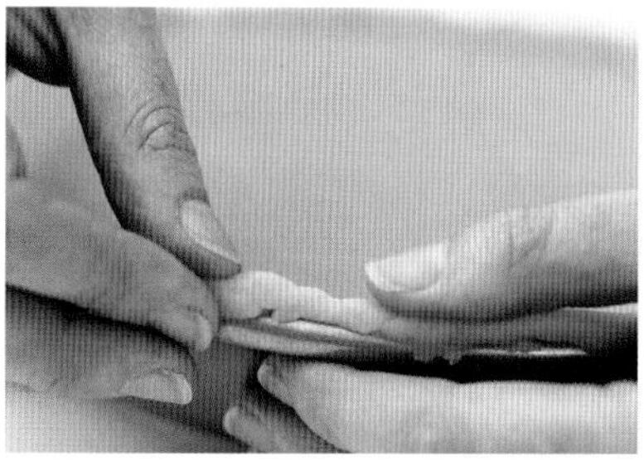

4 Roll out one-third of the pastry and use to line a 23cm/9in pie plate. Use any trimmings to make a second layer of pastry around the top edge of the pie plate.

5 To make the filling, peel, core and slice the apples and arrange half of them on the pastry base, then sprinkle over the sultanas and lemon rind, if using. Top with the caster sugar, the remaining apples and butter or water.

6 Roll out the remainder of the pastry to make a circle about 2.5cm/1in larger than the pie plate. Dampen the pastry edging on the rim and lay the top over the apples, draping it gently over any lumps to avoid straining the pastry. Press the rim well to seal. Knock up the edge with a knife, and pinch the edges neatly with the fingers to make a fluted edge.

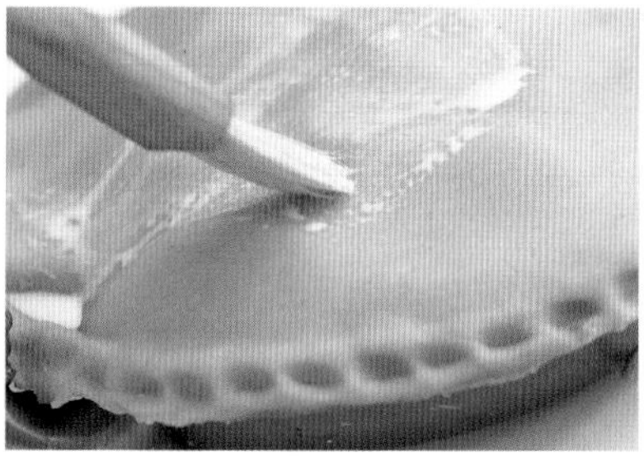

7 Brush the pastry lightly with milk and bake the pie in the preheated oven for about 30 minutes, or until the pastry is nicely browned and crisp, and the fruit is cooked.

8 To serve, dust the pastry with icing sugar and serve hot, warm or cold, but not straight from the refrigerator.

Variation The same filling may be used to make a deep pie in a 25cm/10in deep oval pie dish, although only about three-quarters of the quantity of pastry will be needed for the topping.

Per portion Energy 393Kcal/1650kJ; Protein 4.1g; Carbohydrate 56.3g, of which sugars 27.7g; Fat 18.4g, of which saturates 11.4g; Cholesterol 46mg; Calcium 68mg; Fibre 2.5g; Sodium 136mg

Apple and blackberry crumble

Autumn in Ireland heralds the harvest of apples and succulent soft fruits. Apple trees grow all over the country and brambles provide the delicious blackberries. The pinhead oatmeal in the topping makes this traditional hot dessert especially crunchy and flavoursome. Serve hot with chilled crème fraîche or ice cream.

Serves 6–8

900g/2lb cooking apples

450g/1lb/4 cups blackberries

squeeze of lemon juice (optional)

175g/6oz/scant 1 cup granulated sugar

For the topping

115g/4oz/½ cup butter

115g/4oz/1 cup wholemeal (whole-wheat) flour

50g/2oz/½ cup fine or medium pinhead oatmeal

50g/2oz/¼ cup soft light brown sugar

a little grated lemon rind (optional)

1 Preheat the oven to 200°C/400°F/Gas 6. To make the crumble topping, rub the butter into the flour, and then add the oatmeal and brown sugar and continue to rub in until the mixture begins to stick together, forming large crumbs. Mix in the grated lemon rind, if using.

2 Peel, core and slice the cooking apples into wedges.

3 Put the apples, blackberries, lemon juice (if using), 30ml/2 tbsp water and the sugar into a shallow ovenproof dish, about 2 litres/3½ pints/9 cups capacity.

4 Cover the fruit with the topping. Sprinkle with a little cold water. Bake in the oven for 15 minutes, then reduce the heat to 190°C/375°F/Gas 5 and cook for another 15–20 minutes until crunchy and brown on top. Serve hot.

Per portion Energy 470Kcal/1974kJ; Protein 5.1g; Carbohydrate 78.2g, of which sugars 60.3g; Fat 17.2g, of which saturates 10g; Cholesterol 41mg; Calcium 71mg; Fibre 7g; Sodium 128mg

Autumn pudding

Although summer pudding is made more often, Autumn pudding is equally easy to make, using seasonal fruit that is abundant in Ireland during September and October, instead of the soft fruits of summer. This juicy dessert is very simple to make, but it looks superb. Serve with lightly whipped chilled cream, or crème fraîche.

Serves 6–8

1 loaf white bread, 2 or 3 days old

675g/1½lb/6 cups mixed soft fruit, such as blackberries, autumn raspberries, late strawberries, and peeled and chopped eating apples

115g/4oz/generous ½ cup caster (superfine) sugar or 75ml/5 tbsp honey

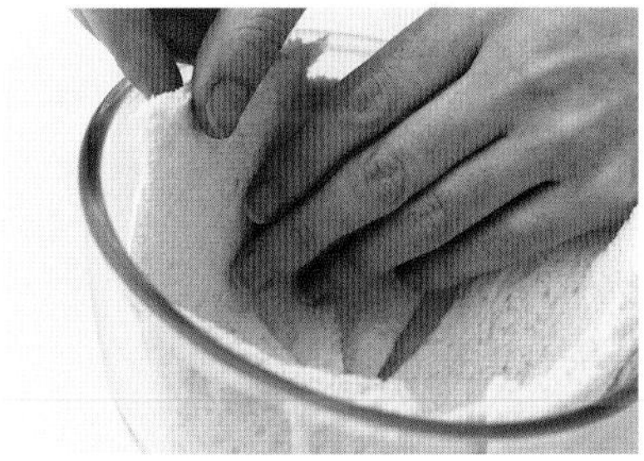

1 Remove the crusts from the loaf and slice the bread thinly. Use several slices to line the base and sides of a 900ml–1.2 litres/1½–2 pints/3¾–5 cup pudding bowl or soufflé dish, cutting them so that the pieces fit closely together.

2 Put all the fruit into a wide, heavy pan, sprinkle the sugar or honey over and bring very gently to the boil. Cook for 2–3 minutes, or until the sugar has dissolved and the juices run.

3 Remove the pan from the heat and set aside 30–45ml/2–3 tbsp of the juices. Spoon the fruit and the remaining juices into the prepared bread-lined dish and cover the top closely with the remaining slices of bread. Put a plate that fits neatly inside the top of the dish on top of the pudding and weigh it down with a heavy tin or jar. Leave in the refrigerator for at least 8 hours, or overnight.

4 Before serving the dish, remove the weight and plate, cover the bowl with a serving plate and turn upside down to unmould the pudding.

5 Use the reserved fruit juice to pour over any patches of the bread that have not been completely soaked and coloured by the fruit juices. Serve cold cut into wedges with lightly whipped chilled cream or crème fraîche.

Per portion Energy 261Kcal/1112kJ; Protein 7.7g; Carbohydrate 57.5g, of which sugars 27.1g; Fat 1.7g, of which saturates 0.4g; Cholesterol 0mg; Calcium 153mg; Fibre 4.2g; Sodium 398mg

Apple snow

This fluffy nursery dish is as simple as it is delicious – and best made with late-cropping Bramley's Seedling cooking apples, which grow abundantly in Ireland and "fall" when cooked, to make a fluffy purée. Serve with crisp cookies, or sponge fingers.

Serves 6

675g/1½lb cooking apples, preferably Bramley's Seedling

a little thinly peeled lemon rind

about 115g/4oz/generous ½ cup caster (superfine) sugar

3 egg whites

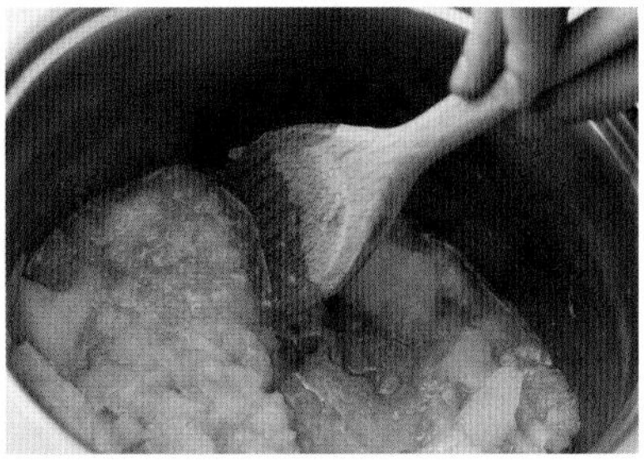

1 Peel, core and slice the apples. Turn into a pan with 45ml/3 tbsp water and the lemon rind. Cover and simmer gently for 15 minutes, or until the apples become fluffy. Remove from the heat, take out the lemon rind and sweeten to taste with caster sugar.

2 Beat the apples well with a wooden spoon to make a purée, or rub through a sieve (strainer) if a smoother texture is preferred. Leave to cool.

3 When the purée is cold, whisk the egg whites until stiff.

4 Fold the egg whites into the apple using a metal spoon. Whisk together until the mixture is thick and light.

5 Turn into a serving bowl, or divide between six individual dishes, and chill until required.

Per portion Energy 121Kcal/516kJ; Protein 1.8g; Carbohydrate 30.1g, of which sugars 30.1g; Fat 0.1g, of which saturates 0g; Cholesterol 0mg; Calcium 7mg; Fibre 1.8g; Sodium 34mg

Apple and barley flummery

The Celtic countries share this old dish, which is usually a cooked cold sweet based on oatmeal. This Irish variation is based on barley and also includes apples; sago or tapioca could replace the barley.

Serves 4–6

- 90ml/6 tbsp pearl barley
- 675g/1½lb cooking apples, such as Bramley's Seedling
- 50g/2oz/¼ cup caster (superfine) sugar
- juice of 1 lemon
- 45–60ml/3–4 tbsp double (heavy) cream

1 Put 1 litre/1¾ pints/4 cups of water into a pan. Add the barley and bring gently to the boil.

2 Peel, core and slice the apples. Add them to the pan and continue cooking gently until the barley is soft and apples are cooked.

3 Liquidize (blend) the mixture, or press through a sieve (strainer), and return to the rinsed pan.

4 Add the sugar and lemon juice and bring back to the boil.

5 Remove from the heat and allow to cool. Turn into individual glasses or a serving dish, and chill until required. Stir in the cream and serve cold.

Variations

- Other garden produce, such as blackcurrants, blackberries or rhubarb, could be used instead of apple.
- For an extra special flavour add 30ml/2 tbsp Irish whiskey to the flummery with the double cream.

Per portion Energy 245Kcal/1040kJ; Protein 2.5g; Carbohydrate 47.1g, of which sugars 28.3g; Fat 6.6g, of which saturates 3.8g; Cholesterol 15mg; Calcium 24mg; Fibre 2.7g; Sodium 7mg

Fraughan mousse

Wild or cottage-garden fruits, or a combination of both, have long been used to make simple desserts such as mousses, creams and fools. This bilberry dish is an attractive and impressive finish for a dinner party. Serve chilled with whipped cream and sponge fingers.

Serves 6–8

450g/1lb cooking apples

450g/1lb/4 cups fraughans (bilberries)

115g/4oz/generous ½ cup caster (superfine) sugar

juice of 1 lemon

1 sachet powdered gelatine

2 egg whites

60ml/4 tbsp double (heavy) cream, to serve

1 Peel, core and slice the cooking apples, then put them into a large pan with the fraughans (bilberries), 150ml/¼ pint/⅔ cup water and 75g/3oz/scant ½ cup of the sugar. Cook gently for 15 minutes, until tender. Remove from the heat.

2 Strain the lemon juice into a cup, sprinkle the gelatine over and leave it to soak. Add the cake of soaked gelatine to the fruit and stir until it has dissolved. Turn into a nylon sieve (strainer) over a large mixing bowl and press the fruit through it to make a purée; discard anything that is left in the sieve. Leave the purée to stand until it is cool and beginning to set.

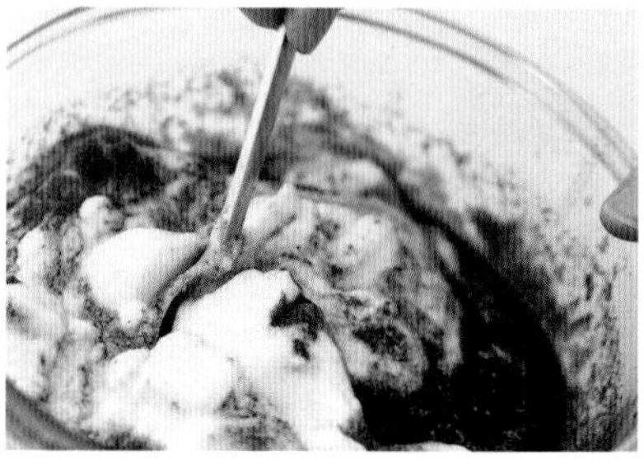

3 Whisk the egg whites stiffly, sprinkle in the remaining sugar and whisk again until glossy. Using a metal spoon, fold the whites gently into the fruit purée to make a smooth mousse. Turn into serving glasses and chill until set. Serve topped with double cream.

Variation Bilberries, also known as whortleberries and by their Irish name, *fraughan*, grow prolifically in bogs and moorland areas all over Ireland in late summer, and bilberry picking makes a great family day out. This modern recipe stretches a modest amount of wild fruit, and can be used to make a mousse with other soft summer fruits, notably the bilberry's larger cultivated cousin, the blueberry, and it works equally well with blackberries.

Per portion Energy 118Kcal/498kJ; Protein 1.9g; Carbohydrate 28.7g, of which sugars 28.7g; Fat 0.2g, of which saturates 0g; Cholesterol 0mg; Calcium 44mg; Fibre 3.2g; Sodium 24mg

Blackcurrant fool

The strong flavour and deep colour of this easily grown fruit makes it especially suitable for fools and ices, although this is an adaptable recipe which can be made using other soft fruits too. The fool can also be used to make an easy no-stir ice cream.

Serves 6

350g/12oz/3 cups blackcurrants

about 175g/6oz/scant 1 cup caster (superfine) sugar

5ml/1 tsp lemon juice

300ml/½ pint/1¼ cups double (heavy) cream

Variation To make Blackcurrant Ice Cream, turn the completed fool into a freezerproof container. Cover and freeze (preferably at the lowest setting). Transfer from the freezer to the refrigerator 10–15 minutes before serving to allow the ice cream to soften. Serve with whipped cream and cookies.

1 Put the blackcurrants into a small pan with 45ml/3 tbsp water, and cook over a low heat until soft. Remove from the heat, add the sugar according to taste, and stir until dissolved.

2 Leave to cool, then liquidize (blend) or strain to make a purée. Set aside and cool. Add the lemon juice and stir well.

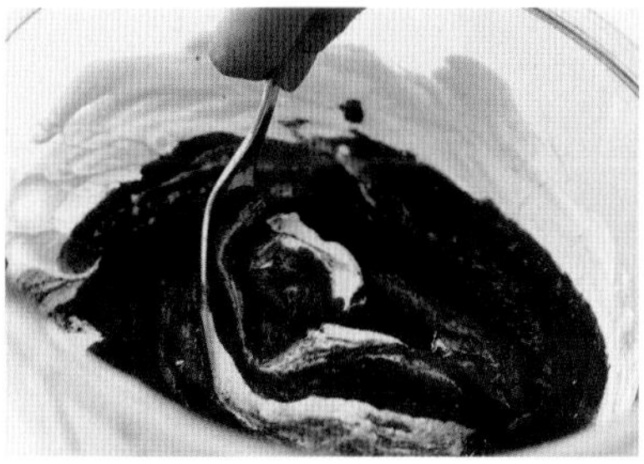

3 Whip the double cream until it is fairly stiff and, using a metal spoon, carefully fold it into the blackcurrant purée, losing as little volume as possible.

4 Turn the mixture into a serving dish or six individual serving glasses and leave to set. Chill in the refrigerator until ready to serve.

Per portion Energy 379Kcal/1581kJ; Protein 1.5g; Carbohydrate 35.2g, of which sugars 35.2g; Fat 26.9g, of which saturates 16.7g; Cholesterol 69mg; Calcium 75mg; Fibre 2.1g; Sodium 15mg

Meringue layer cake with raspberries

This delicious dessert is made with a basic meringue mixture. For the best results avoid very fresh eggs (two to three days old is best) and use them at room temperature.

Serves 8–10

4 egg whites

225g/8oz/generous 1 cup caster (superfine) sugar

For the filling

300ml/½ pint/1¼ cups whipping cream

caster (superfine) sugar, to taste

3–4 drops of vanilla essence (extract) or 2.5ml/½ tsp liqueur, such as Kirsch or Crème de Framboise

about 450g/1lb/2¾ cups raspberries

icing (confectioners') sugar, for dusting

1 Preheat the oven to 150°C/300°F/Gas 2. Line two baking sheets with non-stick baking parchment and draw two circles: one 23cm/9in in diameter and the other 20cm/8in. Fit a piping (icing) bag with a 1cm/½in star nozzle.

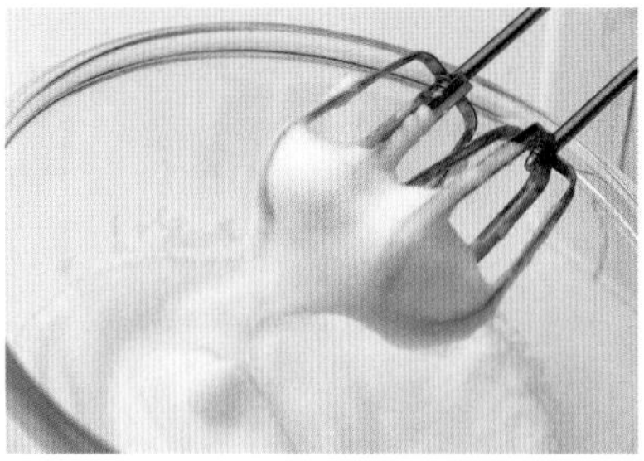

2 Whisk the egg whites until stiff peaks form. Keeping the machine running, add half of the sugar, 15ml/1 tbsp at a time; keep whisking until the mixture stands in stiff peaks.

3 Using a metal spoon, carefully fold in the remaining sugar to mix thoroughly without the loss of volume.

4 Use most of the mixture to spread or pipe inside the prepared circles, then put the remaining meringue into the piping bag and use to pipe nine miniature meringues on to the surrounding baking parchment.

5 Cook in the preheated oven for 50–60 minutes, until lightly coloured and quite dry (the small ones will take less time). Peel off the parchment, cool the meringues on wire racks and, when cold, store immediately in airtight tins.

6 Whip the cream until soft peaks form, sweeten lightly with caster sugar and flavour with a few drops of vanilla essence or liqueur.

7 Lay the larger meringue circle on a serving dish. Spread with three-quarters of the cream and three-quarters of the raspberries, reserving the best berries for the top. Add the smaller meringue circle, spread with the remaining cream, and arrange the small meringues around the edge. Decorate the top with the remaining fruit. Dust lightly with icing sugar.

Cook's tip Don't leave cooked meringues exposed to the air, as they will absorb moisture from the air and "weep".

Per portion Energy 298Kcal/1252kJ; Protein 3.2g; Carbohydrate 39.5g, of which sugars 39.5g; Fat 15.3g, of which saturates 9.5g; Cholesterol 39mg; Calcium 55mg; Fibre 1.4g; Sodium 44mg

Irish whiskey trifle

This luxuriously rich trifle is made the old-fashioned way, with real sponge cake, fresh fruit and rich egg custard, but with Irish whiskey rather than the usual sherry flavouring.

Serves 6–8

1 x 15–18cm/6–7in sponge cake

225g/8oz raspberry jam

150ml/¼ pint/⅔ cup whiskey

450g/1lb ripe fruit, such as pears and bananas

300ml/½ pint/1¼ cups whipping cream

blanched almonds, glacé cherries and angelica, to decorate (optional)

For the custard

450ml/¾ pint/scant 2 cups full cream (whole) milk

1 vanilla pod (bean) or a few drops of vanilla essence (extract)

3 eggs

25g/1oz/2 tbsp caster (superfine) sugar

1 To make the custard, put the milk into a pan with the vanilla pod, if using, and bring almost to the boil. Remove the pan from the heat. Whisk the eggs and sugar together lightly. Remove the pod. Gradually whisk the milk into the egg mixture.

Variation Good-quality tinned fruit, such as peaches or pears, can be used instead of fresh fruit.

2 Rinse out the pan with cold water, return the mixture to it and stir over low heat until it thickens enough to cover the back of a wooden spoon; do not allow the custard to boil. Alternatively, for a very slow method of cooking, use a double boiler, or a bowl over a pan of boiling water.

3 Turn the custard into a mixing bowl and add the vanilla essence, if using. Cover the custard and set aside until ready to assemble the trifle.

4 Halve the sponge cake horizontally, spread with the raspberry jam and make a sandwich. Using a sharp knife cut into slices and use them to line the bottom and lower sides of a large glass serving bowl.

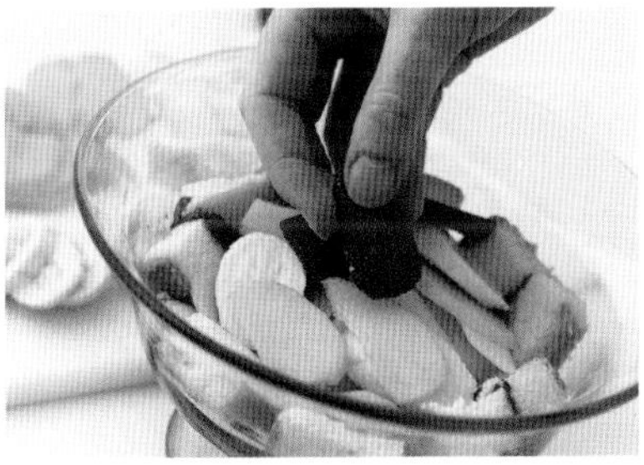

5 Sprinkle with the whiskey. Peel and slice the fruit, then spread it out over the sponge to make an even layer. Pour the custard on top, cover with clear film (plastic wrap) to prevent a skin forming, and leave to cool and set. Chill until required. Before serving, whip the cream and spread it over the set custard. Decorate with the almonds, glacé cherries and angelica, if you like.

Per portion Energy 710Kcal/2959kJ; Protein 12.1g; Carbohydrate 58g, of which sugars 42.6g; Fat 43.2g, of which saturates 14.4g; Cholesterol 171mg; Calcium 194mg; Fibre 2.3g; Sodium 336mg

Burnt cream

Now more elegantly known as Crème Brulée, this classic sweet appears on many an Irish restaurant menu – and the contrast between the crunchy topping and the smooth luxuriously creamy custard underneath it is irresistible.

Serves 6

4 egg yolks

15ml/1 tbsp caster (superfine) sugar plus 115–150g/4–6oz for the topping

600ml/1 pint/2½ cups double (heavy) cream

1 vanilla pod (bean), or a few drops of vanilla essence (extract)

Cook's tip A salamander – a long iron rod with a cast-iron disk at one end and a wooden handle at the other – can also be used to brown the top of the burnt cream.

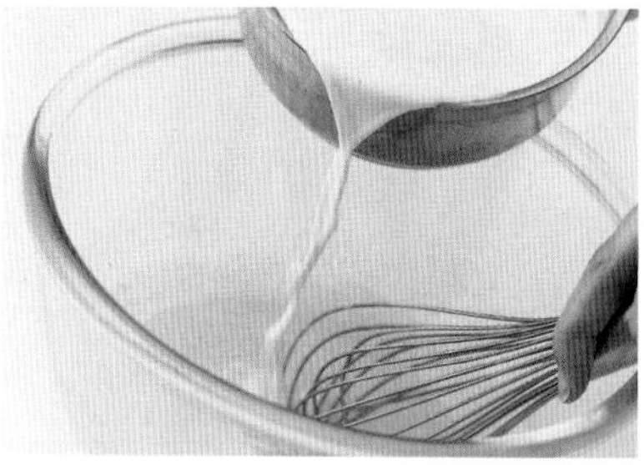

1 Preheat the oven to 140°C/275°F/ Gas 1. Mix the yolks well with 15ml/ 1 tbsp sugar. Put the cream and vanilla pod, if using, in a pan, bring up to scalding point, remove the pod and pour the hot cream on to the yolks, blending well. Add the vanilla essence, if using.

2 Return the mixture to a double boiler, or a bowl over a pan of hot water, and cook carefully, stirring or whisking constantly, until the mixture thickens; do not allow it to boil.

3 Strain the custard into a gratin dish, or divide it among six ramekins. Cook the custard in the oven for 15 minutes or just long enough to let a skin form on the top, but do not allow it to colour. This stage may be omitted if you wish, as the custard is already cooked. Cooking in the oven will set it further.

4 Allow to cool, then leave to chill for several hours, preferably overnight.

5 To finish: preheat the grill (broiler). Sprinkle the custard evenly with the remaining sugar so that it is completely covered, but not too thick. Grill (broil) as close as possible to the heat for 2–3 minutes, or until the sugar melts and caramelizes, then remove from the heat and leave in a cold place for up to 2–3 hours before serving.

Variation This rich dessert is traditionally served with fresh or poached fruit. Alternatively, add a few teaspoons of a soft fruit, such as bilberries (fraughan), strawberries or raspberries to each ramekin before adding the vanilla custard.

Per portion Energy 547Kcal/2251kJ; Protein 3.6g; Carbohydrate 4.3g, of which sugars 4.3g; Fat 57.4g, of which saturates 34.4g; Cholesterol 272mg; Calcium 66mg; Fibre 0g; Sodium 28mg

Baked caramel custard

The Irish have long enjoyed baked custards either served on their own with a sprinkling of grated nutmeg or to accompany simple poached fruits. Baked caramel custard is simply a dressed-up version of this homely dish. Serve it as it is, or with cream.

Serves 6

75g/3oz/scant ½ cup granulated sugar

600ml/1 pint/2½ cups milk

vanilla pod (bean) or a few drops of vanilla essence (extract)

6 eggs

75g/3oz/scant ½ cup caster (superfine) sugar

1 Preheat the oven to 160°C/325°F/Gas 3. Put the sugar into a heavy pan and stir over medium heat to make a golden caramel syrup. Remove from the heat and very carefully stir in 15ml/1 tbsp water. Return to the heat.

2 Pour the caramel into an ungreased, heated 900ml/1½ pints/3¾ cup baking dish, or divide among six ramekins. Using oven gloves or a cloth, tilt the dish to coat the base evenly with the hot caramel, then place in a shallow roasting pan.

3 To make the custard, scald the milk in a small pan with the vanilla pod, if using. Lightly beat the eggs and caster sugar in a bowl and, when it is nearly boiling, remove the vanilla pod and whisk in the hot milk. Add the vanilla essence, if using. Pour the custard into the prepared dish.

4 Fill the roasting pan to a depth of about 2.5cm/1in with cold water, cover the dishes with buttered baking parchment and bake in the centre of the oven until the custard has set, about 1–1½ hours, if baking one large dish, or about 30 minutes for individual ones. Leave to cool, and then chill.

5 To serve, loosen around the edge with a knife and tip the dish to ease the custard away from the sides.

6 Select a serving dish that is flat in the middle but with a deep enough rim to contain the caramel syrup. Invert the serving dish over the baking dish and turn upside down. If using ramekins, turn out on to small plates. Serve.

Cook's tip Baked caramel custard is popular throughout Europe and this dish is very similar to the French pudding *crème caramel*. In Italy it is known as *crema caramella*, and in Spain as *flan*.

Per portion 233Kcal/983kJ; Protein 11g; Carbohydrate 30.8g, of which sugars 30.8g; Fat 8.4g, of which saturates 2.9g; Cholesterol 234mg; Calcium 168mg; Fibre 0g; Sodium 129mg

Bailey's carrageen pudding

Carrageen, also known as Irish moss, is a purplish variety of seaweed which is found all along the west coast of Ireland. Carrageen pudding is an old-fashioned dessert that is still widely made. This version is made with Bailey's Irish Cream and would be a good choice for a dessert selection at a party.

Serves 8–10

- 15g/½oz carrageen
- 1.5 litres/2½ pints/6¼ cups milk
- 300ml/½ pint/1¼ cups Bailey's Irish Cream
- 2 eggs, separated
- about 60ml/4 tbsp caster (superfine) sugar

1 Soak the carrageen in tepid water for 10 minutes. Put the milk into a pan with the drained carrageen. Bring to the boil and simmer very gently for 20 minutes, stirring occasionally.

2 Strain the mixture and rub all the jelly through the sieve (strainer); discard anything remaining in it. Rinse out the pan and return the mixture to it, over a very low heat. Blend in the Bailey's.

3 Heat the mixture very gently to just below boiling point, and then remove from the heat.

4 Mix the egg yolks and the sugar together and blend in a little of the hot mixture, then stir, or whisk, the egg yolks and sugar into the hot mixture. When the sugar has dissolved, leave the mixture to cool a little, and then whisk the egg whites stiffly and fold in gently.

5 Turn into a serving bowl and leave in the refrigerator to set. Serve alone, or with a dessert selection.

Variation Replace the Bailey's with the same amount of milk for a plain dish, and use as an alternative to cream with desserts, such as poached fruit.

Cook's tip When dried, carrageen is a good thickening agent for puddings, ice cream and soups.

Per portion Energy 2078Kcal/8724kJ; Protein 66.3g; Carbohydrate 201.6g, of which sugars 201.6g; Fat 85.3g, of which saturates 19.8g; Cholesterol 545mg; Calcium 1.95g; Fibre 0g; Sodium 1.08g

Brown bread ice cream

The secret of a good brown bread ice cream is not to have too many breadcrumbs (which makes the ice cream heavy) and, for the best texture and deep, nutty flavour, to toast them until really crisp and well browned. Yeast bread produces a better flavour than soda bread for this recipe. Serve the ice cream either on its own or with a chocolate or fruit sauce.

Serves 6–8

115g/4oz/2 cups wholemeal (whole-wheat) breadcrumbs

115g/4oz/½ cup soft brown sugar

2 large (US extra large) eggs, separated

30–45ml/2–3 tbsp Irish Cream liqueur

450ml/¾ pint/scant 2 cups double (heavy) cream

1 Preheat the oven to 190°C/375°F/Gas 5. Spread the breadcrumbs out on a baking sheet and toast them in the oven for about 15 minutes, or until crisp and well browned. Leave to cool.

2 Whisk the sugar and egg yolks together until light and creamy, then beat in the Irish Cream. Whisk the cream until soft peaks form. In a separate bowl, whisk the egg whites stiffly.

◀ **3** Sprinkle the breadcrumbs over the beaten egg mixture, add the cream and fold into the mixture with a spoon. Fold in the beaten egg whites. Turn the mixture into a freezerproof container, cover and freeze.

Right *The popular holiday destination of Ventry, County Kerry.*

Per portion Energy 561Kcal/2332kJ; Protein 6g; Carbohydrate 37.3g, of which sugars 23g; Fat 43.6g, of which saturates 25.7g; Cholesterol 179mg; Calcium 84mg; Fibre 0.4g; Sodium 196mg

Breads, cakes and bakes

Good home baking has always been one of the great strengths of Irish cooking, and restaurants still make a point of serving their own special home-baked breads. The simple soda breads and scones for which Ireland is renowned are easy to make – and are utterly delicious when eaten warm, with lashings of golden Irish butter melting through…

Brown soda bread

Soda bread is best eaten on the day of baking, but it slices better if left to cool and "set" for several hours. It is delicious with good butter, farmhouse cheese and some crisp sticks of celery or a bowl of home-made soup.

Makes 1 loaf

- 450g/1lb/4 cups wholemeal (whole-wheat) flour
- 175g/6oz/1½ cups plain (all-purpose) flour
- 7.5ml/1½ tsp bicarbonate of soda (baking soda)
- 5ml/1 tsp salt
- about 450ml/¾ pint/scant 2 cups buttermilk

Variation Cream of tartar can be added to the dry ingredients to provide the acid instead of buttermilk.

1 Preheat the oven to 200°C/400°F/ Gas 6, and grease a baking sheet. Combine the dry ingredients in a mixing bowl and stir in enough buttermilk to make a fairly soft dough. Turn on to a work surface dusted with wholemeal flour and knead lightly until smooth.

2 Form the dough into a circle, about 4cm/1½in thick. Lay on the baking sheet and mark a deep cross in the top with a floured knife.

3 Bake for about 45 minutes, or until the bread is browned and sounds hollow when tapped on the base. Cool on a wire rack. If a soft crust is preferred, wrap the loaf in a clean dish towel while cooling.

***Above** The beautiful landscape of the river and valleys of Killorglin and Glenbeigh, County Kerry.*

Per loaf Energy 2262Kcal/9643kJ; Protein 88.5g; Carbohydrate 465.4g, of which sugars 31.4g; Fat 18.9g, of which saturates 6.5g; Cholesterol 27mg; Calcium 1.37g; Fibre 34.2g; Sodium 2.18g

White soda bread

Like all soda breads, this loaf is best eaten on the day of baking, but it contains a little butter helping it to keep better than fat-free versions. It is delicious eaten very fresh with lashings of butter and home-made jam.

Makes 1 loaf or 4 farls

450g/1lb/4 cups plain (all-purpose) flour

5ml/1 tsp bicarbonate of soda (baking soda)

7.5ml/1½ tsp cream of tartar

pinch of salt

25g/1oz/2 tbsp butter, at room temperature

1 egg whisked with 300ml/½ pint/1¼ cups buttermilk

1 Preheat the oven to 220°C/425°F/Gas 7 and grease a baking sheet. Sift the dry ingredients into a big bowl. Cut in the butter and rub into the flour until the mixture resembles fine breadcrumbs.

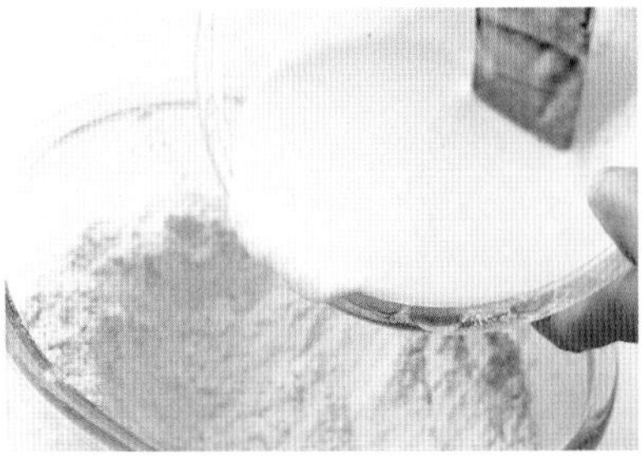

2 Make a well in the centre and pour in the egg and buttermilk mixture. Mix thoroughly to make a soft dough.

3 Turn out on to a floured board and knead lightly for a minute or two. Shape into a round and flatten slightly. Place the loaf on the baking sheet and mark with a deep cross to help it to cook evenly. Bake in the preheated oven for about 30 minutes, until well risen and lightly browned. When cooked, it will sound hollow when tapped on the base.

4 Cool on a wire rack. If a soft crust is preferred, wrap the loaf or farls in a clean dish towel while it is cooling. Serve as soon as possible.

Cook's tip The deep cross cut into traditional round loaves ensures even cooking, and the loaf can then be easily divided into four "farls" (quarters).

Variation For fruit soda bread, a tea-bread popular in the north of Ireland, after rubbing in the butter add 15–30ml/1–2 tbsp sugar, 75g/3oz/½ cup each of currants and sultanas (golden raisins) and 50g/2oz/⅓ cup mixed (candied) peel. Some extra buttermilk may be needed to keep the dough soft. Allow a longer cooking time, about 45 minutes.

Per loaf Energy 1947Kcal/8242kJ; Protein 60.1g; Carbohydrate 363.9g, of which sugars 21g; Fat 38.2g, of which saturates 19g; Cholesterol 299mg; Calcium 1.03g; Fibre 13.9g; Sodium 378mg

Basic yeast bread

Make this dough into any shape you like, such as braids, cottage loaves or rolls. Use strong bread flour as it has a high gluten content making a more elastic dough that rises better.

Makes 4 loaves

25g/1oz fresh yeast

10ml/2 tsp caster (superfine) sugar

900ml/1½ pints/3¾ cups tepid water, or milk and water mixed

15ml/1 tbsp salt

1.3kg/3lb/12 cups strong white bread flour, preferably unbleached

50g/2oz/scant ¼ cup white vegetable fat (shortening) or 50ml/2fl oz/¼ cup vegetable oil

1 Cream the yeast and caster sugar together in a measuring jug (cup), add about 150ml/¼ pint/⅔ cup of the measured liquid and leave in a warm place for about 10 minutes to froth up.

2 Meanwhile, mix the salt into the flour and rub in the fat (if using oil, add it to the remaining liquid).

3 Using an electric mixer with a dough hook attachment or working by hand in a mixing bowl, add the yeast mixture and remaining liquid to the flour, and work it in to make a firm dough which leaves the bowl clean.

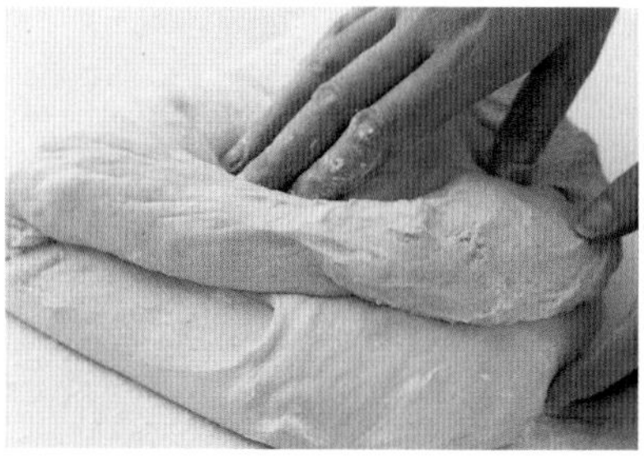

4 Knead well on a floured surface, or in the mixer, until the dough has become firm and elastic. Return to the bowl, cover lightly with a dish towel and leave in a warm place to rise for an hour, or until it has doubled in size. The dough will be springy and full of air. Meanwhile oil four 450g/1lb loaf tins (pans).

5 Turn the dough out on to a floured work surface and knock back (punch down), flattening it out with your knuckles to knock the air out. Knead lightly into shape again, divide into four pieces and form into loaf shapes. Place the dough in the loaf tins, pushing down well to fit into the corners, then leave to rise again for another 20–30 minutes. Meanwhile, preheat the oven to 230°C/450°F/Gas 8.

6 When the dough has risen just above the rims of the tins, bake the loaves in the centre of the oven for 30 minutes, or until browned and shrinking a little from the sides of the tins; when turned out and rapped underneath they should sound hollow. Cool on wire racks.

Variations

• You can form the dough into loaf shapes or about 36 rolls and bake on greased baking trays. Baking time for rolls will be 15–20 minutes.

• For granary bread, replace the white flour with granary flour, or half and half granary and strong white bread flour.

Per loaf Energy 1223Kcal/5185kJ; Protein 30.7g; Carbohydrate 256.4g, of which sugars 7.5g; Fat 15.2g, of which saturates 6.3g; Cholesterol 0mg; Calcium 457mg; Fibre 10.1g; Sodium 1.48g

Buttermilk scones

These deliciously light scones are a favourite for afternoon tea, served fresh from the oven with butter and home-made jam.

Makes about 12 large or 18 small scones

- 450g/1lb/4 cups plain (all-purpose) flour
- 2.5ml/½ tsp salt
- 5ml/1 tsp bicarbonate of soda (baking soda)
- 50g/2oz/¼ cup butter, at room temperature
- 15ml/1 tbsp caster (superfine) sugar
- 1 small egg, lightly beaten
- about 300ml/½ pint/1¼ cups buttermilk

1 Preheat the oven to 220°C/425°F/ Gas 7 and grease two baking trays.

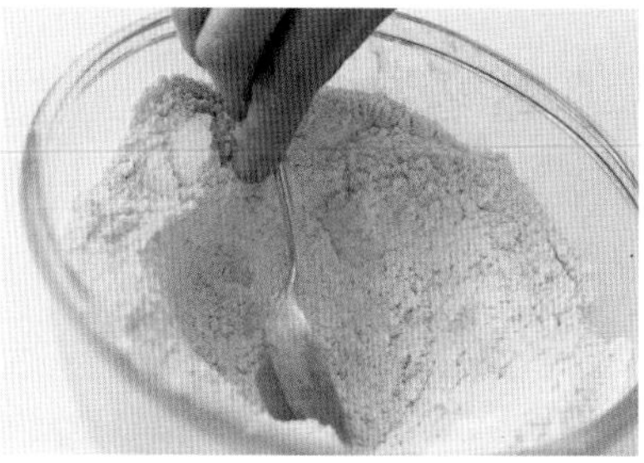

2 Sift the flour, salt and bicarbonate of soda into a mixing bowl. Cut in the butter and rub in until the mixture resembles fine breadcrumbs. Add the sugar and mix well. Make a well in the middle and add the egg and enough buttermilk to make a soft dough.

3 Turn on to a floured work surface and knead lightly into shape. Roll out to about 1cm/½in thick.

4 Cut out 12 large or 18 small scones with a fluted cutter, gathering the trimmings and lightly re-rolling as necessary. Arrange the scones on the baking trays, spacing well apart.

5 Bake in the preheated oven for about 15–20 minutes, until the scones are well risen and golden brown, reversing the position of the trays halfway through. Cool on wire racks. Serve warm.

Variations

- To make wheatmeal scones, use half white and half fine wholemeal (whole-wheat) flour.
- For sultana scones, add 50–115g/ 2–4oz/⅓–⅔ cup sultanas (golden raisins) with the sugar.

***Right** Old-style milk churns left by the roadside in the west of Ireland in County Mayo.*

Per scone Energy 181Kcal/767kJ; Protein 4.9g; Carbohydrate 31.6g, of which sugars 3.1g; Fat 4.8g, of which saturates 2.6g; Cholesterol 26mg; Calcium 86mg; Fibre 1.2g; Sodium 125mg

Oven-baked potato cakes

Potato cakes are widely made in Ireland and come in a variety of forms, but they're all at their best if made with freshly cooked potatoes, preferably while still warm. Serve straight from the oven, split open and buttered while hot.

Makes about 12

- 225g/8oz/2 cups self-raising (self-rising) flour
- 2.5ml/½ tsp baking powder
- 50g/2oz/¼ cup butter, diced
- a pinch of salt
- 175g/6oz freshly cooked mashed potato
- 15ml/1 tbsp chopped fresh chives
- 200ml/7fl oz/scant 1 cup buttermilk

1 Preheat the oven to 220°C/425°F/Gas 7 and lightly grease a baking tray with butter.

2 Sift the flour and the baking powder into a bowl and rub in the butter. Season with salt. Add the mashed potato and chives. Mix well, and then incorporate enough buttermilk to make a soft dough. Turn on to a floured work surface, knead lightly into shape then quickly roll out.

3 Cut into squares with a sharp floured knife or stamp out into rounds with a 5cm/2in cutter.

4 Place on the baking tray and bake in the preheated oven for about 20 minutes or until well risen, golden brown and crisp.

Per cake Energy 108Kcal/455kJ; Protein 2g; Carbohydrate 16.5g, of which sugars 0.4g; Fat 4.3g, of which saturates 2.6g; Cholesterol 11mg; Calcium 68mg; Fibre 0.7g; Sodium 99mg

Oatmeal biscuits

Although not as neat as bought ones, these home-made oatmeal biscuits make up in flavour and interest anything they might lose in presentation – and they make the ideal partner for most Irish farmhouse cheeses.

Makes about 18

75g/3oz/⅔ cup plain (all-purpose) flour

2.5ml/½ tsp salt

1.5ml/¼ tsp baking powder

115g/4oz/1 cup fine pinhead oatmeal

65g/2½oz/generous ¼ cup white vegetable fat (shortening)

1 Preheat the oven to 200°C/400°F/Gas 6 and grease a baking sheet.

2 Sift the flour, salt and baking powder into a mixing bowl. Add the oatmeal and mix well. Rub in the fat to make a crumbly mixture, then blend in enough water to make a stiff dough.

3 Turn on to a worktop sprinkled with fine oatmeal and knead until smooth and manageable. Roll out to about 3mm/⅛in thick and cut into rounds, squares or triangles. Place on the baking sheet.

4 Bake in the preheated oven for about 15 minutes, until crisp. Cool the biscuits on a wire rack.

5 When absolutely cold, store the biscuits in an airtight container lined with baking parchment. Check for crispness before serving; reheat for 4–5 minutes in a preheated oven at 200°C/400°F/Gas 6 to crisp up if necessary.

Per biscuit Energy 72Kcal/301kJ; Protein 1.2g; Carbohydrate 7.9g, of which sugars 0.1g; Fat 4.2g, of which saturates 1.8g; Cholesterol 3mg; Calcium 9mg; Fibre 0.6g; Sodium 57mg

Shortbread

This easy all-in-one recipe makes a very light, crisp shortbread with an excellent flavour, and it keeps well. Serve with tea or coffee, or to accompany light desserts.

Makes about 48 fingers

275g/10oz/2½ cups plain (all-purpose) flour

25g/1oz/¼ cup ground almonds

225g/8oz/1 cup butter, softened

75g/3oz/6 tbsp caster (superfine) sugar

grated rind of ½ lemon

1 Preheat the oven to 180°C/350°F/ Gas 4 and oil a large Swiss roll tin (jelly roll pan), or baking tray.

2 Put the flour, ground almonds, softened butter, caster sugar and lemon rind into a mixer or food processor and beat until the mixture comes together. (To make by hand see below.)

3 Place the mixture on the oiled tray and flatten it out until even all over. Bake in the preheated oven for 20 minutes, or until pale golden brown.

4 Remove from the oven and immediately mark the shortbread into fingers or squares while the mixture is soft. Allow to cool a little, and then transfer to a wire rack and leave until cold. If stored in an airtight container, the shortbread should keep for up to two weeks.

To make by hand Sift the flour and almonds on to a pastry board or work surface. Cream the butter and sugar together in a mixing bowl, until it is soft and light. Turn the creamed mixture on to the flour and almonds, then work it together using the fingers to make a smooth dough. Continue as above from step 3.

Variation Replace the lemon rind with the grated rind of two oranges, if you like.

Per finger Energy 64Kcal/266kJ; Protein 0.7g; Carbohydrate 6.1g, of which sugars 1.8g; Fat 4.2g, of which saturates 2.5g; Cholesterol 10mg; Calcium 11mg; Fibre 0.2g; Sodium 29mg

Gur cake

This spicy fruit "cake" used to be available very cheaply from Dublin bakers, who made it with their day-old bread and cakes. It is still made, although now usually sold as "Fruit Slice".

Makes 24 slices

- 8 slices of stale bread, or plain cake
- 75g/3oz/⅔ cup plain (all-purpose) flour
- pinch of salt
- 2.5ml/½ tsp baking powder
- 10ml/2 tsp mixed (apple pie) spice
- 115g/4oz/generous ½ cup granulated sugar, plus extra for sprinkling
- 175g/6oz/¾ cup currants or mixed dried fruit
- 50g/2oz/¼ cup butter, melted
- 1 egg, lightly beaten
- milk to mix

For the shortcrust pastry

- 225g/8oz/2 cups plain (all-purpose) flour
- 2.5ml/½ tsp salt
- 115g/4oz/½ cup butter

1 To make the shortcrust pastry, mix together the plain flour, salt and the butter in a large mixing bowl. Using the fingertips or a pastry (cookie) cutter, rub the butter into the flour until the mixture resembles fine breadcrumbs.

2 Mix in 30–45ml/2–3 tbsp cold water and knead the mixture lightly to form a firm dough. Wrap the dough in clear film (plastic wrap) and chill in the refrigerator for 30 minutes.

3 Preheat the oven to 190°C/375°F/Gas 5 and grease and flour a square baking tin (pan).

4 Remove the crusts from the bread and make the remainder into crumbs, or make the cake into crumbs. Put the crumbs into a mixing bowl with the flour, salt, baking powder, mixed (apple pie) spice, sugar and dried fruit. Mix well to combine.

5 Add the butter and egg to the dry ingredients with enough milk to make a fairly stiff, spreadable mixture.

6 Roll out the pastry and, using the baking tin as a guide, cut out one piece to make the lid. Use the rest, re-rolled as necessary, to line the base of the tin. Spread the pastry with the mixture then cover with the pastry lid.

7 Make diagonal slashes across the top. Bake in the oven for 50–60 minutes, or until golden. Sprinkle with sugar and leave to cool in the tin. Cut into slices.

Per slice Energy 156Kcal/656kJ; Protein 2.4g; Carbohydrate 24.2g, of which sugars 10.5g; Fat 6.2g, of which saturates 3.7g; Cholesterol 23mg; Calcium 43mg; Fibre 0.8g; Sodium 128mg

Quick barm brack

The traditional yeasted Hallowe'en barm brack contains all kinds of symbolic tokens, of which the best known is a ring. Serve this version sliced and buttered while warm.

Makes 2 loaves

- 450g/1lb/4 cups plain (all-purpose) flour
- 5ml/1 tsp mixed (apple pie) spice
- 2.5ml/½ tsp salt
- 2 sachets easy blend (rapid-rise) dried yeast
- 75g/3oz/6 tbsp soft dark brown sugar
- 115g/4oz/½ cup butter, melted
- 300ml/½ pint/1¼ cups tepid milk
- 1 egg, lightly beaten
- 375g/13oz/generous 2 cups dried mixed fruit
- 25g/1oz/⅓ cup chopped mixed (candied) peel
- 15ml/1 tbsp caster (superfine) sugar

1 Butter two 450g/1lb loaf tins (pans). Mix the flour, spice, salt, yeast and sugar in a large bowl and make a well in the centre. Mix the butter with the tepid milk and lightly beaten egg and add to the bowl.

2 Add the mixed fruit and peel and mix well. Turn the mixture into the loaf tins. Leave in a warm place for about 30 minutes to rise. Meanwhile, preheat the oven to 200°C/400°F/Gas 6.

3 When the dough has doubled in size, bake in the hot oven for about 45 minutes, or until the loaves begin to shrink slightly from the sides of the tins; when turned out and rapped underneath they should sound hollow.

4 Make a glaze by mixing the caster sugar with 30ml/2 tbsp boiling water. Remove the loaves from the oven and brush over with the glaze. Return them to the oven for 3 minutes, or until the tops are a rich shiny brown. Turn on to a wire rack to cool.

Per loaf Energy 2019Kcal/8524kJ; Protein 34.9g; Carbohydrate 364.6g, of which sugars 193.2g; Fat 57g, of which saturates 32.8g; Cholesterol 246mg; Calcium 704mg; Fibre 11.7g; Sodium 590mg

Seed cake

Caraway seeds have long been a feature of Irish baking and this old-fashioned cake remains popular on farmhouse tea tables.

Makes 1 cake

- 225g/8oz/2 cups plain (all-purpose) flour
- 115g/4oz/½ cup butter, at room temperature
- 115g/4oz/generous ½ cup caster (superfine) sugar
- 2 large (US extra large) eggs
- 5ml/1 tsp baking powder
- 15ml/1 tbsp caraway seeds
- 30–45ml/2–3 tbsp milk, if necessary

1 Preheat the oven to 180°C/350°F/Gas 4. Butter and base line a 18cm/7in deep cake tin (pan) with buttered baking parchment.

2 Sift the flour. Cream the butter and sugar together in a large bowl until light and fluffy, then add the eggs, a little at a time, with a spoonful of flour with each addition. Add the baking powder and most of the caraway seeds to the remaining flour, reserving a few seeds to sprinkle over the top of the cake.

3 Add the flour and caraway seeds mixture to the butter mixture, and blend in lightly but thoroughly; add a little milk to make a soft mixture if it seems too stiff.

4 Turn the mixture into the prepared tin and sprinkle with the reserved caraway seeds. Put the cake in the preheated oven and bake for 15 minutes. Reduce the temperature to 160°C/325°F/Gas 3 and bake for a further 1 hour, or until the cake is well risen and golden brown.

5 Leave the cake to cool in the tin for about 10 minutes, then remove and finish cooling on a wire rack. When cold, remove the baking parchment and store in an airtight tin.

Cook's tip Aromatic caraway seeds come from a herb in the parsley family. They have a delicate aniseed flavour and are often used in baking.

Variation To make a traditional Irish Spice Cake, omit the caraway seeds and replace with 7.5ml/1½ tsp of mixed (apple pie) spice (ground cloves, cinnamon and nutmeg) sifted into the flour.

Per cake Energy 2252Kcal/9448kJ; Protein 37.4g; Carbohydrate 295.7g, of which sugars 124.2g; Fat 110.8g, of which saturates 64.1g; Cholesterol 702mg; Calcium 465mg; Fibre 7g; Sodium 879mg

Irish apple cake

This moist cake – also known as Kerry Apple Cake in the south of the country – is perhaps best in autumn, when home-grown apples are in season. It has a lovely crunchy top and can be served cold, as a cake, or warm with chilled cream or custard as a dessert.

Makes 1 cake

225g/8oz/2 cups self-raising (self-rising) flour

good pinch of salt

pinch of ground cloves

115g/4oz/½ cup butter, at room temperature

3 or 4 cooking apples, such as Bramley's Seedling

115g/4oz/generous ½ cup caster (superfine) sugar

2 eggs, beaten

a little milk to mix

granulated sugar to sprinkle over

1 Preheat the oven to 190°C/375°F/Gas 5 and butter a 20cm/8in cake tin (pan).

2 Sift the flour, salt and ground cloves into a bowl. Cut in the butter and rub in until the mixture is like fine breadcrumbs. Peel and core the apples. Slice them thinly and add to the rubbed in mixture with the sugar.

3 Mix in the eggs and enough milk to make a fairly stiff dough, then turn the mixture into the prepared tin and sprinkle with granulated sugar.

4 Bake in the preheated oven for 30–40 minutes, or until springy to the touch. Cool on a wire rack. When cold store in an airtight tin until ready to serve.

Per cake Energy 2315Kcal/9717kJ; Protein 37g; Carbohydrate 312.5g, of which sugars 145.3g; Fat 110.9g, of which saturates 64.1g; Cholesterol 702mg; Calcium 948mg; Fibre 10.7g; Sodium 1.68g

Pratie apple cake

Both sweet and savoury versions of this potato apple cake exist; the sweet one, here, was the high point of many a farmhouse high tea, especially when using home-grown apples in autumn. At Hallowe'en it might be served instead of a Barm Brack, with a ring inside.

Makes 2 farls; serves 4–6

450g/1lb freshly cooked potatoes in their skins, preferably still warm

pinch of salt

25g/1oz/2 tbsp butter, melted

about 115g/4oz/1 cup plain (all-purpose) flour

For the filling

3 large or 4 small cooking apples, such as Bramley's Seedlings

a little lemon juice (optional)

about 50g/2oz/¼ cup butter in thin slices

50–115g/2–4oz/¼ – generous ½ cup caster (superfine) sugar, or to taste

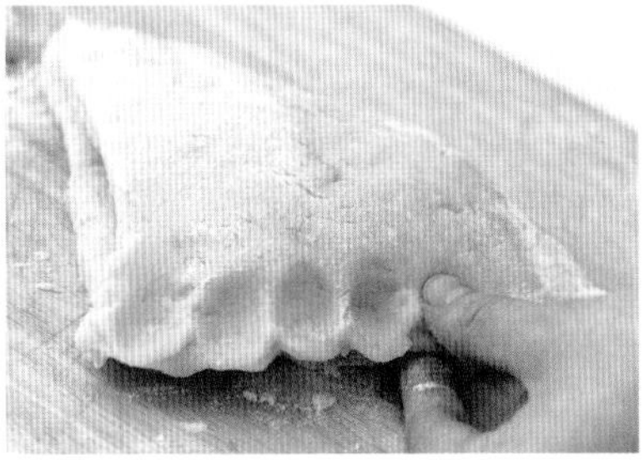

1 Preheat the oven to 200°C/400°F/Gas 6. Peel the potatoes and mash them in a large heavy pan until very smooth. Season to taste with the salt, and drizzle the melted butter over. Knead in as much plain flour as necessary to make a pliable dough (waxy potatoes will need more flour than naturally floury ones, such as Kerr's Pink). The dough should be elastic enough to roll out, but do not knead more than necessary.

2 Roll the potato mixture out into a large circle and cut into four farls (triangular pieces).

3 To make the filling, peel, core and slice the apples and pile slices of the raw apple on to two of the farls. Sprinkle with a little lemon juice, if you like. Dampen the edges of the farls, place the other two on top, and "nip" with your fingers around the edges to seal them together. Cook in the preheated oven for about 15–20 minutes (when the cake is nicely browned, the apples should be cooked).

4 Slit each cake around the side and turn the top back. Lay thin slices of butter over the apples, until they are almost covered, and then sweeten with sugar. Replace the top and return to the oven until the butter and sugar have melted to make a sauce. Cut each farl into pieces and serve.

Per farl Energy 786Kcal/3307kJ; Protein 9.5g; Carbohydrate 121.9g, of which sugars 40.5g; Fat 32.4g, of which saturates 19.9g; Cholesterol 80mg; Calcium 117mg; Fibre 6.1g; Sodium 253mg

Porter cake

Porter was a key ingredient in many traditional Irish dishes, both sweet and savoury, adding colour and richness of flavour without being over-dominant. Stout is a good substitute in recipes like this one, although it is sometimes better diluted.

Makes 1 20cm/8in round cake

- 225g/8oz/1 cup butter, at room temperature
- 225g/8oz/1 cup soft dark brown sugar
- 350g/12oz/3 cups plain (all-purpose) flour
- pinch of salt
- 5ml/1 tsp baking powder
- 5ml/1 tsp mixed (apple pie) spice
- 3 eggs
- 450g/1lb/2⅓ cups mixed dried fruit
- 115g/4oz/½ cup glacé (candied) cherries
- 115g/4oz/⅔ cup mixed (candied) peel
- 50g/2oz/½ cup chopped almonds or walnuts
- about 150ml/¼ pint/⅔ cup stout, such as Guinness

1 Preheat the oven to 160°C/325°F/Gas 3. Grease and base line a 20cm/8in round deep cake tin (pan).

2 Cream the butter and sugar in a bowl, until light and fluffy. Sift the flour, salt, baking powder and spice into another bowl.

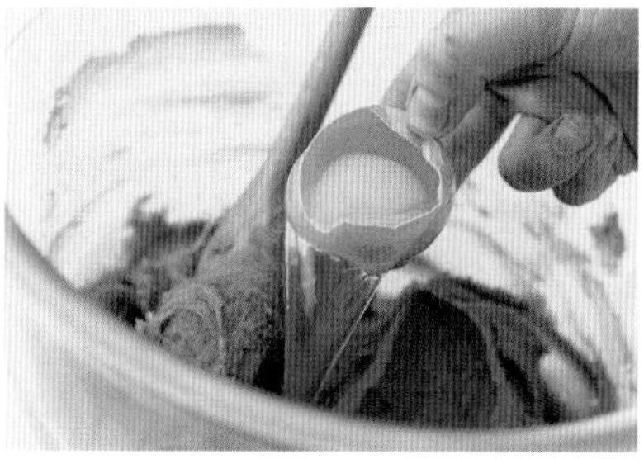

3 Add the eggs to the butter and sugar mixture, one at a time, adding a little of the flour mixture with each egg and beating well after each addition. Mix well and blend in any remaining flour. Add the fruit and nuts and enough stout to make quite a soft consistency. Mix well.

4 Turn the mixture into the prepared tin and bake in the preheated oven for 1 hour. Reduce the heat to 150°C/300°F/Gas 2 and cook for a further 1½–2 hours, or until the top is springy to the touch and a skewer pushed into the centre comes out clean. Cool the cake in the tin.

5 When cold, remove the lining paper, wrap in fresh baking parchment and store in an airtight container for at least a week before eating.

Cook's tip Porter cake is made by many methods, ranging from rubbed-in teabreads to the creaming method, as here.

Per cake Energy 6130Kcal/25807kJ; Protein 80.2g; Carbohydrate 964.9g, of which sugars 696.9g; Fat 240.2g, of which saturates 125.7g; Cholesterol 1.16g; Calcium 1.42mg; Fibre 31g; Sodium 2.23g

Christmas cake

Rich cakes need at least a month to mature, so Christmas cakes are best made by about Hallowe'en. The same recipe can be used to make a wedding cake. It may be finished in the traditional way with almond paste and white icing, or simply glazed with fruit and nuts.

Makes 1 20cm/8in round or 18cm/7in square cake

225g/8oz/2 cups plain (all-purpose) flour

pinch of salt

7.5ml/1½ tsp mixed (apple pie) spice

900g/2lb/5 cups mixed dried fruit

50g/2oz/½ cup slivered almonds

115g/4oz/⅔ cup glacé (candied) cherries, halved

115g/4oz/⅔ cup chopped mixed (candied) peel

225g/8oz/1 cup butter, at room temperature

225g/8oz/1 cup soft dark brown sugar

15ml/1 tbsp black treacle (molasses)

finely grated rind of 1 orange

5ml/1 tsp vanilla essence (extract)

4 large (US extra large) eggs

150ml/¼ pint/⅔ cup whiskey

1 Prepare a 20cm/8in round or an 18cm/7in square loose-based cake tin (pan) by lining it with three layers of greased baking parchment, extending 5cm/2in over the top of the tin. Attach a thick band of folded newspaper or brown paper around the outside of the tin using string to secure it.

2 Sift the flour, salt and spice in a bowl. Put the dried fruit in a large bowl with the almonds, cherries, mixed peel and 15ml/1 tbsp of flour taken from the measured amount.

3 In another bowl, cream the butter and sugar until light and fluffy, then add the treacle, orange rind and vanilla essence. Beat well. Add the eggs, one at a time adding a little of the flour mixture with each egg and beating well after each addition. Fold in the fruit mixture and the remaining flour with 30ml/2 tbsp of the whiskey. Mix well.

4 Put the mixture into the prepared tin, smoothing down well with the back of a spoon and leaving a slight hollow in the centre. At this stage, the cake can now be left overnight or until it is convenient to start baking.

5 Preheat the oven to 160°C/325°F/Gas 3. Place the cake in the centre of the oven and bake for about 1½ hours, or until just beginning to brown. Reduce the heat to 150°C/300°F/Gas 2 and continue to bake for another 3 hours, or until cooked. Protect the top of the cake from over-browning by covering loosely with foil or brown paper.

6 When cooked, the top of the cake will feel springy to the touch and a skewer pushed into the centre will come out clean. Leave the cake to cool, then remove the papers and turn upside down.

7 Using a skewer, make small holes all over the base of the cake and pour in the remaining whiskey. Leave the cake to soak up the whiskey. When soaked, wrap the cake in a double layer of baking parchment followed by a layer of foil. Store in an airtight tin in a cool place until about two weeks before Christmas, if you wish to add a topping.

Per cake Energy 9834Kcal/41,553kJ; Protein 89.9g; Carbohydrate 1846.1g, of which sugars 1673.2g; Fat 247g, of which saturates 127.3g; Cholesterol 1.39g; Calcium 2.24g; Fibre 46g; Sodium 2.8g

Sponge cake with strawberries and cream

This classic treat is delicious in the summer, filled with soft fruit, or with the new season's jam. Have all ingredients at warm room temperature for this recipe. Unless using an electric mixer, whisk the eggs and sugar over hot water to get the required volume.

Serves 8–10

- white vegetable fat (shortening), for greasing
- 4 eggs
- 115g/4oz/generous ½ cup caster (superfine) sugar, plus extra for dusting
- 90g/3½oz/¾ cup plain (all-purpose) flour, sifted, plus extra for dusting
- icing (confectioners') sugar for dusting

For the filling

- 300ml/½ pint/1¼ cups double (heavy) cream
- about 5ml/1 tsp icing (confectioners') sugar, sifted
- 450g/1lb/4 cups strawberries, washed and hulled
- a little Cointreau, or other fruit liqueur (optional)

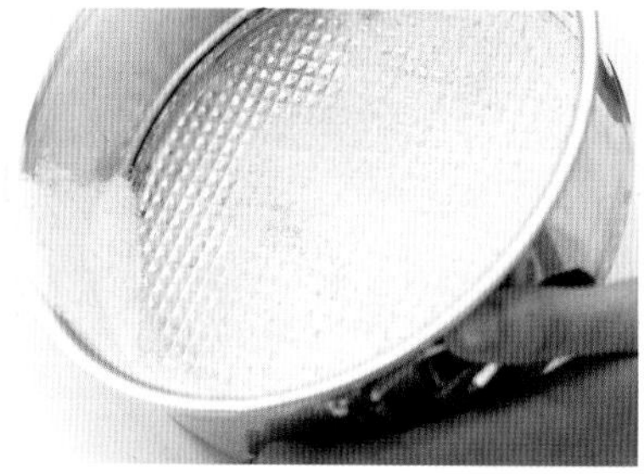

1 Preheat the oven to 190°C/375°F/Gas 5 and grease a loose-based 20cm/8in deep cake tin (pan) with white vegetable fat, and dust it with 5ml/1 tsp caster sugar mixed with 5ml/1 tsp flour. Shake off any excess sugar and flour mixture and discard.

2 Put the eggs and sugar into the bowl of an electric mixer and whisk at high speed until it is light and thick, and the mixture leaves a trail as it drops from the whisk. Alternatively, whisk by hand, or with a hand-held electric whisk; set the bowl over a pan a quarter filled with hot water and whisk until thick and creamy, then remove from the heat.

3 Sift the flour evenly over the whisked eggs and carefully fold it in with a metal spoon, mixing thoroughly but losing as little volume as possible.

4 Pour the mixture into the prepared cake tin. Level off the top and bake in the preheated oven for 25–30 minutes, or until the sponge feels springy to the touch.

5 Leave in the tin for 1–2 minutes to allow the cake to cool a little and shrink slightly from the sides, then loosen the sides gently with a knife and turn out on to a rack to cool.

6 When the sponge is completely cold, make the filling. Whip the double cream with a little icing sugar until it is stiff enough to hold its shape. Slice the sponge across the middle with a sharp knife and divide half of the cream between the two inner sides of the sandwich.

7 Select some well-shaped even-sized strawberries for the top of the cake, and then slice the rest. Lay the bottom half of the sponge on a serving plate and arrange the sliced strawberries on the cream. Sprinkle with liqueur, if using. Cover with the second half of the cake and press down gently so that it holds together.

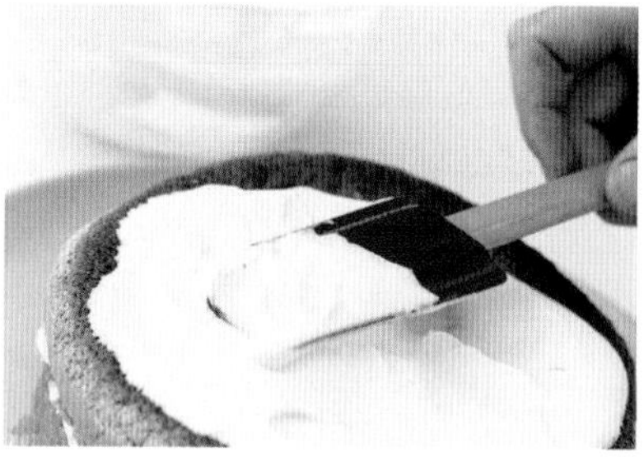

8 Spread the remaining cream on top of the cake, and arrange the reserved strawberries, whole or halved according to size, on top. Set aside for an hour or so for the flavours to develop, then dust lightly with icing sugar and serve as a dessert.

Cook's tips

- Like all fatless sponges, this cake is best eaten on the day of baking.
- The fruits used can be varied according to availability, but strawberries and raspberries are always popular.

Per portion Energy 333Kcal/1387kJ; Protein 5.3g; Carbohydrate 27.8g, of which sugars 19.2g; Fat 23.1g, of which saturates 13.3g; Cholesterol 147mg; Calcium 65mg; Fibre 1g; Sodium 48mg

Irish whiskey cake

This light, moist cake has the subtle flavours of lemon and cloves, rather like Hot Irish Whiskey – making it seem especially tempting in winter.

Makes 1 18cm/7in round cake

- 225g/8oz/1⅓ cups sultanas (golden raisins)
- grated rind of 1 lemon
- 150ml/¼ pint/⅔ cup Irish whiskey
- 175g/6oz/¾ cup butter, softened
- 175g/6oz/¾ cup soft light brown sugar
- 175g/6oz/1½ cups plain (all-purpose) flour
- pinch of salt
- 1.5ml/¼ tsp ground cloves
- 5ml/1 tsp baking powder
- 3 large (US extra large) eggs, separated

For the icing

- juice of 1 lemon
- 225g/8oz/2 cups icing (confectioners') sugar
- crystallized lemon slices, to decorate (optional)

1 Put the sultanas and grated lemon rind into a bowl with the whiskey and leave overnight to soak.

2 Preheat the oven to 180°C/350°F/Gas 4 and grease and base line a loose-based 18cm/7in deep cake tin (pan).

3 Cream the butter and sugar until light and fluffy. Sift the flour, salt, cloves and baking powder together into a bowl.

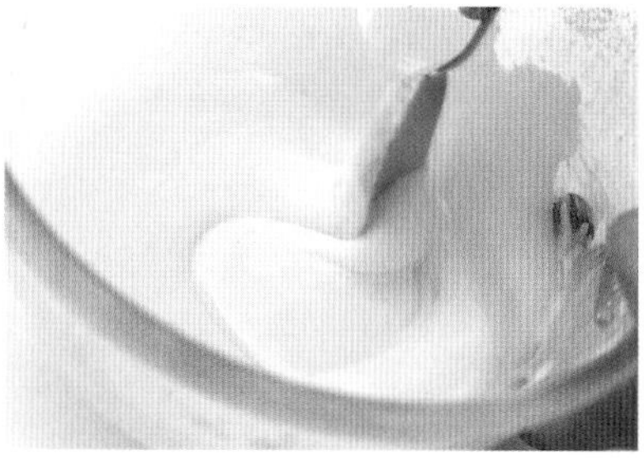

4 Beat the yolks into the butter and sugar one at a time, adding a little of the flour with each egg and beating well after each addition. Gradually blend in the sultana and whiskey mixture, alternating with the remaining flour. Do not overbeat at this stage.

5 Whisk the egg whites until stiff and fold them into the mixture with a metal spoon. Turn the mixture into the prepared tin and bake in the preheated oven for 1½ hours, or until well risen and springy to the touch. Turn out and cool on a rack.

6 Meanwhile, make the icing: mix the lemon juice with the sifted icing sugar and enough warm water to make a pouring consistency. Lay a plate under the cake rack to catch the drips and pour the icing over the cake a spoonful at a time, letting it dribble down the sides. Any icing dripping on to the plate may be scooped and put on top again. When the icing has set, it can be decorated with lemon slices, if you like.

Per cake Energy 4691Kcal/19,730kJ; Protein 48.1g; Carbohydrate 711.2g, of which sugars 577.8g; Fat 167g, of which saturates 97.1g; Cholesterol 1.06g; Calcium 735mg; Fibre 9.9g; Sodium 1.38g

Chocolate cake with coffee icing

This easy all-in-one recipe is a favourite and can be quickly dressed up to make a cake that looks special. The coffee icing complements the rich chocolate flavour of the cake.

Makes 1 18cm/7in round cake

- 175g/6oz/1½ cups self-raising (self-rising) flour
- 25ml/1½ tbsp cocoa powder (unsweetened)
- pinch of salt
- 175g/6oz/¾ cup butter, softened, or easy-spread margarine
- 175g/6oz/¾ cup soft dark brown sugar
- 50g/2oz/½ cup ground almonds
- 3 large (US extra large) eggs, lightly beaten

For the coffee butter icing

- 175g/6oz/¾ cup unsalted (sweet) butter, at warm room temperature
- 350g/12oz/3 cups sifted icing (confectioners') sugar
- 30ml/2 tbsp coffee essence (extract)
- whole hazelnuts or pecan nuts, to decorate (optional)

1 Preheat the oven to 180°C/350°F/ Gas 4 and butter two 18cm/7in diameter sandwich tins (pans).

2 Sift the flour, cocoa and salt into a mixing bowl. Cut in the butter or margarine and add the sugar, ground almonds and eggs.

3 Mix with a wooden spoon for 2–3 minutes, until thoroughly mixed; the mixture should be smooth, with no traces of butter remaining.

4 Divide the mixture between the prepared tins and bake in the centre of the preheated oven for 25–30 minutes, or until springy to the touch. Turn out and cool on a wire rack. Meanwhile make the icing: cream the butter well, then gradually beat in the sifted icing sugar and the coffee essence.

5 When the cakes are cold, sandwich them together with some of the icing and cover the top and sides with most of the remainder. Pipe the remaining icing around the top in rosettes, if you like, and decorate with whole hazelnuts or pecan nuts.

Variation For a deliciously rich touch, 15–30ml/1–2 tbsp of Bailey's Irish Cream can be included in the icing – beat in with the coffee essence at the end of stage 4.

Per cake Energy 5899Kcal/24,684kJ; Protein 56.2g; Carbohydrate 691.1g, of which sugars 556.9g; Fat 343.1g, of which saturates 193.7g; Cholesterol 1.43g; Calcium 1.06g; Fibre 12.2g; Sodium 3.28g

Preserves and sweet treats

Seasonal fruits make excellent preserves to accompany the homely bakes for which the Irish kitchen is rightly renowned and also to serve with savoury foods like wild game. Apples, the most abundant garden fruit, lead the way, and are often used with wild blackberries, bilberries and elderberries – all of which make delicious preserves.

Apple and sultana chutney

Use wine or cider vinegar for this chutney to give it a subtle and mellow flavour. For a mild chutney, add only a little cayenne, for a spicier one increase the quantity to taste. The chutney is perfect served with farmhouse cheese and freshly made soda bread.

Makes about 900g/2lb

350g/12oz cooking apples

115g/4oz/⅔ cup sultanas (golden raisins)

50g/2oz onion

25g/1oz/¼ cup almonds, blanched

5ml/1 tsp white peppercorns

2.5ml/½ tsp coriander seeds

175g/6oz/scant 1 cup sugar

10ml/2 tsp salt

5ml/1 tsp ground ginger

450ml/¾ pint/scant 2 cups cider vinegar

1.5ml/¼ tsp cayenne pepper

red chillies (optional)

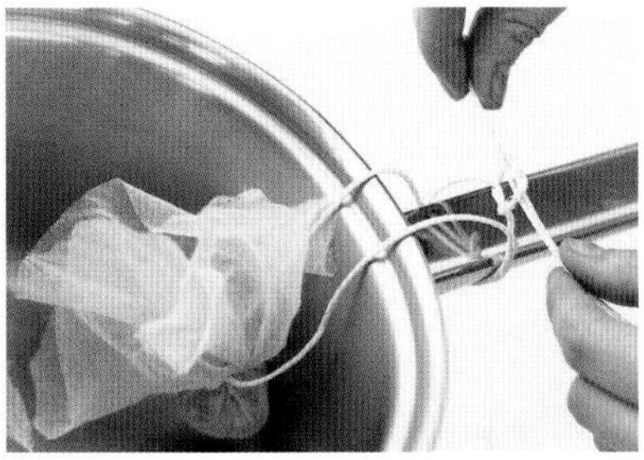

1 Peel, core and chop the apples. Chop the sultanas, onion and almonds. Tie the peppercorns and coriander seeds in muslin (cheesecloth), using a long piece of string, and then tie to the handle of a preserving pan or stainless steel pan.

2 Put the sugar, salt, ground ginger and vinegar into the pan, with the cayenne pepper to taste. Heat gently, stirring, until the sugar has completely dissolved.

3 Add the chopped fruit. Bring to the boil and simmer for 1½–2 hours, or until most of the liquid has evaporated.

4 Spoon into warmed, sterilized jars and place one chilli in each jar, if using. Leave until cold, then cover, seal and label. Store in a cool dark place. The chutney is best left for a month to mature before use and will keep for at least 6 months, if correctly stored.

Per 900g/2lb Energy 1299Kcal/5525kJ; Protein 10.9g; Carbohydrate 299.5g, of which sugars 297.7g; Fat 14.9g, of which saturates 1.1g; Cholesterol 0mg; Calcium 254mg; Fibre 10.4g; Sodium 3.97g

Garden jam

Soft fruit is widely grown in Irish gardens and, after the first flush of early fruit is over, much of it is used for preserves, including this useful mixed fruit jam.

Makes about 3.6kg/8lb

450g/1lb/4 cups blackcurrants (stalks removed)

450g/1lb/4 cups blackberries, or whitecurrants or redcurrants

450g/1lb/2⅔ cups raspberries or loganberries

450g/1lb/4 cups strawberries

1.8kg/4lb/9 cups granulated sugar, warmed

Cook's tip To reduce the risk of mould forming during storage, cover and seal home-made preserves while they are either very hot or when absolutely cold – if covered while they are lukewarm, condensation will form and a layer of mould will grow on the surface.

1 Put the blackcurrants into a large preserving pan and add 150ml/¼ pint/⅔ cup water. Bring to the boil and simmer until almost cooked. Add the rest of the fruit and simmer gently, stirring occasionally, for about 10 minutes, or until the fruit is just soft.

2 Add the warm sugar to the pan and stir over a gentle heat until it is completely dissolved.

3 Bring to the boil and boil hard until setting point is reached. To test, put a spoonful of jam on to a cold saucer. Cool slightly, then push the surface. It is ready if a skin has formed. If not, boil for longer and keep testing until it sets.

4 Remove any scum from the jam and pour into sterilized, warm jars. Cover and seal. Store in a cool, dark place for up to 6 months.

Per 3.6kg/8lb Energy 7583Kcal/32,328kJ; Protein 23.9g; Carbohydrate 1991.7g, of which sugars 1991.7g; Fat 1.4g, of which saturates 0g; Cholesterol 0mg; Calcium 1.44g; Fibre 31.1g; Sodium 203mg

Blackberry and apple jam

This old favourite recipe is ideal for the late summer and early autumn when a family day out blackberrying can supply the berries, and windfall apples are plentiful.

Makes about 4.5kg/10lb

1.3kg/3lb cooking apples or windfalls

1.8kg/4lb/16 cups blackberries

2.75kg/6lb/13½ cups sugar, warmed

1 Remove any bad bruises from the cooking apples before weighing, then peel, core and cut them up roughly. Put into a large pan. Add half of the water, bring to the boil and simmer until the apples are soft.

2 Meanwhile pick over the blackberries, wash them gently and drain well.

3 Put the blackberries into a preserving pan with 300ml/½ pint/1¼ cups water and cook gently until tender. If you want a seedless jam, press the cooked berries through a sieve (strainer), then return to the rinsed preserving pan. Add the apples and the sugar to the berries.

4 Stir over a low heat until the sugar has completely dissolved, and then bring to the boil. Boil hard for about 15 minutes, or until setting point is reached. To test, put a spoonful of jam on to a cold saucer. Allow to cool slightly, and then push the surface of the jam with your finger. Setting point has been reached if a skin has formed. If not, boil a little longer and keep testing until it sets.

5 Skim if necessary, then pour into warmed, sterilized jars. Cover, seal and store in a cool, dark place until required. The jam will store well for at least 6 months, if correctly stored.

Per 4.5kg/10lb Energy 11,740Kcal/50,063kJ; Protein 33.9g; Carbohydrate 3081.3g, of which sugars 3081.3g; Fat 4.9g, of which saturates 0g; Cholesterol 0mg; Calcium 2.29g; Fibre 76.6g; Sodium 227mg

Raspberry jam

For many this is the best of all jams: it is delicious with scones and cream. Raspberries are low in pectin and acid, so they will not set firmly – but a soft set is perfect for this jam.

Makes about 3.1kg/7lb

1.8kg/4lb/10⅔ cups firm raspberries

juice of 1 large lemon

1.8kg/4lb/9 cups sugar, warmed

Cook's tip To test if jam or jelly has set, put a spoonful of jam or jelly on to a cold saucer. Allow it to cool slightly, and then push the surface of the jam with your finger. Setting point has been reached if a skin has formed and it wrinkles. If not, boil for a little longer and keep testing regularly until it sets; the flavour will be better if the boiling time is short.

1 Put 175g/6oz/1 cup of the raspberries into the preserving pan and crush them. Add the rest of the fruit and the lemon juice, and simmer until soft and pulpy. Add the sugar and stir until dissolved, then bring back to the boil and boil hard until setting point is reached, testing after 3–4 minutes.

2 Pour into warmed, sterilized jars. When cold, cover, seal and store in a cool, dark place until required. The jam will store well for 6 months.

Variation For a slightly stronger flavour, 150ml/¼ pint/⅔ cup redcurrant juice can be used instead of the lemon juice.

Per 3.2kg/7lb Energy 7542Kcal/32,220kJ; Protein 34.2g; Carbohydrate 1963.8g, of which sugars 1963.8g; Fat 5.4g, of which saturates 1.8g; Cholesterol 0mg; Calcium 1.40g; Fibre 45g; Sodium 162mg

Elderberry jelly

This country jelly uses hedgerow produce that would otherwise go to waste. It is easy to make and tastes wonderful served as an accompaniment to roast chicken or with scones.

Makes about 1.8–2.25kg/4–5lb

1.6kg/3½lb cooking apples, or windfalls

900g/2lb elderberries

1.2 litres/2 pints/5 cups water

450g/1lb/2¼ cups sugar to 600ml/1 pint/2½ cups juice, warmed

Cook's tip To test the jelly, put a spoonful of jam on to a cold saucer. Allow to cool slightly, and push the surface of the jam with your finger. Setting point has been reached if a skin has formed. If not, boil a little longer and keep testing until it sets.

Variation For bramble jelly follow the recipe but substitute blackberries.

1 Cut up the cooking apples roughly, without peeling the skin. Sort through the elderberries, removing any damaged berries and stalks, and wash and drain them. Put the apples into a large pan with the elderberries and add 1.2 litres/2 pints/5 cups water. Bring to the boil and cook to a pulp. Allow to cool a little, then strain the fruit mixture through a jelly bag.

2 Measure the juice and allow 450g/1lb/2¼ cups sugar for each 600ml/1 pint/2½ cups. Return the juice and sugar to the rinsed pan and heat gently until the sugar has completely dissolved. Bring to the boil. Boil hard until setting point is reached. Pour into warmed, sterilized jars. Cover, seal and store in a cool, dark place until required. The jelly will store well for 6 months.

Per 2.25kg/5lb Energy 2585Kcal/11,070kJ; Protein 15.1g; Carbohydrate 672g, of which sugars 672g; Fat 1.6g, of which saturates 0g; Cholesterol 0mg; Calcium 843mg; Fibre 58g; Sodium 86mg

Rowan jelly

This astringent jelly is made from the orange fruit of mountain ash trees, which flourish in areas where deer run wild. It is a traditional accompaniment to game, especially venison.

Makes about 2.25kg/5lb

- 1.3kg/3lb/12 cups rowan berries
- 450g/1lb crab apples, or windfall cooking apples
- 450g/1lb/2¼ cups sugar per 600ml/1 pint/2½ cups juice, warmed

Cook's tip For a less astringent jelly, an equal quantity of apples and berries may be used, such as 900g/2lb of each.

1 Cut the rowan berries off their stalks, rinse them in a colander and put them into a preserving pan.

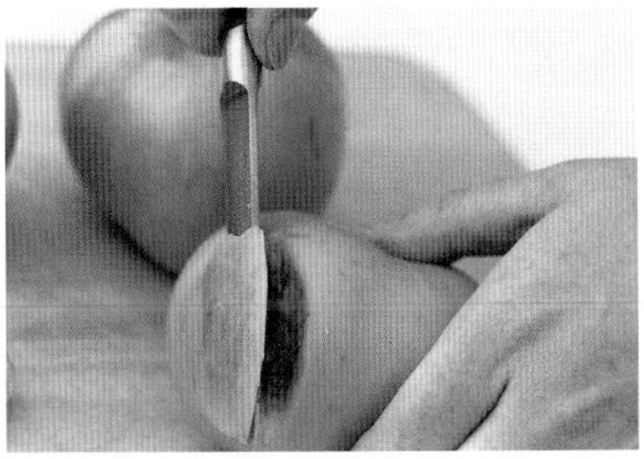

2 Remove any badly damaged parts from the apples before weighing them, then cut them up roughly without peeling or coring. Add the apples to the pan, with 1.2 litres/2 pints/5 cups water, which should just cover the fruit.

3 Bring to the boil and simmer for about 45 minutes, until the fruit is soft, stirring occasionally and crushing the fruit with a wooden spoon to help extract the pectin. Strain the fruit through a jelly bag or a fine sieve (strainer) into a bowl overnight.

4 Measure the juice and allow 450g/1lb/2¼ cups sugar per 600ml/1 pint/2½ cups juice. Return the juice to the rinsed preserving pan and add the measured amount of sugar.

5 Stir over a low heat until the sugar has dissolved, and then bring to the boil and boil hard for about 10 minutes until setting point is reached. To test, put a spoonful of jam on to a cold saucer. Allow to cool slightly, and then push the surface of the jam with your finger. Setting point has been reached if a skin has formed. If not, boil a little longer and keep testing until it sets.

6 Skim, if necessary, and pour into warmed, sterilized jars. Cover, seal and store in a cool, dark place until needed. The jelly will store well for 6 months.

Variations

- The thinly peeled rind and juice of a lemon can be included for a firmer set; reduce the amount of water slightly to allow for the lemon juice.
- For sloe jelly, substitute 1.3kg/3lb sloes (black plums) for the rowan berries and use 675g/1½lb apples.

Per 2.25kg/5lb Energy 2340Kcal/9993kJ; Protein 15.8g; Carbohydrate 606.4g, of which sugars 606.4g; Fat 0.5g, of which saturates 0g; Cholesterol 0mg; Calcium 1.03g; Fibre 54g; Sodium 80mg

Irish whiskey marmalade

Real home-made marmalade tastes delicious, and flavouring it with whiskey makes it a special treat. This is an adaptation of the commercial method, in which marmalade is matured in old whiskey barrels and takes the flavour from the wood.

Makes 3.6–4.5kg/8–10lb

1.3kg/3lb Seville oranges

juice of 2 large lemons

2.75kg/6lb/13½ cups sugar, warmed

about 300ml/½ pint/1¼ cups Irish whiskey

1 Scrub the oranges using a nylon brush and pick off the disc at the stalk end. Cut the oranges in half and squeeze the juice, retaining the pips. Quarter the peel, cut away and reserve any thick white pith, and shred the peel – thickly or thinly depending on how you prefer the finished marmalade.

2 Cut up the reserved pith roughly and tie it up with the pips in a square of muslin (cheesecloth) using a long piece of string. Tie the bag loosely, so that water can circulate in the bag during cooking and will extract the pectin from the pith and pips. Hang the bag from the handle of the preserving pan.

3 Add the cut peel, strained juices and 3.5 litres/6 pints/15 cups water to the pan. Bring to the boil and simmer for 1½–2 hours, or until the peel is very tender (it will not soften further after the sugar has been added).

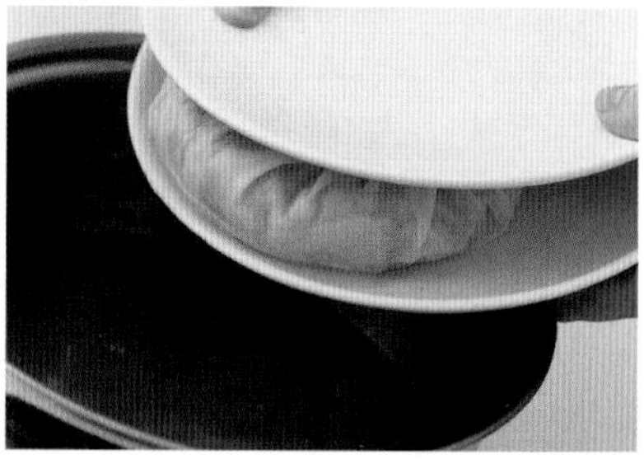

4 Lift up the bag of pith and pips and squeeze it out well between two plates over the pan to extract as much pectin as possible. Add the sugar to the pan and stir over a low heat until it has completely dissolved.

5 Bring to the boil, and then boil hard for 15–20 minutes or until setting point is reached. To test, put a spoonful of marmalade on to a cold saucer. Allow to cool slightly, and then push the surface of the marmalade with your finger. Setting point has been reached if a skin has formed. If not, boil a little longer and keep testing until it sets.

6 Skim, if necessary, and leave to cool for about 15 minutes, then stir to redistribute the peel. Divide the whiskey among 8–10 warmed, sterilized jars and swill it around. Using a small heatproof jug (pitcher), pour in the marmalade.

7 Cover and seal while still hot. Label when cold, and store in a cool, dark place until required. The marmalade will keep well for at least 6 months.

Per 4.5kg/10lb Energy 10,736Kcal/45,734kJ; Protein 22.8g; Carbohydrate 2657.8g, of which sugars 2657.8g; Fat 1.3g, of which saturates 0g; Cholesterol 0mg; Calcium 1.74g; Fibre 15.6g; Sodium 187mg

Chocolate citrus candies

Home-candied peel makes a superb sweetmeat, especially when dipped in chocolate. You can also use bought candied peel for this recipe, but make sure it is the very best quality. If you can buy it in one piece it can then be simply sliced and dipped.

Makes about 100g/4oz petits fours

1 orange or 2 lemons

25g/1oz/2 tbsp sugar

about 50g/2oz good quality plain (semisweet) chocolate

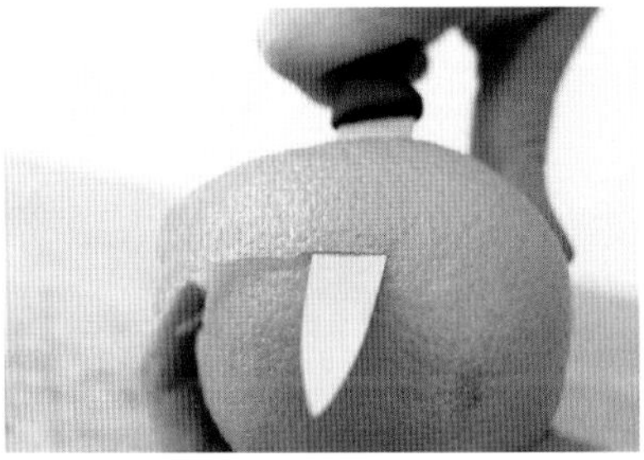

1 Using a vegetable knife, peel the rind from the fruit, without taking too much of the pith. Slice into matchsticks.

2 Blanch in boiling water for 4–5 minutes, until beginning to soften, then refresh under cold water and drain thoroughly.

3 In a small pan, heat the sugar and 30ml/2 tbsp water gently together until the sugar has dissolved. Add the strips of rind and simmer for about 8–10 minutes, or until the water has evaporated and the peel is transparent.

4 Lift out the peel with a slotted spoon and spread out on baking parchment to cool. When cold the peel can be stored in an airtight container for up to 2 days before using, if required.

5 To coat, melt the chocolate carefully in a double boiler or in a bowl over a pan of hot water. Spear each piece of peel on to a cocktail stick (toothpick) and dip one end into the chocolate.

6 To dry the candies, stick the cocktail sticks into a large potato. When the chocolate is completely dry, remove the sticks and then arrange the citrus candies attractively on a dish to serve as petits fours.

Variations

- The candied peel can be coated with caster (superfine) sugar instead of chocolate. Roll the peel in the sugar before spreading out on baking parchment to dry.
- Crystallized ginger is also good coated with melted plain chocolate: scrape off some of the rough sugar coating and dip in chocolate and dry as above.
- A mixture of the three types – chocolate- and sugar-coated peel, and ginger – makes an attractive petits fours selection for a special festive occasion such as Christmas or a large party celebration.

Per 100g/4oz Energy 438Kcal/1845kJ; Protein 4.4g; Carbohydrate 74g, of which sugars 72.6g; Fat 15.8g, of which saturates 8.9g; Cholesterol 15mg; Calcium 208mg; Fibre 3.6g; Sodium 270mg

Yellowman

This toffee-like confection is a bit of a curiosity and has always been associated with the Auld Lammas Fair at Ballycastle, County Antrim, which is held in August.

Makes about 900g/2lb

- 115g/4oz/½ cup butter
- 30ml/2 tbsp vinegar
- 225g/8oz/scant ⅔ cup treacle (molasses)
- 225g/8oz/scant ⅔ cup golden (light corn) syrup
- 450g/1lb/2 cups demerara (raw) sugar
- 2.5ml/½ tsp bicarbonate of soda (baking soda), sifted

Cook's tip Test by dropping a small amount of the mixture into a saucer of cold water, if it is ready it should become crisp.

1 Grease a marble slab or a baking tin (pan). Melt the butter in a pan and add the vinegar, treacle, syrup and sugar. Stir over a gentle heat until the sugar has completely dissolved, and then raise the heat and bring to the boil.

2 Boil steadily until the mixture reaches soft crack stage (151°C/304°F on a sugar thermometer).

3 Remove from the heat and stir in the bicarbonate of soda. When it foams up, stir again, then pour on to a greased marble slab or baking tin and, using a spatula, keep working the edges into the centre until the mixture is pale.

4 If poured on the marble slab break into pieces, if poured into the tin, mark up into squares.

Per 900g/2lb Energy 3877Kcal/16,404kJ; Protein 6.3g; Carbohydrate 799.9g, of which sugars 799g; Fat 94.5g, of which saturates 59.9g; Cholesterol 245mg; Calcium 1.53g; Fibre 0g; Sodium 1.74g

Vanilla fudge

Perennially popular, home-made fudge ends a meal beautifully when served as a petit four, – this meltingly good vanilla version is sure to become a favourite.

Makes about 60 pieces

- 175g/6oz/¾ cup butter
- 900g/2lb/4 cups soft light brown sugar
- 400g/14oz can condensed milk
- 2.5ml/½ tsp vanilla essence (extract), or to taste

1 Butter a shallow tin (pan), about 18 x 28cm/7 x 11in. Put the butter and 150ml/¼ pint/⅔ cup water into a large, heavy pan and warm very gently over a low heat until the butter melts.

2 Add the sugar and stir over a low heat until it has completely dissolved. Raise the heat and bring the mixture to the boil. Without stirring, let the mixture cook at a slow rolling boil until it reaches the soft ball stage (114°C/238°F on a sugar thermometer). This will take about 10 minutes.

3 Remove from the heat and beat in the condensed milk with a wooden spoon. Return to a medium heat, stirring, for a few minutes. Remove from the heat again, add the vanilla essence, and beat again with a spoon until glossy. Pour the mixture into the tin. Leave to cool.

4 Cut the fudge into cubes and store in an airtight tin until required. Place in petits fours cases to serve.

Variation For Coffee Fudge, add 30ml/2 tbsp coffee essence (extract).

Per portion Energy 103Kcal/435kJ; Protein 0.7g; Carbohydrate 19.4g, of which sugars 19.4g; Fat 3.1g, of which saturates 1.9g; Cholesterol 9mg; Calcium 28mg; Fibre 0g; Sodium 28mg

Drinks

Milk and buttermilk have always been the great country drinks – and a good cup of tea is now probably "the national drink". But today Ireland is perhaps most widely associated with famous alcoholic drinks like stout (Guinness, Beamish, Murphy's), porter, whiskey and cream liqueurs such as Bailey's. And then there are the cocktails, which are well and truly back in style...

Lemonade

Fresh lemonade is a traditional country drink for many generations, drunk on farms to refresh the workers during harvest. Now, although still popular in rural areas, it is just as likely to be on the menu in a smart contemporary café.

Serves 4–6

3 lemons

115g/4oz/generous ½ cup sugar

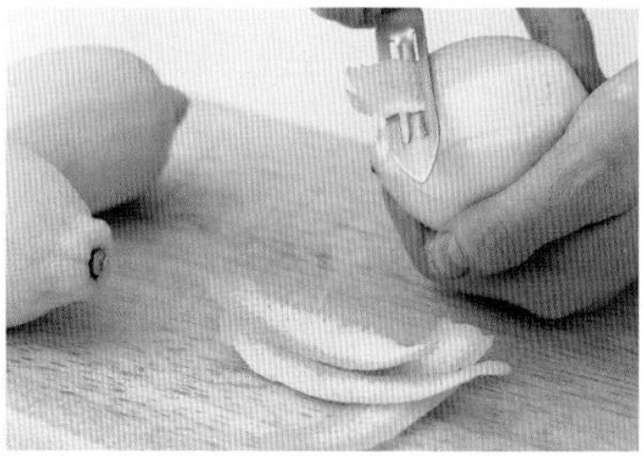

1 Pare the skin from the lemons with a vegetable peeler and squeeze the juice from the lemons.

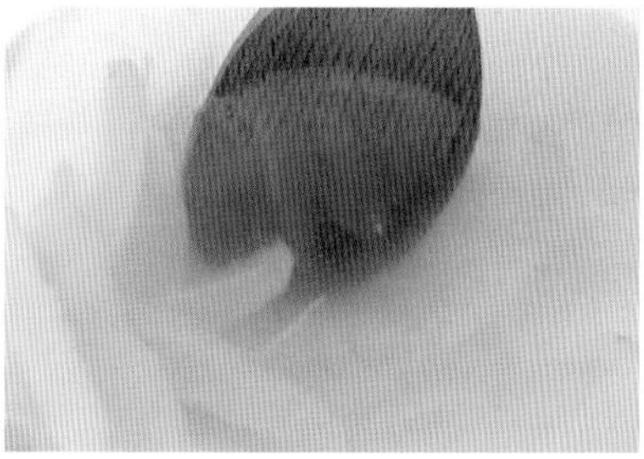

2 Put the lemon rind and sugar into a bowl, add 900ml/1½ pints/3¾ cups boiling water and stir well until the sugar has dissolved. Cover and leave until cold.

3 Add the lemon juice, mix well and strain into a jug (pitcher). Chill.

4 Serve with plenty of ice.

Variation Old-fashioned lemonade made with freshly squeezed lemons is a far cry from the carbonated commercial varieties. It can be topped up with soda water if you want some fizz.

Per glass Energy 115Kcal/489kJ; Protein 0.2g; Carbohydrate 30.4g, of which sugars 30.4g; Fat 0g, of which saturates 0g; Cholesterol 0mg; Calcium 17mg; Fibre 0g; Sodium 2mg

Barley water

Like lemonade, barley water has long been widely enjoyed as a refreshing summer drink and, until a generation ago, it would have been home-made. Barley water is usually served cold, but is also delicious as a hot drink.

Makes about 10 glasses

50g/2oz/⅓ cup pearl barley

1 lemon

sugar, to taste

ice cubes and mint sprigs, to serve

1 Wash the pearl barley, then put it into a large stainless steel pan and cover with cold water. Bring to the boil and simmer gently for two minutes, then strain the liquid. Return the barley to the rinsed pan.

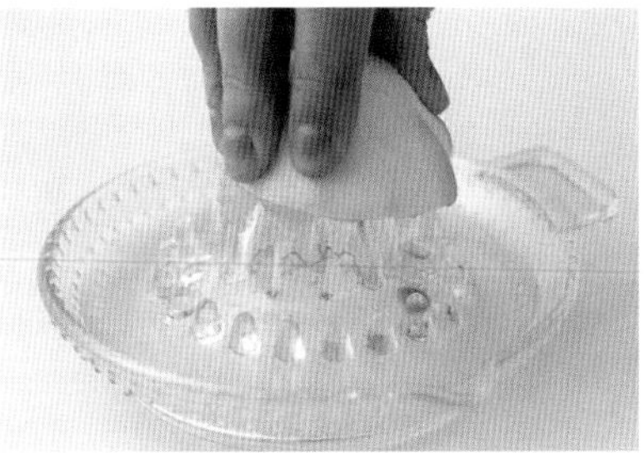

2 Wash the lemon and pare the rind from it with a vegetable peeler. Squeeze the juice.

3 Add the lemon rind and 600ml/1 pint/2½ cups cold water to the pan containing the barley. Bring to the boil over a medium heat, then simmer the mixture very gently for 1½–2 hours, stirring occasionally.

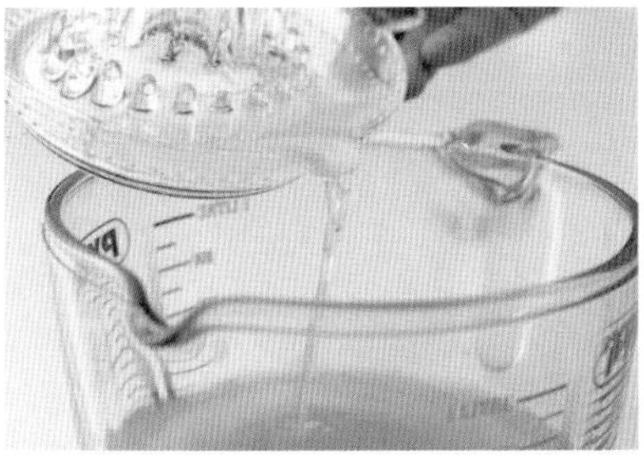

◀ **4** Strain the liquid into a jug (pitcher), add the lemon juice, and sweeten to taste. Leave to cool. Pour the liquid into a bottle and keep in the refrigerator to use as required.

5 To serve, dilute to taste with cold water, and add ice cubes or crushed ice and a sprig of mint, if you like.

Variations

- The barley water can also be used with milk, in which case omit the lemon juice as it would curdle the milk.
- Make up the barley water with hot water to be drunk as a cold remedy.

Per glass Energy 37.9Kcal/161.6kJ; Protein 0.43g; Carbohydrate 9.44g, of which sugars 5.26g; Fat 0.08g, of which saturates 0g; Cholesterol 0mg; Calcium 3.8mg; Fibre 0g; Sodium 0.5mg

Drivers' special

Several small Irish producers make delicious natural pressed apple juice – use it if possible when making this bubbly non-alcoholic cocktail.

Makes about 10 glasses

- 1.2 litres/2 pints/5 cups unsweetened apple juice
- juice of 1 lemon
- 4 small red-skinned eating apples
- 1.2 litres/2 pints/5 cups ginger beer
- ice cubes, to serve
- lemon slices or mint sprigs, to decorate

1 Mix the apple juice and lemon juice in a large glass jug (pitcher).

2 Wash and core the apples, but do not peel them. Slice thinly and add the slices to the jug.

3 Stir well and, to prevent browning, check that all the slices are immersed. Cover and set aside in the refrigerator to chill until required.

4 Shortly before serving, add some ice cubes and the ginger beer to the jug, and decorate with lemon slices, or sprigs of mint. Serve in tall glasses.

Above *Red and green apples.*

Per glass Energy 82Kcal/352kJ; Protein 0.2g; Carbohydrate 21.4g, of which sugars 21.4g; Fat 0.2g, of which saturates 0g; Cholesterol 0mg; Calcium 15mg; Fibre 0.4g; Sodium 11mg

Black velvet

This modern classic always provokes debate – but those who feel it is a waste of good champagne usually get to like it if sparkling wine is substituted for the bubbly.

Serves 8

1 bottle of champagne, chilled

about 750ml/1¼ pints Guinness, or to taste

1 Mix the champagne with an equal quantity of Guinness, or to taste, in eight tall glasses.

2 Drink immediately, while very bubbly.

Above *Musicians playing traditional Irish music at Peader O'Donnell's pub, Derry City, County Londonderry.*

Per glass Energy 98Kcal/406kJ; Protein 0.7g; Carbohydrate 6.2g, of which sugars 6.2g; Fat 0g, of which saturates 0g; Cholesterol 0mg; Calcium 12mg; Fibre 0g; Sodium 10mg

Sloe gin

The small, purple sloes grow widely in the Irish hedgerows and are not much used except, perhaps, for Sloe Gin, which is drunk as a liqueur. Remember to allow at least three months for it to mature – sloes picked in September will make a special Christmas drink.

Makes 2–3 bottles

450g/1lb/4 cups ripe sloes (black plums)

225g/8oz/generous 1 cup caster (superfine) sugar

1 litre/1¾ pint/4 cups Cork Dry Gin

1 Check through the sloes and discard any damaged or unsound fruit. Rinse the sloes and remove the stalks.

2 Prick each sloe with a silver or stainless steel fork or use a cocktail stick (toothpick).

3 Select several wide-necked screw-top or easy to seal sterilized jars and arrange alternate layers of fruit and sugar in them. Top up the jars with gin, and close them tightly. Store for at least 3 months in a cool, dark place.

4 Shake the jars gently every now and then to help extract and distribute the flavour evenly. When ready, strain into a jug (pitcher) and then pour into sterilized bottles and store for another 3 months if possible.

Per bottle Energy 1554Kcal/6486kJ; Protein 0.6g; Carbohydrate 117.6g, of which sugars 117.6g; Fat 0g, of which saturates 0g; Cholesterol 0mg; Calcium 60mg; Fibre 0g; Sodium 7mg

Irish cream liqueur cocktails

Bailey's is the best known of the Irish cream liqueurs that have taken the world by storm. There are several other excellent brands available too, and they make good cocktail ingredients. These liqueurs slip down easily, however, and should be taken in moderation.

Irish flag

Serves 1

A layered cocktail that is just the thing for St Patrick's day.

Pour 25ml/1½ tbsp green crème de menthe and 25ml/1½ tbsp Bailey's Irish Cream into a shot glass. Float 25ml/1½ tbsp brandy on the top to mimic the green, white and orange of the Irish national flag.

Bailey's dream shake cocktail

Serves 1

Almost an ice cream!

Put some ice into a cocktail shaker. Add 50ml/2fl oz/¼ cup Bailey's Irish Cream, 2 scoops vanilla ice cream and 25ml/1½ tbsp of single cream. Shake until the shaker is too cold to hold. Serve in long, chilled glasses.

Per glass Irish Flag Energy 215Kcal/896kJ; Protein 0g; Carbohydrate 11.8g, of which sugars 11.8g; Fat 3.9g, of which saturates 0g; Cholesterol 0mg; Calcium 5mg; Fibre 0g; Sodium 24mg
Bailey's Dream Shake Energy 476Kcal/1987kJ; Protein 6.2g; Carbohydrate 41.6g, of which sugars 40g; Fat 25.4g, of which saturates 12.2g; Cholesterol 50mg; Calcium 181mg; Fibre 0g; Sodium 142mg

Whiskey cocktails

Cocktails are a big hit in many of Ireland's contemporary bars, and they're a fun way to give any party a kick-start. Whiskey makes a good foundation for cocktails and these three are especially suitable for making with Jameson, which is widely available. Instructions are for one serving, but you can scale up the shaken cocktails to serve in jugs.

Jameson hourglass

Serves 1

This pink cocktail contains cranberry juice – refreshing and not too strong either, as there are four measures of juice (plus ice) to one of whiskey.

Pour 25ml/1½ tbsp whiskey into a tall glass and add ice. Pour in two measures of cranberry juice and two measures of orange juice. Stir and finish with a dash of fresh lime.

Jameson WTR (What's the rush?)

Serves 1

A long, refreshing drink that's simple to make and easy to drink.

Pour 25ml/1½ tbsp whiskey into a tall glass and add ice. Add 75ml/5 tbsp lemonade and a dash of apple juice. Stir and decorate with a slice of orange.

Whiskey sour

Serves 1

Glasses should be chilled ahead and a cocktail shaker is useful for this classic Irish cocktail or you can simply make it in the glass.

To 25ml/1½ tbsp whiskey, add 5ml/1 tsp caster sugar and the juice of 1 lemon. Shake over ice and strain, then pour into a chilled glass. Twist a strip of lemon peel over the drink and drop into the glass. Serve with a maraschino (cocktail) cherry on a cocktail stick (toothpick).

Cook's tip Murphy's, Paddy, Dunphy's and Tullamore Dew whiskeys are all made mostly around Dublin or Cork.

Per glass Hourglass Energy 104Kcal/436kJ; Protein 0.3g; Carbohydrate 11.6g, of which sugars 4.4g; Fat 0.1g, of which saturates 0g; Cholesterol 0mg; Calcium 5mg; Fibre 0.1g; Sodium 5mg
Jameson WTR Energy 72Kcal/300kJ; Protein 0g; Carbohydrate 4.3g, of which sugars 4.3g; Fat 0g, of which saturates 0g; Cholesterol 0mg; Calcium 4mg; Fibre 0g; Sodium 5mg
Whiskey sour Energy 74Kcal/308kJ; Protein 0.1g; Carbohydrate 4.7g, of which sugars 4.7g; Fat 0g, of which saturates 0g; Cholesterol 0mg; Calcium 5mg; Fibre 0g; Sodium 1mg

Hot whiskey, or whiskey punch

Also known as a "hot toddy" this traditional "cure" for colds is more often drunk for pleasure as a nightcap, particularly to round off a day's winter sporting activities, and it is a great drink to hold and sip on cold, damp winter evenings.

Serves 1

- 4–6 whole cloves
- 60ml/4 tbsp Irish whiskey
- 1 thick slice of lemon, halved
- 5–10ml/1–2 tsp demerara (raw) sugar, to taste

Cook's tip All three types of Irish whiskey (single malt, pure pot stilled and a column-and-pot still blend of grain and malt) work well in this recipe.

1 Stick the cloves into the lemon slice, and put it into a large stemmed glass (or one with a handle) with the whiskey and the sugar.

2 Put a teaspoon in the glass, to prevent the hot water from cracking it, then top it up with boiling water. Stir well to dissolve the sugar and serve.

Per glass Energy 149Kcal/619kJ; Protein 0g; Carbohydrate 4.2g, of which sugars 4.2g; Fat 0g, of which saturates 0g; Cholesterol 0mg; Calcium 2mg; Fibre 0g; Sodium 0mg

Hot claret

A hot wine cup is now unlikely to be made with claret, but the name dates back hundreds of years to the time when it was plentiful, and probably not very special.

Makes about 10 glasses

1 bottle red wine

175g/6oz/scant 1 cup sugar, or to taste

1 lemon

5cm/2in piece of cinnamon stick

lemon slices, to decorate (optional)

1 Put the red wine, 300ml/½ pint/1¼ cups water and the sugar into a large stainless steel pan.

2 Peel the lemon thinly with a vegetable peeler and add the peel to the pan with the cinnamon stick. Slowly heat this mixture over a low heat, stirring to dissolve the sugar, until almost boiling.

3 Remove from the heat, cover and leave for 10 minutes to infuse (steep). Strain into a heated jug (pitcher) and pour the hot mulled wine into warmed glasses, each garnished with a half-slice of lemon, if you like.

Per glass Energy 120Kcal/506kJ; Protein 0.2g; Carbohydrate 18.4g, of which sugars 18.4g; Fat 0g, of which saturates 0g; Cholesterol 0mg; Calcium 15mg; Fibre 0g; Sodium 6mg

Mulled cider

This hot cider cup is easy to make and traditional at Hallowe'en, but it makes a good and inexpensive warming brew for any winter gathering.

Makes about 20 glasses

2 lemons

1 litre/1¾ pints/4 cups apple juice

2 litres/3½ pints/9 cups medium sweet cider

3 small cinnamon sticks

4–6 whole cloves

slices of lemon, to serve (optional)

1 Wash the lemons and pare the rinds with a vegetable peeler. Blend all the ingredients together in a large stainless steel pan.

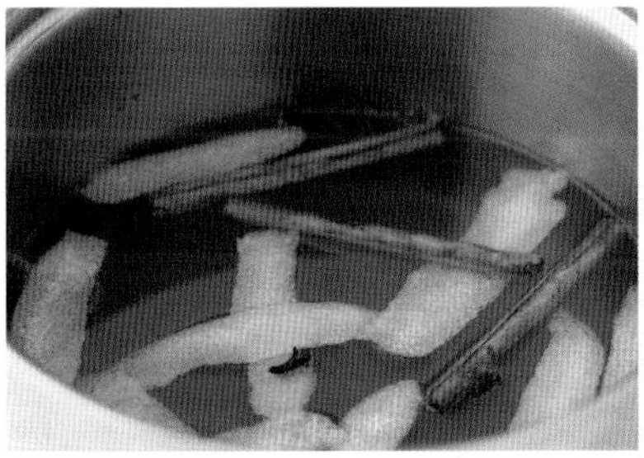

2 Set over a low heat and heat the mixture through to infuse (steep) for 15 minutes; do not allow it to boil.

3 Strain the liquid and serve with extra slices of lemon, if you like.

Per glass Energy 61Kcal/258kJ; Protein 0.1g; Carbohydrate 9.3g, of which sugars 9.3g; Fat 0.1g, of which saturates 0g; Cholesterol 0mg; Calcium 12mg; Fibre 0g; Sodium 8mg

Blas meala

This traditional recipe is even more like a dessert than Gaelic coffee. It is debatable whether it should be drunk or eaten with a spoon!

Serves 1

50ml/2fl oz/¼ cup freshly squeezed orange juice

5ml/1 tsp honey

25ml/1½ tbsp Irish whiskey

a little lightly whipped cream

a little toasted pinhead oatmeal

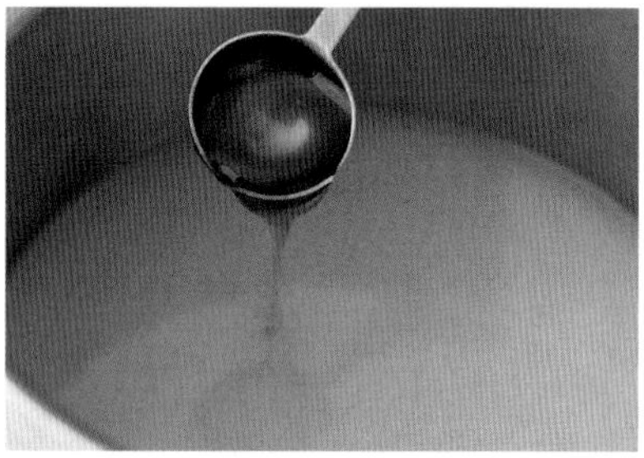

1 In a small pan, heat the orange juice to just below boiling point, then add the honey and stir.

2 Pour into a glass, add the whiskey and top with a layer of whipped cream.

3 Sprinkle with the freshly toasted oatmeal, and drink straight away.

Per glass Energy 227Kcal/943kJ; Protein 1.4g; Carbohydrate 14.2g, of which sugars 11.3g; Fat 12.5g, of which saturates 7.6g; Cholesterol 32mg; Calcium 25mg; Fibre 0.3g; Sodium 15mg

Gaelic coffee

A good Gaelic coffee, also called Irish coffee, is an exercise in contrast and a rare treat indeed – and often taken as an alternative to dessert.

Serves 1

25ml/1½ tbsp Irish whiskey

about 150ml/¼ pint/⅔ cup hot strong black coffee

demerara (raw) sugar, to taste

about 50ml/2fl oz/¼ cup lightly whipped chilled cream

1 Measure the whiskey into a stemmed glass, or one with a handle. Pour in enough freshly made strong black coffee to come to about 1cm/½in from the top.

2 Sweeten to taste and stir vigorously to dissolve the sugar and create a small whirlpool in the glass.

◀ **3** Top the coffee with the lightly whipped cream, poured over the back of the teaspoon. It will settle on the top to make a distinct layer in creamy contrast to the dark coffee underneath. (It is important that the coffee should be very hot to contrast with the chilled cream.) Serve immediately and do not stir in the cream.

Above *Enjoying a glass of Guinness by the open fire in a traditional Irish bar – Martin's bar – in County Donegal.*

Per glass Energy 262Kcal/1081kJ; Protein 1g; Carbohydrate 5.5g, of which sugars 5.5g; Fat 20.1g, of which saturates 12.6g; Cholesterol 53mg; Calcium 31mg; Fibre 0g; Sodium 13mg

Shopping information

Ireland

The Burren Smokehouse
Lisdoonvarna, Co Clare
Tel: 65 7074432
www.burrensmokehouse.ie

Clonakilty Food Company
16 Pearse St
Clonakilty, West Cork
Tel: 23 8834835
www.clonakiltyblackpudding.ie

Country Choice
25 Kenyon St
Nenagh, Co Tipperary
Tel: 67 32596
www.countrychoice.ie

The Irish Store
Unit 134 Slaney Close,
Dublin Industrial Estate,
Glasnevin,
Dublin 11
Tel: 353 1 8611590
www.theirishstore.com

Irish Gourmet
www.irishgourmet.co.uk

Irish Provincial Hampers
www.irishhampers.net

Natural Ireland
www.naturalireland.ie

Wrights of Howth
www.wrightsofhowth.com

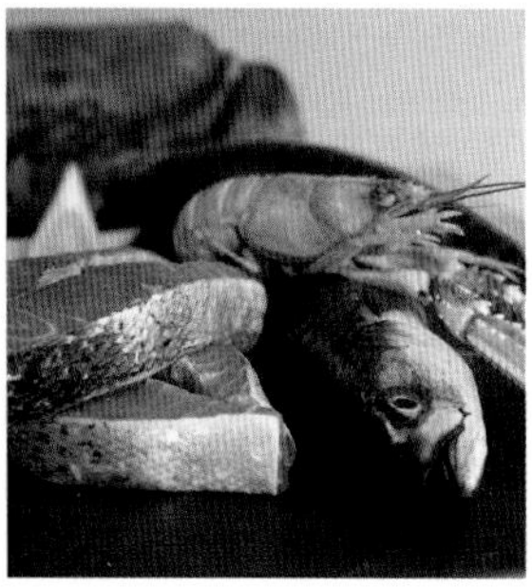

United Kingdom

A selection of Irish foods can be sourced in a large number of stores in London. Irish beef – clearly identifiable with an Irish beef logo – can be sourced from all leading multiple retail outlets. A full range of Irish consumer foods are also available in many UK supermarkets. Irish farmhouse cheeses and other artisan products such as speciality meats, smoked salmon and handmade chocolates can be sourced from the following outlets.

Bayley & Sage
60 High Street
London SW19 5EE
Tel: 020 8946 9904
www.bayley-sage.co.uk

C Lidgates
110 Holland Park Avenue
London W11 4UA
www.lidgates.com

CST Irish Imports
Unit 2 The Waterside
Trading Centre,
Trumpers Way,
London W7 2QD
Tel: 020 8574 7377

Fortnum & Mason
181 Piccadilly
London W1A 1ER
Tel: 0845 300 1707
www.fortnumandmason.com

Hamish Johnston
48 Northcote Road
London SW11 1PA
Tel: 020 7738 0741
www.hamishjohnston.com

Harrods Food Hall
87 Brompton Road
Knightsbridge
London SW1X 7XL
Tel: 020 7730 1234
www.harrods.com

Harvey Nichols Food Hall
109 Knightsbridge
London SW1X 7RJ
Tel: 020 7235 5000
www.harveynichols.com

The Irish Shop
Coventry Retail Market,
Stall No 39-40, Queen
Victoria Road, CV1 3HT
Tel: 02476 630118
www.theirishshop.co.uk

Jeroboams
43 Portland Road
London W11 4LJ
www.jeroboams.co.uk

Mise-en-Place
2nd Floor
240 High Holborn
London WC1V 7DN
Tel: 020 7430 9811
www.miseenplace.co.uk

Mortimer & Bennett
33 Turnham Green Terrace
London W4 1RG
Tel: 020 8995 4145
www.mortimerandbennett.com

Neals Yard Dairy (wholesale)
108 Druid Street
London SE1 2HH
Tel: 020 7500 7654
www.nealsyarddairy.co.uk

O'Kane Irish Foods
8 Quad Road
East Lane Business Park
Middlesex HA9 7NE
Tel: 020 8385 1771
www.okaneirishfoods.co.uk

Paxton & Whitfield
Unit 6 Willow Court
Bourton Industrial Park
Bourton on the Water
Glos GL54 2HQ
Tel: 01451 823460
www.paxtonandwhitfield.co.uk

Selfridges Ltd
400 Oxford Street
London W1A 1AB
Tel: 0800 123 400
www.selfridges.com
Teddington Cheese Online
Tel: 020 8977 6868
E-mail: cheese@teddington cheese.co.uk
www.teddingtoncheese.co.uk

Tom's Deli
226 Westbourne Grove
London W11 2RH
Tel: 020 7243 3341
www.newtoms.co.uk

For further information on Irish products, please visit loveirishfood.ie, www.foodireland.com or www.bordbia.ie

United States

Bewley Irish Imports
1130 Greenhill Road
West Chester, PA 19380
Tel: 1 888 239 5397
www.bewleyirishimports.com

Crown Pacific
8809, S 190th St
Kent, WA 98031
Tel: 425 251 8750
www.cpff.net

DPI Northwest
12360 SW Leveton Dr.
Tualatin, OR 97062
Tel: 503 692 0662
www.dpispecialtyfoods.com

Food Ireland
230 East Third Street
Mount Vernon, NY 10553
Tel: 914 699 5000
www.foodireland.com

Gaelic Imports
6346 W. Gunnison St.
Chicago, Illinois 60630
Tel: 773 792 1905
gaelicimportschicago.com

Gourmet Merchants International
16511 S. Main Street
Gardena
California 90248
Tel: 310 808 0960
www.gmidist.com

Irish Breakfast USA
13 Highview Avenue
Orangeburg
New York 10962
Tel: 1 888 846 7335
irishbreakfastusa.com

Irish Dairy Board, Inc.
1007 Church Street
Suite 314 Evanston
IL 60201
Tel: 847 492 8036

Irish Food Distributors
The James Trading Group
13 Highview Avenue
Orangeburg NY 10962
Tel: 1 800 541 5004
www.irishfooddistributors.com

McElroy Imports
92 Wendy Lane
Glen Mills
PA 19342-1123
Tel: 610 361 0354
Fax: 610 361 0985
Contact: Mr Martin McElroy

O'Connor's Deli and Market
7280 West Devon Ave
Chicago, IL 60631
Tel: 773 631 0747
www.oconnorsdeli.com

Posh Nosh Imports
1 Jacobus Ave, Suite 120
South Kearny
NJ 07032
Tel: 973 274 9444
posh-nosh.com

Tommy Moloney's
P.O. Box 780019
Maspeth, NY 11378
Tel: 1 800 431 6365
www.tommymoloneys.com

www.igourmet.com
Tel: 877 446 8763
Specialist cheese suppliers

Authors' Acknowledgements

The authors would like to thank the following people and organizations for their invaluable help in researching this book: Bord Bia (Irish Food Board), Bord Glas (Irish Horticulture Board), Bord Iascaigh Mhara (Irish Sea Fisheries Board), Cáis (Irish Farmhouse Cheesemaker's Association), Associated Craft Butchers of Ireland, Euro-Toques (The European Community of Chefs) and Ireland's Blue Book. Thanks are due also to the many creative chefs around Ireland who have inspired some of the modern recipes, many of them members of Euro-Toques, and the Slow Food Movement.

Publisher's Acknowledgements

Thanks to the following for kindly supplying pictures:
36t Ross Lewis/Chapter One.
36b Ray Byrne/Wineport Lodge.
37t Enniscoe House.
37b Catherine Dundon/Dunbrody Country House Hotel.

All photographs are by Craig Robertson except the following:
50b, 60b © Caroline Jones.
7b © Mick Rock, 48b © Wine Magazine/Cephas Picture Library.
9b © Sandro Vannini, 10b © Geray Sweeney, 11b © Richard Cummins, 33t, 33b © Jacqui Hurst/Corbis.
10t, 14, 20t; 22b, 28br, 32 © Fáilte Ireland.
7t © Peter Zoeller, 8b © Gareth McCormack, 9t © Eddie Dunne, 16b © Ivan O' Driscoll, 17t © Geray Sweeney, 20b © George Munday, 21b © Billy Clarke, 22t © LP Pictures, 22b, 44b © Tim Hannen, 52b © Liam Blake, 167br © Billy Clarke, 177br © Seoirse de Luan, 209b © Peter Zoeller/Irish Image Collection.
23b, 45tl, 46t, 49b, 51t, 52t, 54t, 56b, 57b, 59bl, 59br, 62t © iStock.
189br © Jameson Irish Whiskey Picture Library.
18, 24t, 25b, 28bl © Mary Evans Picture Library.
8t © Michael Jenner, 15br © A Woolfitt, 17b © D Harcourt-Webster, 17t © Michael Jenner/Robert Harding Picture Library.
12t, 12b, 16t, 24b, 25t, 26b, 27, 29, 31t, 34t, 34b, 35b, 58b, 93b, 106br, 140b, 147br, 241bl, 249bl © Chris Hill/SceniclrelAND.com.
30 © Shane McElroy.
15bl © Shannon Heritage.
19t, 77br, 84br, 95br, 102br, 104br, 108bl, 116br, 124b, 143br, 144b, 180br, 183br, 203br, 206br © Stockbyte/Punchstock.
11t © Georg Gerster, 35t © Ken Walsh/Powerstock; 26t © SuperStock; 53b © SuperStock/Powerstock.
13t, 13b, 17b, 28t © Werner Forman Archive.

Index